"At a time when many people are questioning the ways in which our ideas about ourselves, others, and the world are formed, *That Is Not Your Mind!* is an invaluable guide, offering deep insight along the Buddhist path of self-realization. Framing the teaching of the Surangama Sutra within the context of Zen practice and everyday experiences of the contemporary world, Bob Rosenbaum draws on his years of experience as a neuropsychologist and Zen practitioner, bringing to light the fundamental teachings of how our minds come to frame our perceptions of the world."

—Diane Eshin Rizzetto, author of
Waking Up to What You Do and *Deep Hope*

"As a Zen teacher, Taoist student, neuropsychologist, and psychotherapist, my dharma brother Bob Rosenbaum brings a lifetime of training to the beloved Surangama Sutra, a seminal Mahayana text only recently available in English. With warmth, keen insight, and great clarity, Rosenbaum writes at the intersection of ancient but perennial Buddhist wisdom and his own human yearning to awaken. This Sutra of the Heroic March can now be a reliable map on our own enlightening journey."

—Hozan Alan Senauke, author of
Turning Words: Transformative Encounters with Buddhist Teachers

THAT IS NOT YOUR MIND!

Zen Reflections on the Surangama Sutra

ROBERT ROSENBAUM

FOREWORD BY NORMAN FISCHER

SHAMBHALA

Shambhala Publications, Inc.
2129 13th Street
Boulder, Colorado 80302
www.shambhala.com

Cover art: from *Varieties of Lychee Fruit*, Unidentified artist, Song Dynasty, from the Collection of A. W. Bahr, Purchase, Fletcher Fund, 1947
Cover design: Katrina Noble
Interior design: Jordan Wannemacher

9 8 7 6 5 4 3 2 1

First Edition
Printed in the United States of America

Shambhala Publications makes every effort to print on acid-free, recycled paper. Shambhala Publications is distributed worldwide by Penguin Random House, Inc., and its subsidiaries.

Library of Congress Cataloging-in-Publication Data
Names: Rosenbaum, Robert, author.
Title: That is not your mind!: Zen reflections on the Surangama Sutra / Robert Rosenbaum; foreword by Norman Fischer.
Description: Boulder: Shambhala, 2022.
Identifiers: LCCN 2021050383 | ISBN 9781645470793 (trade paperback)
Subjects: LCSH: Tripiṭṭaka. Sūtrapiṭṭaka. Śūraṅgamasamādhisūtra—Commentaries. | Liberty—Religious aspects—Buddhism. | Zen Buddhism.
Classification: LCC BQ2127 .R67 2022 | DDC 294.3/82—dc23/eng/20220128
LC record available at https://lccn.loc.gov/2021050383

I dedicate this book with deep gratitude

to the memory of my root teachers,

Sojun Mel Weitsman and Hui Liu Chiang.

In truth no eloquent articulation

can ever capture, quite, in art

the wonders of a plain, mundane sensation.

CONTENTS

FOREWORD

NORMAN FISCHER

Most Buddhist books published these days skirt the edges of what we have come to call the "self-help" market—Buddhism as a way to cope, be happy, even thrive, in this very mixed-up world (the world has always been mixed-up, but never before have we had a book industry so adept at churning out texts to address the confusion). I am not complaining. We need help.

And the truth is, Buddhism *is* a form of self-help, a way to overcome pervasive human suffering. As the Buddha is said to have remarked, "I teach only one thing: suffering and the end of suffering."

But how do you end suffering? Well, first you identify its cause. Early iterations of the Second Noble Truth list desire as the cause of suffering. Because we want what we cannot possibly have—for instance, among other things, to live and not to die—we are doomed to suffer. Overcoming suffering is overcoming desire.

But as Buddhist thought and practice developed, sages revised this. What is desire, after all? Why does it arise? Is there something prior that produces it?

The Buddhist sages saw that desire is not the ultimate problem. Our biological desires are natural and can be a source of joy. To desire to eat when we are hungry is not suffering. And our desire to love and benefit others isn't suffering. But when desire is based on misapprehension, when we desire the impossible without realizing it is impossible, we suffer. The true cause of suffering, then, the cause of desire, is misknowledge. Given this, Buddhism developed a complex and detailed phenomenological and philosophical analysis of reality, not in an effort to accurately describe it but as a necessary step in bringing suffering to an end. Seeing reality as it is, we bring desire into alignment.

There is where texts like the Surangama Sutra fit in. Along with other important Buddhist texts like the Diamond Sutra, the Heart Sutra, the Lankavatara Sutra, Nagarjuna's Middle Verses, the Thirty Verses of Vasubandu—and many, many others—the Surangama Sutra is a philosophical text that touches on issues of epistemology, the phenomenology of perception, language, and what we probably have to call metaphysics. It is a work of intellectual exploration at a very sophisticated level—quite unlike most self-help books.

Although Buddhist thought and Buddhist practice might seem like two different things, in fact they are not. Practicing Buddhism with people for a lifetime, I have seen that there's an intellectual dimension to spiritual transformation. Practice changes our life, and this turns out to mean not only that it increases our sense of contentment and patience with things, and our wisdom in the world, but also, possibly most importantly, that it effects a revolution in the way we see and think about things. We come to understand ourselves, others, and the world radically differently.

This is why all versions of traditional Buddhist practice include some philosophical teaching beyond instructions for practice per se. Even the Zen that Robert Rosenbaum and I have both practiced for many years—a tradition that seems to denigrate thinking as counterproductive—includes a daily Dharma talk. As one of my Zen teachers once told me, "Yes, you have to sit long and hard, but someone has to tiptoe up to you at some point and whisper in your ear." Despite the reductionist implications of recent brain research, Buddhism, as it turns out, is a culture, not just a set of psychophysical operations that change your brain.

I love the Surangama Sutra. It is, like other Buddhist texts that were particularly important in Chinese Buddhism (like the Lotus Sutra and the Platform Sutra), sometimes lighthearted and fanciful. Some scholars suggest that the sutra was a Chinese production passed off as Indian. Its opening scene recounts an incident, the springboard for the teaching that follows, that couldn't, it seems to me, originate from pious India. Ananda, the Buddha's cousin and chief disciple (who appears, in Zen, as a clueless quasicomical figure, despite the fact that—or perhaps because of it—he memorized all the teachings the Buddha ever gave), is about to take off his Buddhist robes to make love to a courtesan who has just seduced him. Ananda is a monastic: he can't do this! But, apparently, he can't help it. But, not to worry—the Buddha, who is elsewhere, clairvoyantly sees this impending catastrophe and easily handles it. With his Buddha magic, he instantaneously whisks Ananda away and, for much of the rest of the sutra, explains to him that desire is a conceptual error, that there is nothing to desire. Ananda's apparent moral lapse is based on a deeply ingrained misunderstanding endemic in all humans. Understanding the error (without, as you will read, having any concept of "understanding") and therefore undoing it is the ultimate Buddhist self-help.

Although Bob Rosenbaum and I haven't practiced Zen together, we have known each other for many years and have had the same teacher, our dear Sojun Mel Weitsman, who passed away in 2021 at the age of ninety-one, after having served as an example of steady wise practice for more than fifty years. Bob, as you will soon see, is astonishingly well suited to explicate this text. His love of it, which matches mine I am sure, shines on every page. That's the main thing—to love, not merely explain, what you are teaching. But, more than this, Bob brings many special gifts to the text. A lay Zen teacher with decades of practice under his belt, he is, in addition, a qigong instructor (so he understands the Chinese way of embodying the thinking of the teachings), a psychotherapist (so he understands the everyday hang-ups and sufferings of ordinary people like you and me), a scientist (as a neuropsychologist, he is conversant with how the brain works and has a working knowledge of other relevant sciences, like physics and cosmology), and, perhaps most importantly, a really lively and trustworthy writer.

That Is Not Your Mind. Indeed! That's the trouble, isn't it? We are so sure of what our mind is, and, especially, that it is ours. The Surangama Sutra, held in Bob's capable hands, shows us otherwise. Bob wisely divides the text into two main parts: "Mind," focusing on the sutra's important philosophical and phenomenological teachings, and "Heart," the spirit of compassion and kind conduct that these teachings foster when we fully appreciate them. In this latter part, he writes movingly of the bodhisattva Avalokiteshvara, hearer of the cries of the world, and of the practice of Zen's bodhisattva precepts, which, as time goes on, have become more and more central in Western Zen practice.

It's possible that it takes a longtime Buddhist teacher with an intellectual bent (like Bob or me) to fall in love with the Surangama Sutra. But that's the beauty of the book you are about to read—it makes this great and neglected text fully available to many readers in lucid and friendly fashion, bringing out its brilliance and applying it to Buddhist practice as we live it now. You will savor this wonderful book. And it will help.

THAT IS NOT YOUR MIND!

INTRODUCTION

Nothing is hidden, but there is an infinite field we cannot see. Horizons stretch ahead, behind, below, and above. Lights infrared and ultraviolet shine beyond form and emptiness. Within our range of vision, everything we see is refracted through the corneas and vitreous humors of our eyes, bent by the lenses of our minds.

That Is Not Your Mind! is an exploration of the Surangama Sutra, an ancient Buddhist text that alerts us to the ubiquity of our illusions, along with the means to dispel them and realize the Mind of the Great Sage of India. Although the Surangama, like many Mahayana sutras, features esoteric worlds and incredible events, it also resonates with contemporary findings in neuroscience and psychology. The sutra offers a bridge from our deeply ingrained "unseen" habits to the liberating touch of genuine intimacy. Its invitation to walk across that bridge begins with looking at how our erroneous imaginations are so all-encompassing that we have difficulties seeing the illusory sources of our fears.

The Bay Bridge spans the gap between Oakland and San Francisco. One day when my firstborn daughter, Anna, was three years old, we were driving toward the bridge when she started crying for no apparent reason. She stopped crying as soon as we got off the bridge, but from then on, every time we drove over the bridge, she became more and more distressed. We tried questioning her, distracting her, soothing her, sitting next to her, but each time her crying became increasingly frantic. She was terrified, hyperventilating with panic attacks, but we couldn't see what was bothering her.

Finally, one day as we approached the bridge and she started to get upset, my wife turned to her and said, "Anna, are you worried London Bridge is falling down?"

"Yesss!" sobbed Anna.

"This isn't London Bridge," said my wife.

"No?" asked Anna, starting to quiet down.

"No," said my wife. "It won't fall down."

"Oh!" said Anna, taking a deep breath. The bridge was no longer a hindrance; without any hindrance, her fears ceased to exist.

How did my wife see what she (and I) could not see so that she could comfort our daughter? First, she had to loosen the grip of an adult mind stuck on the illusion of "This is the Bay Bridge; everyone can see it's a solid structure." Letting go of her idea of the bridge helped my wife close the gap between her perceptions and how Anna experienced the bridge—not with her eyes but with her nursery-rhyme mind. A pliable imagination allowed her to relieve Anna's suffering by dispelling the mental constructions that had given rise to her fearful illusion.

Yet we cannot find true liberation from suffering by substituting one false illusion ("The Bay Bridge is London Bridge") for another equally false but more comforting one ("This bridge is solid and safe"). My daughter's perception of London Bridge falling down was an illusion, but so are all our assumptions of permanence and stability. During the earthquake of 1989, six years after this incident with my daughter, a substantial portion of the Bay Bridge collapsed.

Buddhist practice is a bridge we traverse from suffering to suchness, *tathata*, the "as-is-ness" of the moment. The adult variations of our nursery-rhyme minds obscure suchness with the seemings of our senses: we naively believe what we see, hear, touch, feel, desire, and think are true depictions of the world and ourselves. When we enter meditation practice, we begin to get an inkling that all is not as it appears. We become like Neo in the film *The Matrix*, confronting the possibility that we are caught in a simulation of experience masquerading as reality.

Are you willing to explore the precariousness of your perceptions? Will you take the red pill offered by the Surangama Sutra? If you do, it will introduce you to the Matrix of the Thus-Come-One—the mind that sees unseeing, hears all beings crying to be seen, and responds with wise compassion to liberate us from suffering and confusion. This mind orients toward ungraspable—hence, unbreakable—truth.

The Buddhist practices in the sutra can teach us to approach each moment of our lives as a bridge: each of our thoughts is but a bridge from one idea to the next, each of our sensations but a bridge from one part of the body to the next. You and I are bridges to a world of interbeing. Bodhisattvas are bridges to buddhas.

The Surangama Sutra provides us with a vivid encounter with the Buddha's enlightened Mind. Awareness by itself is insufficient for liberation; we need to reach the enlightened *basis* of awareness, penetrate all illusion, and realize that all the solid realities and mental impressions we take for granted are airy bridges. They sway in the winds, bend under their burdens, and are subject to aging and decay. When conditions sound their resonant frequencies, these bridges of the mind oscillate, tremble, and fall apart.[1]

Buddhas, though, are not bridges, so they cannot be broken by earthquakes of any sort. The Surangama Sutra helps us realize that earthquakes and bridges are buddhas.

One of the most difficult aspects of Buddhist practice is wrapping our minds around how every moment is both a deceptive seeming and also a true gateway to awakening. Suffering arises from craving; craving arises when we get caught in the forms, feelings, perceptions, formations, and consciousnesses that pile up to become the constituents of our experience. To confuse these signs with what they point to is to confuse the finger pointing at the moon with the moon itself.

Often, we cannot see the moon, but the moon is constantly expressing itself in tides high and low. The same kinds of limitations that limit our eyesight apply to all our forms of awareness. Our hearing is bounded by frequencies beyond our range. We cannot catch the supersonic waves navigated by dolphins and bats or sing along with the infrasonic melodies of whales and elephants. Our consciousness is constrained by our limited taste of the world. Verse 12 of the *Tao Te Ching* reminds us:

> *Five colors blind our seeing.*
> *Five notes deafen our hearing.*
> *Five flavors blunt our palate.*

The Surangama Sutra melds this Taoist wisdom of ancient China with the Buddhadharma that originated in India. The sutra reminds us, as we swim through the seas of sights, sounds, tastes, touches, and thoughts that constitute our experience, not to mistake these for the ocean that provides them with a place to be. One name for that ocean is Buddha-Mind, but our sense impressions (including our thoughts) are so vivid, so "in-your-face," that we often mistake them for the mind itself.

It can be difficult to understand this with the discriminating, conceptualizing mind—the mind that functions via comparisons and judgments, by analyzing bits and pieces in an attempt to understand the whole. One response arose in Tang dynasty China, where the encounter between Indian Mahayana Buddhism and Chinese Taoism brought forth Chan (later, in Japan, Zen). Chan Buddhism developed practices to cultivate True Mind, immersing its practitioners in concrete experience instead of mental conceptualizations.

We cannot think our way to mindfulness because thinking is based on analytical discriminations. Even when we leave off conceptualizing and return to "bare" awareness, we are easily misled: sight, sound, touch are not truly bare. We confuse hearing with sounds, seeing with sights, consciousness with thoughts. We confuse the objects of mind with the mind itself.

As a neuropsychologist, I know how prone we are to faulty beliefs and distorted perceptions. In the popular media, the brain is often portrayed as a kind of computer whose empathy is located in one area and memory in another; awareness becomes a simple matter of generating the proper EEG pattern. In contrast, modern neuroscience is closer to Buddhist notions of dependent co-arising: small-hub brain networks flicker, expressing the impermanent nature of nervous system structures continually coming into being and dissolving.

We still live mostly in a culture of body-mind dualism, physiological materialism, and I realism. I was fortunate to find an antidote to such reductionistic "isms" when I first encountered the Surangama Sutra in the eighty-eighth koan of the *Shoyoroku* (*Book of Serenity*):

> The *Surangama* scripture says, "When I don't see, why don't you see my not seeing?
>
> If you see my not seeing, that is naturally not the characteristic of not seeing.
>
> If you don't see my not seeing, it's naturally not a thing—how could it not be you?"[2]

As a neuropsychologist, I was intrigued. As a Zen teacher and practitioner, I was aware that it's not through our eyes that we perceive our original face before we were born. As a psychotherapist, I knew that people yearn to be seen even as they hide behind masks of fear.

ORIGINS OF THE SURANGAMA SUTRA

People are not static things. Neither are sutras, which alter over time, appear in multiple versions and different translations, and speak differently to people of disparate cultures and historical eras. Sutras are reincarnated whenever readers study, recite, or reinterpret how they apply to current practice.

The Surangama Sutra is particularly prone to being regarded differently in different cultures. Even its name is less than straightforward.[3] The full title of the sutra is *Da foding rulai miyin xiuzheng liaoyi zhupusa wanxing shouleng-yan jing*. Merging the translations offered by the Buddhist Text Translation Society and by Buddhist studies scholar James Benn, this might be rendered in English as "Sutra of the Paramount Heroic March, the Surangama Mantra Spoken from above the Crown of the Great Buddha's Head, and on the Hidden Basis of the Bodhisattva's Myriad Practices for Cultivating, Verifying, and Realizing the Tathagatha's Ultimate Truth." The Surangama Sutra is frequently confused with the Surangamasamadhi Sutra, an early Indian Mahayana text of known provenance that describes a myriad of the Buddha's supernatural powers.

The provenance of the Surangama Sutra, in contrast, has long been controversial. Chinese tradition holds that it was translated from an Indian Sanskrit text by a monk around 705 C.E. and subsequently polished, edited, and issued around the end of the reign of Empress Wu Zetian (624–705 C.E.). The sutra became a canonical part of Chinese Chan, used for the training of monastics and linked with the enlightenment of several Chinese Chan masters. The sutra gave rise to a ritual that became standard by the time of the Song dynasty (960–1279 C.E.) and is still practiced today: the semiannual Surangama Assembly. From the Song dynasty onward, the Surangama Sutra was widely studied by all Chinese Buddhist schools. Since it draws on a variety of Buddhist philosophies, includes teachings on proper behavior, and features a female central character, it was particularly popular in syncretic circles and with laywomen practitioners.

The sutra remains important in modern Chinese Chan. "For both clergy and lay practitioners in the Chinese Buddhist tradition . . . it continues to be the object of devout study, recitation, and memorization," and many Chinese Buddhists recite the Surangama mantra—a critically important part of the text, as we shall see—"every morning as an essential aspect of daily practice."[4] The sutra was a focus for the teaching of Master Hsuan Hua (1918–1995), an important figure in the transmission of Chinese Buddhism to the United States. We owe the only modern English translation of the sutra, with commentaries by Master Hua, to the Buddhist Text Translation Society (BTTS).[5] This is the edition I use for all quotations in this book. (James Benn of McMaster University has a new translation forthcoming.)

The Surangama Sutra received a very different reception in Japan, where controversy over its authenticity arose when it first arrived during the Nara period (710–784 C.E.). Eihei Dogen (1200–1253 C.E.), founder of the Soto school in Japan, had doubts about its authenticity and quality. Recently, the Zen teacher and scholar Shohaku Okumura has suggested that Dogen critiqued the sutra out of concerns that it provides a non-Buddhist view of essential mind-nature as permanent.[6] The Surangama mantra is unknown to most Japanese lay practitioners, but it is chanted during retreats at some contemporary Rinzai Zen temples and on a daily basis by Zen monastics from the lesser-known Obaku tradition, which was established in Japan in 1661 by Chinese masters and still bears their influence. In the United States, both the City of Ten Thousand Buddhas and the Shasta Abbey Buddhist Monastery in Northern California observe the Surangama ceremony.

James Benn has identified specific elements in the sutra that are indigenous to China—blind jellyfish and wasps, using metal mirrors to ignite moxa—but do not appear in Indian Sanskrit Buddhist writings. Benn also shows how the sutra takes themes common in Chinese Taoist literature and casts them in a Buddhist framework.[7] In contrast, while scholar Ronald Epstein acknowledges doctrinal inconsistencies, Chinese classical language, and "creeping Taoism" in the sutra, he also points to indications of an Indic origin.[8]

Among Buddhist scholars, the current consensus seems to be that the sutra is a Chinese apocryphal composition that draws on Sanskrit sources. As I am not a Buddhist scholar, I don't have the technical capacity to assess the sutra's provenance. All told, it seems likely that the Surangama Sutra is some admixture of Indian Sanskrit sources filtered through Chinese Buddhist perspectives prevalent in Tang dynasty China. Ultimately, as a Zen practitioner, I'm less concerned with a sutra's provenance than with the teachings it presents: What skillful means does it offer us to help us realize our enlightenment, together with all beings, here this moment?

Other Zen and Chan texts—for example, the Platform Sutra—enrich our practice and understanding even when it is clear they were not written by their purported authors but several generations later, then backdated and ascribed to a revered ancestor. Although Eihei Dogen had doubts about the Surangama Sutra, he also noted that the question of "authenticity" is moot since his own teacher, Rujing, as well as other Zen masters, have quoted the text: "Because these words have been turned by buddha ancestors and have turned buddha ancestors, even if this sutra is spurious, it has become a genuine buddha sutra and ancestor sutra, an intimate and familiar dharma wheel."[9]

Benn summarizes as follows:

> In the later Chinese Buddhist tradition, one text above all others has been extolled for the profundity of its ideas, the beauty of its language, and its insight into the practice of

> meditation—this is the scripture popularly known as the *Lengyan jin* or Śūramgama Sūtra. . . .
>
> The Śūramgama is elegantly constructed and beautifully written, a text that we might easily rank among the masterpieces of medieval Chinese literature. . . . That it is not a translation of an Indian original by no means discredits its spiritual value.
>
> Buddhism from its origins was adaptable to local circumstances, and the Śūramgama is but another example. . . . [I]t pursues the serious endeavor of achieving a comprehensive vision that can account for the multifarious nature of reality—a Buddhist answer to the perennial question of how unity and multiplicity are related.[10]

OVERVIEW OF THE SUTRA

The Surangama Sutra begins—unusually for a sutra—with the siren of sex. Ananda, the Buddha's cousin and primary attendant, is wrapped in the arms of a beautiful woman courtesan from the Matanga tribe. He has succumbed to a spell and is about to break his vows of celibacy! Shakyamuni pours forth light from the crown of his head, producing the powerful Surangama mantra to rescue both Ananda and the Matanga woman. Once back at the sangha, Ananda is mortified by his lapse and requests instruction.

The Buddha responds by identifying the root of Ananda's problem: he is vulnerable to being ensnared by sense cravings because he has not understood the nature of mind. Like most of us, Ananda believes his sense-impressions are true representations of an external reality. He fails to realize these are illusions. In true reality, every apparent thing, every apparent where, every apparent when, is the fully awakened Mind of all buddhas.

Shakyamuni engages Ananda in what Western traditions might term Socratic questioning until Ananda admits he cannot say the mind is inside his body, outside his body, somewhere in between, or anywhere else. The Buddha then brings forth a number of examples of visual and auditory perception to demonstrate that awareness is not dependent on objects and that, by meditating on the enlightened basis of awareness, it's possible to dispel illusions and experience the true nature of Buddha-Mind. The Buddha teaches that although the forms through which we perceive the world are illusory, they are fundamentally identical with the Matrix of the Thus-Come-One. Illusion leads us to look everywhere for what we feel we've lost, not perceiving that it is always right at hand.

Having heard the Buddha's discourse, Ananda asks how he should practice to realize the truth of the teaching. Shakyamuni asks twenty-five of the sages in attendance to explain the spiritual means they practiced that enabled them to break through to enlightened reality. Each of the sages responds with an account of practicing with one of the elements of perception or of the primary elements: in each case, they needed to rely on the enlightened basis of awareness. Avalokiteshvara gives the final account, saying he began by focusing on hearing, then—by turning hearing to the fundamentally enlightened basis of hearing—all sounds disappeared, and he heard the cries of the world.

After this offering of an array of meditative practices, the Buddha emphasizes that none of them are sufficient without cultivating moral behavior. He describes four core precepts, explains how to set up a place for awakening, provides the Surangama mantra, and describes its many benefits.

In the last sections of the sutra, the Buddha describes twelve classes of beings, three gradual steps, and fifty-seven stages of the bodhisattva's path. The Buddha then warns practitioners to be on their guard against fifty demonic states of mind that can arise in meditation practice, describing the mental phenomena in detail. Most are harmless if the practitioner dismisses the states as being of no importance, but if the practitioner takes them as a sign of personal enlightenment and pursues them, the consequences will be severe. Finally, in accord with the traditional ending of Mahayana sutras, the Buddha describes the immense benefits that come from practicing and teaching the Surangama Sutra and its mantra.

I hope this brief review of the sutra is intriguing enough to tempt you into exploring it further. The full sutra covers a wide range of topics in its substantial length (the single-volume BTTS version runs to 464 pages). It is divided into ten sections, each consisting of a minimum of four and a maximum of thirteen chapters. It is rich in conceptual theory, drawing on several major schools of Mahayana teachings: the *Yogacara* (Consciousness-Only) school, the *Tathagata-garbha* (Matrix of the Thus-Come-One) school, and the *Vajrayana* (Esoteric) school. It is also down-to-earth and concrete in the myriad practices it recommends, extending even to dietary matters—in the spirit of its cultural context, it warns against eating onions.

Given its length and the complexity of its philosophy, along with the lack of an English translation until recently, the Surangama Sutra has not occupied a prominent place in American and

European meditation practice. The chaos of twentieth-century Chinese history also created difficulties in the transmission of this jewel of Chinese Buddhism to the West.

In its English-language edition by the Buddhist Text Translation Society, the Surangama sutra consists of sixty-one chapters organized into ten sections.[11] I find the sutra also falls naturally into a first part that deals with the nature of the mind and a second part that provides specific practices to foster behaviors and intentions to enable practitioners to realize the Buddha Way. Accordingly, I have divided this book into Part One (Mind) and Part Two (Heart).

A comprehensive study of the depth of the Surangama Sutra's teachings is beyond the scope of this book, but I hope it may serve as an introduction to the sutra for Western Buddhist practitioners and stimulate further interest in the deep benefits of its teachings. To that end, rather than provide full explanations and interpretations of the sutra's teachings—a task for scholars more well-versed in the text's underlying philosophies than I am—I treat the sutra as a springboard for my own reflections and explorations. My chapters mostly follow the ten sections of the sutra, but in some cases I have devoted two chapters to a single section; occasionally, for clarity's sake I include material in a chapter that appears earlier or later in the original sutra. By drawing on my background as a psychologist and neuropsychologist I attempt to make the sutra's teachings accessible to concrete issues readers will find personally relevant.

I've found the Surangama Sutra to be a treasure trove for contemporary practitioners. Reverend Heng Sure, who studied the sutra deeply with his teacher Master Hsuan Hua, expresses it well in his introduction to the BTTS edition of the sutra:

> Over the years, when I have need[ed] advice in cultivation, I have referred to the Śūraṅgama Sūtra for authoritative information. I go to the "Fifty Demonic States of Mind" (part 10) to check on strange states in meditation. I go to the "Twenty-Five Sages" (part 6) for encouragement on the path from the voices of Bodhisattvas. I go to the "Four Clear and Definitive Instructions on Purity" (part 7) for clarity on interaction with the world.[12]

I hope you accept this invitation to join me in studying the Surangama Sutra. If you do, you're likely to encounter meditation techniques previously unknown to you; philosophical conundrums about the nature of reality that challenge assumptions you may not have been aware you were carrying; insights for deepening your experiences with all you encounter; and a powerful mantra offering you protection from harms past, present, and future.

The sutra can be daunting—and great fun. Join me in exploring:

- Why London Bridge *is* falling down
- What resides *under* understanding
- How to find freedom from "is" and "is not"
- Where your mind and eyes actually are
- When to unravel which knot
- Whose mind is not that, but "just this"

May we awaken together with all beings.

PART ONE

Mind

Ānanda, what are the two fundamentals? The first is the mind that is the basis of death and rebirth and that has continued since time without beginning. This mind is dependent on perceived objects, and it is this mind that you and all beings make use of and that each of you consider to be your own nature.

The second fundamental is full awakening, which also has no beginning; it is the original and pure essence of nirvana. It is the original understanding, the real nature of consciousness. All conditioned phenomena arise from it, and yet it is among those phenomena that beings lose track of it.

1

The Request for Dharma

Practice—What and Why?

Near the beginning of the Surangama Sutra, Ananda petitions the Buddha to explain the practices that enabled Shakyamuni to awaken completely. The Buddha does not answer with a meditation instruction or with a discourse on the Four Noble Truths and the Eightfold Path. Instead, he responds to Ananda with his own question: "Ananda: what did you see in my Dharma which motivated you to seek enlightenment?"

> The Buddha said to Ānanda, "You and I are members of the same family, and we share the affection that is natural among relatives. At the time you first made the resolve to become enlightened, what excellent attributes did you see in my Dharma that immediately led you to reject the deep familial affection and conjugal love found in the world?"
>
> Ānanda said to the Buddha, "I saw the thirty-two hallmarks of the Thus-Come-One, which were so supremely wondrous and incomparable that his entire body shone like crystal, with an interreflecting radiance. . . . that is why I

admired the Buddha and why I let the hair fall from my head so I could follow him."[1]

This interchange invites us to look back on our own beginnings. Unlike Ananda, few of us have seen the thirty-two hallmarks of the Thus-Come-One. What motivates us, then, to explore Buddhist practice? How did you come to pursue this path? What prompted you to look inside this book and explore the Surangama Sutra? These are good questions to return to again and again.

We're not always clear about what motivates us. This is true not just for Buddhist practice but for many of the things we do. When you look at your life, how many forks in the road did you come to intentionally via advanced planning, and how many did you (seemingly) stumble into?

Few, if any, of us come to the Dharma seeking nothing at all. In my own case, I had no coherent vision of what I was looking for. I stumbled into Buddhist practice when I was in college. I was miserable a good deal of the time, as only a late adolescent can be, and experimented with all sorts of things without any clear goals in mind. Mind-altering drugs, Freudian depth psychology, music, theater, science—all were enticing. I had my first taste of meditation when I took a course in hatha yoga to fulfill the college's Phys. Ed. requirement; my friends and I explored meditation after hearing Baba Ram Dass exhort us to "Be Here Now" and Alan Watts chuckle over Zen koans. I attended my first Zen meditation retreat in an effort to impress a woman I had met in a class on Japanese religion.

I discovered a college exchange program to study abroad in Japan and, after graduating, stayed in Japan to study *shakuhachi* (a Japanese bamboo flute deeply imbued with Zen aesthetics). I lived in a small Rinzai Zen monastery but became disillusioned with the competitive strivings of monks boasting about how many koans they'd solved. One day my shakuhachi teacher told me the monastery's Zen teacher was very right-wing. I was surprised. Zen teachers could be politically reactionary? "Oh yes," said my shakuhachi teacher. In fact, this particular teacher had been a war criminal and, at the end of WWII, had been given a choice between a term in a Zen monastery or a prison. I felt disillusioned and left the monastery, but—though I couldn't say exactly why—I continued to meditate on my own a few times a week, exploring a variety of methods.

I obtained a PhD and practiced as a psychotherapist and neuropsychologist. I married, and we had two children. Some years later I accepted a Fulbright Professorship to teach clinical psychology at the National Institute for Mental Health and Neurosciences in India. My family thrived; my work was stimulating without being stressful—yet I felt something was lacking. I wasn't depressed or worried or even dissatisfied, but I also couldn't say I actually felt happy. I wanted to find a way to fully appreciate every moment of my life. Not having any better idea, I resumed daily meditation, practicing Soto Zen *shikantaza*, "just sitting," for the first time. After returning to the United States, I started going regularly to the Berkeley Zen Center (BZC). There I met Sojun Mel Weitsman, who would eventually become my root Zen teacher. Initially, though, I approached BZC as one more experiment of "try this and see what you get from it."

What do you see in Buddhadharma that motivates you to seek enlightenment?

People in Asian cultures usually practice Buddhism because they were raised in it; family traditions and cultural norms make this as natural (and as problematical) for them as Christianity, Judaism, and Islam is for people in our society. Most Western practitioners take a more circuitous path, coming to meditation practice out of some personal psychological or spiritual need.

One of the ironies of practice is that people drawn to it from a "spiritual" standpoint usually need to discover their intensely personal hurts and desires before they can realize their more universal aspirations; conversely, people who come to practice from their personal sufferings usually discover these are inextricable from the suffering—and liberation—of all beings. Whatever our original motivations, something unexpected happens: our self-centered goals begin to morph into wider, stranger shapes. Like a Möbius strip, a small twisting-turn changes our topology, and we enter a different dimension; instead of feeling we are on a solitary quest, seeking a Way hidden somewhere in the wilderness, we discover the Way is also, always, seeking us.

Our motivation for practice is rarely solely what we think it is: it is both larger than we are and pettier than we are able to see. As we continue to practice, we find we can never plumb the depths of "practice" or "self" because they are twining vines, continually giving rise to each other past, present, and future.

A central tenet of Soto Zen is that we don't practice to become enlightened. We meditate because it's a natural expression of the fundamental enlightened nature we share with all beings. This is true, but it won't be grounded in the reality of our lives if we don't acknowledge the personal needs that bring us to practice. Whether you are Buddhist, Catholic, Jewish, Sufi, Sunni, Protestant, Ethical Culturist, Unitarian, Marxist, or Existentialist, at some point you must confront the question, what is it that really motivates you? Why bother to seek a Way?

In answer, we need to acknowledge both the spiritual calling that transcends self and the personal issues we need to deal with. If we practice only from the standpoint of devotion, abjuring and denying our personal concerns, we run the risk of sending our psychological and somatic selves underground, where they are likely to rebel and bite back. If we practice only to deal with our personal concerns, we'll run into other problems. For example, if we use meditation primarily as a vehicle for coping with difficulties or curing our emotional ills, we may abandon the practice when it fails to fulfill our fantasies of cure. If we do reach our immediate goal, we may stop practicing until we encounter difficulties again.

Whether we think we practice to realize a spiritual goal or to complete a personal self-improvement project, it's never the whole story. We probably cannot be fully conscious of what ultimately motivates us, but the Buddha encourages us to keep asking the question.

In the Surangama Sutra, after the Buddha asks Ananda what motivated him to seek enlightenment, Ananda responds by citing how he was dazzled by the Buddha's radiant body sparkling with the thirty-two hallmarks of enlightenment. It's easy to become mesmerized by such a glittering display. Shakyamuni, though, does not allow Ananda to rest in a spiritually fabulous hypnotic trance. The Buddha questions him further (all italics are mine):

> "When . . . you first made the resolve to attain full awakening, *what was it that saw* those hallmarks and *who was it that took delight* in them and loved them?"

> Ananda replies: "I delighted in them and loved them with my mind and eyes."
>
> The Buddha says, "... It is as you say: your mind and eyes were the reason for your admiration and delight. Someone who does not know where his mind and eyes are will not be unable to overcome the stress of engagement with perceived objects. When bandits invade a country and the king sends forth his soldiers to drive them out, the soldiers must first know where the bandits are.
>
> *It is the fault of your mind and eyes that you are bound to the circle of birth and death!*
>
> *I am now asking you: precisely where are your mind and eyes?"*[2]

Welcome to the world of the Surangama Sutra! The Buddha presses Ananda—and us—not to stop at a glimpse of the truth and the resulting spiritual high it brings. By asking "what was it that saw" and "who was it that took delight," the Buddha urges us to confront a central question: What is this body-and-mind that experiences and practices? Who are you, really?

First Shakyamuni Buddha acknowledges that Ananda's mind and eyes are the gates for Ananda's delight in the Dharma; they motivate him to practice and seek enlightenment. With his next sentence, though, Shakyamuni tells Ananda his eyes and mind are bandits that rob him of his ability to realize enlightenment; they are culprits binding him to the suffering of an endless cycle of creation and destruction, birth-and-death. Here the sutra brings up a central paradox: realization and delusion depend on each other, arising and dispersing together.

Meditation practice and sutra study help us become more

aware of how our conditioning traps us in habitual distortions. A good deal of the focus in modern practice is on how the curvatures of our thoughts, the crookedness of our actions, and the tangle of our feelings mutually interact and contort us. Our practice needs to be sensible; it will be incomplete if it doesn't examine the concrete sensory and perceptual processes that are fundamental to our existence as embodied beings.

A significant portion of the Surangama Sutra deals with how our sense-perceptions trap us in illusion but also offer gateways for enlightened understanding. I experienced this dual nature of sense-perception on a wintry night about a year after I'd begun practicing yoga.

Yoga was my first awakening to how I habitually felt driven and tightly strung. It gave me an inkling that genuine relaxation and ease might be possible, that my body might be something other than a clumsy container for my mind. On the night in question, I had just missed catching the bus that would have taken me back to my college. The bus stop was by a wooded arboretum a considerable distance from any campus building, so I stood alone in the snowy dark, knowing it would be an hour until the next one came. It was bitterly cold, probably below zero. I started to shiver and then began to catastrophize the situation. I didn't have gloves, and my fingers, even thrust into my pockets, were going numb. I couldn't feel my hands and arms; I worried I'd get frostbite.

At that point I noticed I had tensed my shoulders and was hunching over in a vain effort to keep myself warm. I thought back to a recent yoga relaxation exercise and decided to follow my breath and let my muscles loosen. As I relaxed, I experienced an intriguing cluster of sensations. The surface of my skin felt the cold air more intensely, but my muscles and inner organs began to feel warm. My thoughts calmed, and I could feel my arms and hands again.

I touched an inner warmth I'd previously been unaware of, even though it is my—and everyone's—constant companion. We take our warm-blooded nature for granted, rarely sensing how our body-and-mind maintains a comfortable temperature range for us, providing us access to equanimity.

Cultivating awareness and breathing, I literally "re-membered" myself. "Cold" was not an isolated measurement of the air temperature separate from me but an embodied idea influenced by conditioned habits. I could say it was cold out, and I could say I was cold—but I also could discover the cold moment was me, sustained by an inner warmth.

That night my mind and eyes told me I was freezing in the dark until I discovered there was more to the situation than I'd assumed. Similarly, in the Surangama Sutra, the Buddha teaches Ananda that so long as he unquestioningly believes that his mind and eyes tell him the whole truth of being, he will be limited to the sufferings of birth-and-death.

ILLUSIONS AND THE PSYCHOLOGY OF PERCEPTION

The Surangama Sutra emphasizes that we cannot realize enlightenment so long as we mistake the concepts we create for reality itself. This is not mystical esoterica. Modern neuroscience and perceptual psychology confirm that our nervous systems give us images of the world, not the world itself. There is wide variation in how people apprehend the world, along with surprising ways the world presents itself that defy simple representation. In order to communicate, we form abstract generalizations and label these with words. The word provides a map, but the map is not the world.[3] As the first verse of the *Tao Te Ching* reminds us:

> *The way that can be spoken of is not the eternal Way;*
> *the name that can be named is not the Immortal Name.*
> *Nameless the Source of earth and sky,*
> *names engender every thing.*
>
> *Unfettered by desire, the mystery reveals itself;*
> *wanting this gives rise to that.*
>
> *Beyond named and nameless, reality still flows;*
> *unfathomable the arch, the door, the gate.*[4]

Whether it's possible to have direct access to true reality is a matter of some debate in contemporary philosophy and perceptual neuroscience. Our senses provide an interface—bridges, if you will—for experiences that arise in the crossing. Buddhist psychology goes a little further in this area than conventional Western concepts: mind-consciousness joins seeing, hearing, tasting, touching, smelling as another avenue for "sensing" the world.

In the Surangama Sutra, the Buddha teaches us that through practice it is possible to dispel all delusions and directly contact true reality. Sometimes called "Buddha-Nature," this refers to reality appearing completely, with nothing added and nothing taken away. A related technical Buddhist term is *tathata*, usually translated as "suchness," "thusness," or "just this." The Buddha is sometimes referred to as the Tathagata, the "Thus-Come-One." Chan Buddhism asks us to crack open our doors of perception and rediscover our inner eyes and ears, to drop body-and-mind and truly wake up to the enlightened reality of body-mind, bodhi-mind, "just this."

We practice to become more aware of our bodies and beings, of where our minds and eyes are. That's the first step, but it's *only* a first step. Our senses mislead us. They are inherently incomplete and distorted—otherwise, our nervous systems would be overwhelmed by floods of information beyond their capacity. The problem is that in seeming complete, they foster the illusion that their shorthand summaries of the world, depicted as selves and objects, is the whole story. When we accept the tangible touch and taste of the world as givens, as "real," it's easy to believe our thoughts and feelings are "real" too. Then we are trapped within ideas of ourselves and mistake ourselves for our sensations and desires.

Paradoxically, our senses' illusions of completeness give rise to illusions of separateness. Because we don't see how we fail to see our connectedness, we believe we exist apart from the world that constitutes us.

It seems obvious that I exist "in here," excluded from the beings and things of a world "out there." This illusion is the source of much suffering: to be ultimately isolated from others, to be born and to die inherently alone. We yearn to bridge that painful separation, but, ambivalent, we also fear losing ourselves in the process. Meanwhile, we cannot understand how there can be anything other than what we see and experience. We assume that however we experience the world, others experience the world as we do, since that felt reality is "the world."

This self-centered childishness can be quite amusing. I remember one time visiting a friend who had forbidden her four-year-old son Aaron to have a stick of gum just before dinner.

About ten minutes later, I was chatting with my friend in her kitchen when we heard a wet smacking, chewing sound coming from the adjacent living room. We quietly peeked into the room and saw four-year-old Aaron, his head underneath the sofa, his feet and legs sticking out, surrounded by discarded chewing-gum wrappers. With his head hidden beneath the furniture, he'd stuffed a whole pack of gum in his mouth and was lustily enjoying it. Chomp! Chomp! Chomp! When Carol called him to come out and, trying not to laugh, scolded him for disobeying her, Aaron couldn't figure out how his mother knew what he was doing—she must have some mystic powers! His eyes and mind and mouth were in the dark, and if he couldn't see them, nobody else should be able to.

All of us hide our heads under the furniture we call "myself." Our enlightened nature is sweet and elastic and ordinary as chewing gum, with a flavor that never fades. We're continually chewing on ourselves, making bubbles until . . . *pop*.

When I first began practicing Zen meditation at Berkeley Zen Center, I was still chewing on myself, dazzled by the prospect of obtaining mystic powers that would bring me freedom from pain and confusion. I thought removing my inner obstacles and external stumbling blocks to practice would bring radiance. I didn't understand that the filament glows in the light of its resistance. I'd had a few *kenshos* (enlightenment experiences) but hadn't yet realized how much I was still in the dark.

After a few months at BZC, I signed up for my first *sesshin* (multiday meditation retreat) there. I'd attended Zen sesshins before and thought I knew what to expect. Some of my prior sesshins had been quite rigorous, meditating from 3 A.M. to midnight. When I saw BZC's sesshin schedule was from 5 A.M. to 9 P.M., I privately considered it a little too easy and too loose. Nonetheless, I looked forward to a relaxing five days. I was in a good mood when I arrived at the zendo at 4:45 A.M. the first day; I felt physically relaxed and psychologically calm.

If you're an experienced meditator, you probably can predict what happened next. As soon as I sat down on the cushion, I started to experience waves of anxiety and sadness, along with sharp shooting pains in my back, legs, and knees spreading to many other parts of my body. I was puzzled. I had arrived at the sesshin in good physical shape, from practicing yoga and running daily, and in a reasonably contented mood. I couldn't identify any particular stressors setting off the unpleasant feelings and sensations. The dysphoric emotions weren't accompanied by any distressing memories, worries, or regrets. I shrugged mentally and assumed I'd gradually settle down and have a pleasant time.

Nope. Each day was more painful physically than the last, despite my attempts to soothe my aching body with yoga during rest periods. Each session of zazen was more devastating emotionally than the last, despite my attempts to calm my aching mind with psychological inquiry and coping techniques. I was tossed by waves of intense sadness unalloyed by any thoughts or ideas I could grab hold of.

I felt desolate, grief-stricken, embarrassed by what I thought must be the inadequacy of my meditative technique, angry at a Zen practice that promised enlightenment and brought misery. I cried and cried, without knowing why. This continued through all five days of the sesshin.

On the last day, we had closing *shosan* ceremony: one by one, each of us were given a chance to stand up, go to the center of the meditation hall, face the teacher (Sojun Mel Weitsman), and ask a question from the depth of our heart. Sojun would make a terse reply, aiming to direct us to the fundamental point of our personal practice at that moment.

When my turn came, I told Sojun how I'd come to sesshin feeling wonderful but had plunged immediately into misery. I described my pain, my sadness, and my frustration at having no idea what or why this was happening.

Tearful and in anguish, I asked him, "What *is* this?"

Sojun paused, met my gaze, and answered me directly with one word: "Nirvana."

At that moment, something cracked open within me. I knew, with complete certainty, that Sojun was right. I didn't understand, yet somehow, I knew. Yes, this *is* nirvana.

The Surangama Sutra invites us to allow our usual understandings to crack open, to tolerate not-knowing, and to realize the Way. If you know your reasons for seeking the Way, that's fine. It's also fine if you don't know. It helps to trust that the Way-seeking mind is always at play.

Seeking seeks transparently, realizing itself along the Way, laying down a path by walking.[5] It does this through your feet and spine and heart; through your nose and tongue and skin; through your eyes and ears, body and mind. A good place to start is by attending to these, as the Buddha asks, "Where are your eyes and mind at this moment?"

2

Temptation and Intention

The Context for the Teaching

Have you ever been tempted to do something even though you knew you'd feel badly about it afterward: stress-eating ice cream, telling a white lie, having "just one more" drink, or indulging in a one-night stand? The Surangama Sutra speaks to these situations by framing its discourse, as noted in chapter 1, as the Buddha's response to one of his most beloved followers (almost) succumbing to sexual temptation.

Many of modern society's offerings and indulgences run contrary to our best interests, seducing us with convenience and enticing us with novelty. Even if we support efforts to reduce climate change, when it comes time to buy an automobile, we may choose one with the most comfortable seats rather than opting for the more fuel-efficient model. We may commit ourselves to the ethical principles of a spiritual path, but the undertows and rip currents of desire are powerful—many ministers practice what they preach should not be done.

Psychological research shows we are far more subject to outside influence and the pressures of immediate circumstances than we like to believe.[1] When the refreshments in an office's break room are funded by putting money in a box on the honor system, people don't typically notice the picture on the price list. They submit 2.76 times more cash, however, if the picture is a pair of observant eyes than when it's a posy of ornamental flowers.[2]

We draw moral maps to mark where the dangerous territories are, but we don't always respect the Do Not Enter signs—even when we're the ones who posted them, let alone when we chafe at restrictions imposed by others. Our internal rebukes and warnings falter when our self-talk soothes them with "just this once"; threats of social disapproval or potential punishment lose their sting in the face of "nobody will ever know." Our conditional conscience, our learned habits of "should" and "should not," and even a solemn public commitment to follow the precepts sometimes do not save us from straying. As verse 53 of the *Tao Te Ching* says, "The Great Path is very smooth and straight, but people are fond of bypaths."

A CAUTIONARY TALE

The prologue to the Surangama Sutra tells the story of how Ananda nearly strays from his avowed path. (In the previous chapter, I skipped over this prologue because I wanted to focus on the central question of "Why practice?") One day Ananda is on his daily begging rounds when he comes to a house of courtesans. The Buddha had instructed his monastic followers to beg from each household in turn, without discriminating the worthiness of the inhabitants or whether they were likely to receive a large or small donation. Coming to the brothel, Ananda wants to follow the Buddha's instructions; perhaps he also feels uncomfortable depriving people considered "deluded lowlifes" of the merit they'd accumulate by donating food. So he goes up to the door and holds up his bowl for alms.

> Wielding a spell that Kapila[3] had obtained from a god of the Brahma Heavens, a young Mātaṅga woman seduced Ānanda onto her bed. Then she caressed him lasciviously until the power of his vows was on the verge of being broken.[4]

The Buddha, through his supernatural powers, sees what is unfolding.

> Ānanda was succumbing to the carnal influence of the spell, [so] the Thus-Come-One . . . poured forth invincible light which was as dazzling as a hundred gems. Within that light sat a Buddha in full-lotus posture on a thousand-petaled sacred lotus, proclaiming a spiritually powerful mantra.

Buddha then sends Manjusri to Ananda. Using the spiritually powerful mantra (which we will encounter later in the sutra), Manjusri defeats the evil spell, saving Ananda and also the young Matanga woman from succumbing to their fatal attraction. He brings them back to the grove where Buddha is staying with his disciples. Ananda, weeping, beseeches Shakyamuni to teach him how to become fully awakened so he will not succumb to temptation again.

We can imagine Ananda's shame and regret through our own experiences of remorse after being caught in misbehavior. Furthermore, in the cultural context of the time, any sexual involvement was an obstacle to enlightenment. So was being born a woman. In modern Buddhism, we need to do a lot of work to redress such misogynistic strains. We also need to develop precepts that modulate sexuality beyond the extremes of celibacy and self-indulgence to better fit with current culture. (We'll return to this issue in some of the later chapters.)

For our present purpose, the issue is not so much that Ananda came close to—heaven forbid!—having sex. In Christianity, Islam, and Judaism, misdeeds incur the risk that a divine judge will render a verdict of "guilty" and impose a (possibly eternal) punishment. Buddhism is less judgmental but more pragmatic: everything we do has consequences (a.k.a. karma), so it's important to have our deeds align with our intentions.

When he became a monk, Ananda committed to a set of vows that included among them a vow of celibacy. Taking vows in front of witnesses in a solemn ceremony, sealing the commitment by shaving the head and donning monk's robes, carries significant power. If Ananda violated his vow of celibacy with a sexual liaison, he'd squander the power of his vows and likely encounter hurdles to his practice. He'd have to deal with his own shame, as well as with the responses of others—the courtesan, her associates, his fellow sangha members. All this would take energy and distract him from his meditation practice.

The harm we incur when we break a vow is not just that we do something "bad." When we vow one thing and do another, we undermine ourselves. This lowers our confidence and erodes our trust in ourselves. If we feel discouraged, if we feel we're unable to follow the path faithfully, we may even give up the practice, protesting, "It's too hard." The Buddha kindly called on us to "Please treasure yourselves." It's difficult to follow this teaching when we feel more like turds than treasure.

As a psychotherapist, I often saw clients resolve to make some change, then berate themselves when they did not follow through as they'd intended. They'd feel flawed, blame themselves for being insincere, or worry they lacked some important quality. Their willpower was "too weak," they were "incapable of love" or "not smart enough." Sometimes they'd shift the blame to account for their felt failures by saying they had been too injured by traumas, they had never received the kind of parenting they truly needed, or social circumstances put too many obstacles in their way. Perhaps their horoscope indicated their timing was off.

Their lack of success, though, lay not in their stars *nor* in their selves. People overestimate the power of will, underestimate the need to form and implement specific plans, and often don't take a hard look at the influence (and impermanence) of fluctuating external circumstances. Psychological research shows that goal intentions account for no more than 28 percent of the variance in what people actually end up doing.[5]

Our human delusions of greed and pride bring with them a tendency to overreach, to overestimate our abilities while underestimating the practical difficulties, to expect and grasp at too much too soon. We can be sincerely well-intentioned and sincere in our aspirations, even capable of occasional honest self-observation. However, we have a tendency to conflate imagination with actuation. When we form an intention to be more loving, or more efficient, or less short-tempered, or less ruled by fear, it often comes with a magical tinge: "If I think it, it must/should be so."

HEAPS OF DELUSION

What was it, then, that came between Ananda's well-formed intentions and his behavior with the courtesan? Ananda was nearly seduced by the image of carnal loveliness produced by Kapila's magic spell wielded by the Matanga woman. A significant portion of the Surangama Sutra consists of analyzing how such illusions arise. In a later chapter, the Buddha says to Ananda,

> Ananda, you have not yet understood that the objects we perceive are unreal and illusory. They are subject to change, appearing here and there and disappearing here and there. Yet these illusions, each with its conventional designation, are in fact within the essential, wondrous enlightenment. The same is true of the five aggregates, the six faculties, the twelve sites, and the eighteen constituent elements . . .[6]

But let's not get ahead of ourselves—we are still in the prologue of the sutra. In the next few chapters, the Buddha lays the groundwork for this broad statement by challenging Ananda's (and our) assumptions about what constitutes "reality." For now, let's just take a moment to consider the five aggregates, also called the "heaps," or *skandhas*.

A fundamental tenet of all forms of Buddhism is that everything is composed of collections of heaps, rather than consisting of some fundamental essence. In traditional Western philosophy and science, this evolved into the atomistic approach, which analyzed material compounds into elements, elements into atoms. In the twentieth century, scientists discovered atoms are not indivisible but composed of further heaps of fundamental forces and elementary particles.[7] The radical consequence for both Buddhist and Western physics is the absence of essence: no "thing" exists in and of itself. It's convenient in everyday experience to refer to individual things we can hold, see, and point to, but fundamentally these are illusory appearances. Material things that seem to be static and permanent are arising and disappearing every moment in continuous, dynamic processes.

In Buddhism, the five skandhas are variously translated as follows:

- Form (material image, impression)
- Feelings (or sensations)
- Perceptions
- Formations (mental activity, intention, impulse)
- Consciousness (thought, mind, discernment)

If even the skandhas of form (materiality) and consciousness are components of illusions, we should know that thinking something doesn't make it so. Nevertheless, if we make a mistake and reify our thoughts—saying to ourselves, for example, "I *never* get anything right!"—our belief in this distortion makes it a fact. The fact becomes "our thing" and may cause us to stop making the effort—and, in the process, make the belief a self-fulfilled prophecy. Under the influence of "I never" we can box ourselves and others into despair, forgetting how just a short while ago we managed to tie our shoes, fry an egg, and drive on a crowded freeway without crashing. Cognitive-behavior therapists like to point out the toxic nature of overgeneralization and all-or-nothing thinking in "I never," but the Surangama Sutra will help us appreciate the subtler foundations of our delusions, namely our assumption that things exist as separate entities and our very belief in an essence of "I."

ACTUALIZING

The problem with illusions is how their images distract us from our actual circumstances. A desert traveler who, deceived by a mirage of an oasis just ahead, guzzles the last bit of water from their canteen might regret it when they arrive at the spot and find nothing but sand. Had Ananda succumbed to the magical mirage of loveliness and had sexual intercourse with the Matanga concubine, perhaps he'd have felt postcoital regret blinding him to the real loveliness of the actual woman he'd slept with. The pleasure of a one-night stand often fades with the awkwardness of waking up the following morning to the stranger beside you—and the stranger "within" you. You might have difficulties recognizing yourself in your actions.

Ananda was not only tempted by a vision of loveliness; he was also taken in by an illusory vision of himself as someone who, as an avowed practitioner, would not be susceptible to temptation. Our attachment to ideal visions of ourselves often leads us to discount our limitations and vulnerabilities—at our and others' peril. Many well-meaning spiritual leaders have caused problems for themselves and their communities by transgressing boundaries of power and intimacy.

We need to have the humility to acknowledge our human susceptibilities. Early in my practice at BZC, I witnessed a lesson in this during an exchange between a student and our abbot, Sojun:

> STUDENT: As far as I can tell, you've managed to steer clear of most of the wrongdoings that have ensnared many Zen teachers. How do you avoid falling into the dark alleys?
> SOJUN: By knowing the dark alleys like the palms of my hands.

We need to cultivate this attitude, but we can't rely completely on our own efforts since, by definition, we can't see our own blind spots. Sojun presided over BZC for more than fifty years without any major scandals, but he was helped by having empowered a co-abbot (Alan Senauke), an ethics committee, and longtime senior students he could rely on when misunderstandings and missteps inevitably occurred.

Our ideal visions and aspirations can also get in the way of taking the concrete steps necessary to realize them. Right intention is important, but our intentions can be as seductive as any courtesan, so it's important not to be beguiled by them into forgetting that practice is nitty-gritty. Some years ago, I attended a New Year meditation session where people gave voice to their practice resolutions for the coming year. After listening to folks expressing their sincere intention to meditate in the morning, or to practice one of the *paramitas*, or to attend more retreats, I suggested we might spend some time discussing the specifics of how we planned to implement these lofty goals. I was roundly condemned for dirtying lofty goals with trivial technicalities and casting doubt on peoples' sincerity.

Sincerity and determination are crucial, but they are incomplete without the details of doing. Getting things done is usually much harder than dreaming up what might be done. As T. S. Eliot put it,

> *Between the idea*
> *And the reality*
> *Between the motion*
> *And the act*
> *Falls the shadow.*[8]

The shadow arises when ideas and images substitute for substance. Consider the books on your shelf: they give the appearance to others that you know what's in them. How does their appearance on the shelf affect *your* sense of knowing them? How many of them have you read completely, how many have you skimmed, and how many have you *meant* to read but never got around to?

The danger is that once I form a vision—whether the vision is of reading a book, of being able to withstand the lure of sex, of meditating daily, or of being kind to everyone—the petty details of how to implement the vision in practical, small steps may seem unimportant. This can be due to a combination of pride ("I am able to do this") and optimism ("Nothing's likely to get in the way"). We can mistake the imagined accomplishment as "no sooner said than done." This easily leads to disappointment, pessimism, and shame. Sometimes we simply don't know how to implement a change but feel too embarrassed to ask for help.

Research on the implementation of intentions shows rates of any follow-through are low, and those of sustained follow-through are even lower. Medication compliance rates are around 30–50 percent. That's for something as simple and important as taking a pill—much easier than sitting down on the meditation cushion every day or being generous and kind to everyone we encounter. Breaking a habit such as losing your temper, smoking cigarettes, abusing alcohol, or engaging in inappropriate sexual behavior is even more difficult.

A few years ago, I learned a humbling lesson in the difficulties of changing even a seemingly trivial habit. I became aware that each morning I got into my car, pulled out of the garage, then put my seat belt on when I came to the first stop sign. I thought it would be better to buckle the seat belt first thing, before turning on the ignition. I formed a firm resolve to do so, but the following morning, when I came to the stop sign, I realized I'd forgotten. So I reminded myself: "Next time, don't forget!"

Next time, I forgot. At the stop sign, as I put on the seat belt, I felt frustrated and annoyed at myself. Surely this surge of negative emotion would be enough to help me remember to comply with my intention the next day.

Nope. To make a long story short, I struggled with this for over a year. Sometimes at night, before going to bed, I'd reinforce my commitment and remind myself of my intention. Occasionally this would work, but more often than not it wouldn't overcome my early morning mental fog and urgency of getting to work on time. On the plus side, I did usually succeed in getting my seat belt on a little earlier—by the time I was exiting the garage—but I failed to put it on consistently before starting out.

Then I moved into a new neighborhood where I parked on the street. The area had a higher crime rate, so I purchased a steering wheel lock, The Club. The next day I got into my car, unlocked the steering wheel—and put on my seat belt before turning on the ignition! From then on, I fastened my seat belt as I meant to.

The lock on the steering wheel interrupted my automatic behavior. Until then, I'd been unable to alter my habit. As a psychologist, I was familiar with the concept of automatic chains of behavior, where each link summons the next. I just never thought it would apply to *me*. After all, wasn't I a devoted mindfulness practitioner?

Change is ubiquitous, but changing our conditioned habits requires the humility of step-by-step specificity. We are biological beings who get tired and forget. We are social beings subject to the influences of those around us. We are human beings subject to conditioning and karma. I wonder what would have happened if Ananda had paused in his begging rounds, looked at the house of courtesans, thought of how he'd woken up that morning feeling horny, and decided he might need to make a specific plan to deal with the situation. He could have decided to ask a fellow sangha member to accompany him; he could have chosen to pass by the house and not tempt himself, given the possibility he could be overwhelmed. Such planning could have protected both Ananda and the courtesan but would have required Ananda to be honest enough to acknowledge he had not yet reached the lofty realms of realization of a Vimalakirti.[9]

If Ananda, an esteemed devotee of the Buddha, was easily overwhelmed in his circumstances, how much more do we need the capacity to pause and seek clarity today? In our current society, someone is trying to seduce our attention all the time via billboards, newspapers, social media, and clickbait. We need to be careful to limit our exposure to what we're capable of handling. It's not a great idea for a recovering alcoholic to go into a bar; it's not a great idea for someone whose Buddhist practice has not fully matured to go into a brothel. It takes humility, though, to acknowledge the frailties of our self-control.

We need to support our efforts by relying not just on our personal willpower—limited at best—but also by building resilient structures in our communities, our homes, and our practice methods. One way of building resilience is to introduce what systems theorists call "redundancies," multiple ways of realizing the same goal. If you only practice meditation on the breath, you'll have difficulties meditating when you have pneumonia, asthma, or a panic attack. At such times, it helps to have some experience with meditating on posture, a mantra, or a koan—or, for that matter, a toothbrush—to fall back on.

You can meditate in the morning and hope it will make you sufficiently mindful to inoculate you against stress as you go about your day. But you can also meditate in the morning, recognize your susceptibility to the pressures of daily life, and schedule in time for a lunchtime run or join a friend in a refresher period of contemplation and comradeship. Zen teacher Bernie Glassman used to set his watch to go off at noon to remind him to stop whatever he was doing and take a minute of silence to offer *metta* (loving-kindness) to the world. Perhaps, as you look at your daily calendar and notice a difficult phone call scheduled for 3 P.M., you might make a plan such as, "Before dialing the number, I'll take a deep breath. Then as I touch the numbers, I'll do so gently and cultivate kindness." If you tell a friend of your plan, you'll be even more likely to follow through; sharing your practice widens your community and adds their support to your individual efforts.

When we first start to practice meditation, we may harbor idealistic fantasies that meditation will, by itself, protect us against the infections of greed, hate, and delusion. At some point, we understand that meditation cannot exist by itself. Meditation can only express itself in our relationships with all the beings we interact with, bodies and minds with felicities and flaws.

Realization is about making our practice real. Facing a difficult phone call with a difficult person offers a real opportunity for practicing mindfulness. At that point, though, we still need to construct the specifics of turning our awareness into action so that we can be gracious hosts, greeting the person at the other end of the line as our guest in the practice place we've assembled.

3

The Nature and Location of the Mind

Unreal

When Ananda asks Buddha for instruction, Shakyamuni responds, as we have seen, by asking Ananda what attracted him to the Dharma in the first place. Ananda replies that, having seen with his own eyes the thirty-two radiant hallmarks of the Thus-Come-One shining like crystal, his mind was filled with admiration and delight. Shakyamuni presses him on this: "Precisely where are your mind and eyes?"

Ananda has difficulty responding to the Buddha's question. He proposes one answer after another—the mind is in the body; no, the mind is outside the body; the mind is in the middle; the mind lies within the sense-faculties; the mind arises in response to conditions. Using metaphors and reasoning, the Buddha dismantles each proposition until finally, in desperation, Ananda proposes the mind has no specific location—to which the Buddha replies that if there's no *where* that mind exists, how can it exist at all?

> Does the mind that you suppose has no specific location exist in some place, or else does it exist in no place?

> If it is located nowhere, then it is an absurdity—like a turtle with fur or a hare with horns. How can you speak of something that does not have a specific location?
>
> Suppose, however, things could in fact exist without a definite location. . . . What[ever] does exist has attributes. And whatever has attributes does have a location. How can you say then that the mind has no specific location?
>
> Therefore, you should know that when you say the mind . . . has no specific location, you state what is impossible.[1]

I'm not going to delve into details of Ananda's answers and the Buddha's refutations here. We'll visit some of the issues in more depth further on in the sutra. For now, let's start with a fairly simple example by slightly rephrasing Buddha's question to Ananda. Let me ask you: Where are your thoughts?

BRAINS AND MINDS

If we were to cut open your skull and peer inside while you were pondering, we wouldn't see any thoughts. We'd see a gooey mass of brown-gray-peach-colored flesh marbled with white fibers and reddish blood vessels. You might object, "Well, of course we couldn't *see* the thoughts. They're in the neurons firing, too small for us to see." Thoughts, though, are not inside the neurons nor in the synapses. Despite the media hype in blaring headlines, such as JENNIFER ANISTON STRIKES A NERVE: SINGLE BRAIN CELLS SHOW SELECTIVE RESPONSE TO SPECIFIC CELEBRITY PHOTOS,[2] there's no one-to-one correspondence between any single neuron and a single thought or image arising from it. Sometimes if you stimulate a single neuron repeatedly, a single percept arises. But sometimes when you stimulate a single neuron repeatedly, different percepts arise. And sometimes, stimulating different single neurons leads to the same percept. The brain functions via multiple pathways to the same end, and multiple ends to the same pathway.[3]

Our thoughts are not in our heads. There's a tendency in popular accounts of neuroscience to ascribe everything we're aware of to what happens in our brains. Despite the fact that when we're angry, we can feel our hearts beat faster and our muscles tense, there's a view that points to a single brain structure—the amygdala—as the source of our rage and fear. This not only ignores the contributions of other parts of the body but grossly oversimplifies the situation. The amygdala lights up when a frightening face is seen in a full-frontal view but not when the face is in profile; the amygdala also lights up during pleasant emotional states and in response to novel stimuli.[4]

Don't be misled by pretty pictures of brain scans, which can be very deceptive; they are usually composites of multiple brains, averages that no individual brain completely conforms to. Brain scans are not precise: at their best resolution, each dot in current magnetic resonance imagings (MRIs) represents about 630,000 neurons. If you seek to locate thought in the electrical activity of the brain, you'll find it spread across complex networks far more tangled than the wires of a switchboard. Seeing thoughts as being "in" neurons would be like trying to find the meaning of a paragraph by examining the individual letters of the constituent words.

When you play a flute or clarinet, opening and closing certain combinations of holes produces a specific note, but the entire instrument vibrates. The same is true of the brain: all of it is continually oscillating. Think of how striking one key on a grand piano invokes vibrations on the strings of all the other notes that are engaged, bringing forth harmonics in countless tonal colors. Multiply the eighty-eight keys of the piano by the 85 billion neurons in a human brain, and you begin to get a sense of the vastness of the universe of the mind.

Furthermore, electrical activity is certainly not the whole story in brain functioning. Chemical changes are important, and neurotransmitters don't localize precisely; seepage and spreading occurs across and around areas. Fluid (blood, cerebrospinal, and intracellular) flows play an important role, and subtle shifts in neuron sizes during nerve conduction may also influence the process. The prevailing theory in current neuropsychology suggests that while some functions are prone to be found in certain brain locations more than others, these locations are not static: small hub networks arise temporarily in response to specific situations, then dissipate as the brain rewires itself to process the next set of circumstances. Because so many interacting factors are involved, many neuroscientists believe the subjective experience of conscious thought is an emergent process that cannot be tied to isolated components of the brain. They are therefore skeptical that we will ever be able to locate "where" thoughts occur—or even "what" they are.

All of which is to say: *the brain is not the mind.* The brain is not even the entire central nervous system (CNS). The CNS is not restricted to the space in the skull, as it also occupies the spine and is intimately tied to the peripheral nervous system. All of the nervous system is sensitive to changes in heat and cold, to pressure, to what's circulating in the bloodstream, and to what's occurring in the gut, the bacteria of the mouth, and the health of the skin. This intertwining of nervous system and environment has important implications for our understanding of mind. Mind does not exist separate from minding; mind realizes itself in constant dynamic activity.

"Knowing" thoughts are in our heads leads too many meditators to meditate only from the neck up. Many cultures "know" differently. Some cultures locate thought in the heart. The Chinese and Japanese use the same written character for "heart" and "mind," and many meditation methods are best practiced "in" or "with" the heart (for example, Thich Nhat Hanh suggests cultivating heart-smiles). Many cultures see thinking as a product of what happens in the gut. When I was introduced to meditation in Japan, I was told to put my thoughts in my *hara* (belly, gut, lower *dantien*) or, if that was too hard, to hold my thoughts in the mudra formed by my hands. Even our own culture talks about "gut feelings." Biologists are investigating the gut-brain axis, and the bidirectional communication between the enteric and central nervous systems.

Moving beyond the boundary of the skin, many cultures believe thoughts are present in nature spirits: trees, animals, all the myriad beings—including the seemingly inanimate—with which we share the world. Some of these cultures believe such beings transfer their thoughts to us during our everyday activities, and especially in dreaming and sacred trances.

Recent research on embodied cognition shows the entire body participates in the experience of thinking.[5] For example, when we think about the future, our bodies tend to incline slightly forward, and when we think of the past, our bodies lean slightly back. Our thoughts are subject to environmental factors such as pollutants, heat/cold, music/noise, and the whole of nature. If you meditate under a willow tree, you will have a different experience than meditating next to a pine or sequoia.

The crucial points here are that thoughts have no fixed physical location, and they arise in response to far more than what occurs in our heads. Thoughts are not tangible things. They are more insubstantial and more variable even than clouds—and sometimes heavier and more opaque. Clouds take form as bright cumulus billows and dark pouring rain; thoughts take form as dazzling self-instructions and inky images.

CLOUDS OF WITNESS

It's certainly important to witness the clouds of our mental processes, but we don't always take the next step to examine the clouds that arise through witnessing. In the sutra, the Buddha takes Ananda through a series of questions on the location of the mind to help the latter realize his excessive reliance on conceptual formations. Faced with the nonlocalizable mind that nevertheless is not without location, Ananda exclaims, "All I have done is to become learned, and so I am not yet free!"[6]

Given our modern fascination with thoughts, brains, and neuroscience, we'd be wise to take a lesson from this. Trying to use intellectual understanding to solve all our problems is one of our prime ways of confusing ourselves. When we get lost in mental worlds, we can mistake them for genuine reality without probing further into how—and whether—we can know what we "know."

This is the terrain of epistemology, which refers to the study of the nature, origin, and limits of human knowledge. If I remain unaware of my epistemological assumptions, my meditation practice will be hemmed in by my conditioned habits of knowing. Much of the initial portion of the Surangama Sutra is devoted to the Buddha helping Ananda become aware of the limits of his unexamined assumptions.

The Buddha begins a long epistemological excursion, drawing on centuries of Buddhist analyses of the mind and its vicissitudes. He makes use of the *abhidhamma,* the volumes of Buddhist psychology and philosophy that constitute one of the three parts of the Buddhist canon; teachings from Yogacara, the "consciousness-only" school of Indian Mahayana Buddhism, subsequently developed in East Asia; and teachings from *Madhyamaka*, the "middle way" school most famously associated with Nagarjuna, which became known for its fearsome negation of all conceptual views. Along this journey, readers of the sutra encounter the five aggregates, the six faculties, the twelve sites, the eighteen constituents, and other classical Buddhist teachings about mind and reality.

It's easy to get lost in these philosophical deconstructions or feel they're irrelevant to the issue at hand. After all, while the enticing young Matanga woman is caressing Ananda, he's more likely to be aware of his rapid breathing, his elevated heartbeat, and his hard penis than of the eighteen constituents. The eighteen constituents are just an idea, while the hormones rushing through his bloodstream, the feel of warm flesh, the amber of her eyes, and the red of her lips are *real*, right?

Actually, they're not real. They're also not unreal. But they are so very *convincing* that they easily snare us. Ananda gets tangled up by a confluence of sensations, perceptions, feelings, thoughts, and desires, in part because he fails to fully recognize them as "clouds of witness," transitory manifestations of the skandhas. In Mahayana Buddhism, all five skandhas are empty: *every* impression we have of material solidity (form—the curvaceous, warm flesh of the Matanga woman); *every* perception (the sight of the courtesan, the sound of her song), *every* feeling tone ("She's wonderful!"); *every* formation (the intention and accompanying impulse, "I want her") is a lacuna ultimately void of any core, permanent essence.

Not only form, perception, feeling, and formation are empty; the fifth skandha, mind-consciousness, is empty as well. We tend to overlook this when we overvalue thinking and awareness. One sign of the emptiness of mind, consciousness, and thought is how Buddhist practitioners, Western philosophers, and neuroscientists—whether within each group or between them—can't agree on a definition of "thought," "consciousness," or "mind." At this point in the sutra, though, Ananda is only ready to take a few tentative steps toward Buddha-Mind. Remorseful about his susceptibility to pleasurable sensations, Ananda asks the Buddha to help him purify his mind.

PURIFYING MIND?

We like to think that if we purify our minds, we'll be able to rely on them, that our minds will rule over our wayward senses and thoughts. Ananda had worked on his mind through diligent study, but relying solely on his intelligence left him lost in his learning. Ananda's abstract avowal of chastity faltered when he was touched by a beautiful woman and confronted by actual sexual desire.

Information about the Dharma can only take us so far. Something similar can happen in psychotherapy if there's too much emphasis on understanding oneself and not enough focus on different *doing*. At some point, gathering more and more information becomes fruitless, as "one's self" is not a thing that stays still. Adding information both alters the self and runs the danger of bogging it down in what it "knows" to be true. Verse 48 of the *Tao Te*

Ching points out the danger: "Seek learning? Increase daily. Seek the Way? Decrease daily!"

The problem, the Buddha says, is that Ananda is caught by the "first fundamental": the mind of death-and-birth, the mind dependent on perceived objects. However, there is a second fundamental, beginningless and endless, namely

> the original understanding, the real nature of consciousness.
>
> All conditioned phenomena arise from it, and yet it is among those phenomena that beings lose track of it. They have lost track of this fundamental understanding though it is active in them all day long, and because they remain unaware of it, they make the[ir] mistakes.[7]

The Buddha's teachings in the Surangama Sutra aim to guide us back to this original understanding, to what Zen often calls True Mind, Unconditioned Mind, Big Mind, or "the mind of clover." The Buddha describes this as the pure and luminous mind that understands without mental objects or the processes arising with them. This luminous mind was a major focus of the Chan lineages in China—to understand or intuit something about it, as a first step, and ultimately to realize it for oneself.

The third-century patriarch Jianzhi Seng-ts'an, one of the earliest Chan adepts, gave a fundamental instruction in his famous poem *Hsin-Hsin Ming* (Faith in Mind[8]): "To seek Mind with the discriminating mind is the greatest of all mistakes." It's easy to confuse this fundamental Mind with the conditioned mind, the "mind" with a lowercase *m*. When we assign the properties of small mind to Big Mind, we miss the fundamental point: *Mind is ungraspable.*

Most of us like to imagine we can manage the mind. Many meditators attempt to use the mind to find the mind and wind up chasing their own tails. (So do many psychotherapists.) Some students (and clients) feel they've failed when they cannot control the mind and quiet it sufficiently to attain *samadhi* (or "mental health").

This apparently has been a common experience for a long time, as it's the subject of the forty-first koan of one of the classic koan collections, the *Mumonkan* (*Gateless Barrier* or *Gateless Gate*). The koan describes the legendary first patriarch of Chan, Bodhidharma, sitting facing a wall. He's been meditating for eight years. His future successor, Dazu Huike, has been fruitlessly appealing to Bodhidharma to take him on as a student. Huike stands in the snow to show his resolve, eventually becoming so desperate that he cuts off his arm and presents it to Bodhidharma as a token of sincerity. "Very well," snaps Bodhidharma at the interruption. "What is it?"

> Dazu Huike cries, "My mind is not pacified. Master, pacify my mind."
>
> Bodhidharma promises, "If you bring me that mind, I will pacify it for you."
>
> Dazu Huike complains, "No matter how much I search my mind, I can't grab hold of it to bring it out for you."
>
> Bodhidharma: "Ha! Pacified already!"

According to the story, at this point Dazu Huike immediately experiences *satori*, a full realization of True Mind.

Many students, though, are more puzzled than enlightened. Like Dazu Huike, they complain to their teachers, "I'm terrible at meditation. I keep having thoughts." Reassuring them this is natural usually isn't all that helpful so long as the student continues to view meditation as a technique for controlling the mind to produce an idealized mental state. As soon as you identify certain characteristics necessary for a particularly desirable kind of mind, the specs limit it to being some special *thing*. Special things are, by definition, rare and transient. How could something special be ever-present?

Meditation doesn't aim at creating some special state of mind. Indeed, meditation isn't something to *do* at all. Meditation simply makes room for mind to manifest naturally, to assume any and all of its forms. Usually we have some ideas of how we want mind to be or how mind "should" be. It can be disappointing to discover True Mind is truly nothing special.[9] Any defining characteristics would constrain it. Eihei Dogen, in his essay "The Triple World Is Only Mind," writes (italics are mine),

> *walls, tiles, and pebbles are mind . . .*
> *it has thinking, sensing, mindfulness, and realization*
> *and it is free of thinking, sensing, mindfulness,*
> *and realization . . .*
> *Blues, yellows, reds, and whites are the mind.*
> *The long, the short, the square, and the round are the mind.*
> *Living-and-dying and coming-and-going are the mind.*
> *Years, months, days, and hours are the mind.*
> *Dreams and fantasies, and flowers in space, are the mind.*
> *The spray of water, foam, and flame are the mind.*
> *Spring flowers and the autumn moon are the mind.*
> *Each moment is the mind.* And yet it can never be broken.[10]

I-MIND

As anyone who has spent time in a psychiatric or neurology clinic can tell you, the mind we're most used to—the mind of thoughts and attention, sensations and perceptions, intellect and feeling—can most definitely be broken. The breakable small mind is continually making distinctions we need to navigate the world. The physical brain and the psychological ego[11] look to differentiate what is safe from what is dangerous, what is desirable from what is not, what is achievable from what is impossible. The "free energy" functions of the brain are continuously identifying patterns to predict the organism's needs and allocate resources accordingly, while the psychological ego strives to obtain pleasure and avoid pain. In effect, mind and brain imitate a former New York City mayor, Ed Koch, in his habit of going around asking his constituents, "How am I doing? How am I doing?"

Our conditioning is heavily biased to immediate experience, so we often respond automatically. With extra effort, and especially when things do not go smoothly, we can engage in longer-term planning and error correction. This is sometimes known as "dual process theory" or, more recently, due to the influence of Daniel Kahneman's influential book *Thinking, Fast and Slow* as "System 1" and "System 2" information-processing.[12] In both System 1 and System 2, the ego-mind functions by discriminating analysis, drawing distinctions between things depending on whether they are the same or different: pleasant or unpleasant, in or out, me or you. Ego-mind protects and guards us by making such distinctions, drawing on past experience, comparing it with current environmental conditions, and imagining what will happen next.

We need to highlight one other aspect of ego-mind: we identify closely with it and can even equate ourselves with it. Ego-mind is *my* mind. The most fundamental distinction ego-mind draws is between self and other. The ego-mind points to *my* feelings, *my* body, as separate from yours. To the Cartesian "I think, therefore, I am," ego-mind adds, "I feel (sense, want), therefore, I am."

Our sense of ourselves as separate entities is a function of ego-mind. Ego-mind insists, "I can make up my own mind" while disregarding the question of who is doing the deciding. It revels in fragments and can even say, "I'm not myself today," or "I'm of two minds about that," because it appropriates ownership of "me." Its sense of ownership further confuses us by seeming to separate mind from body when they are two sides to one coin.

What we usually call the mind is this activity of discriminatory thinking that insists, "I am." Using the fancy Latin word *ego* can make it sound like something special or mysterious, so I prefer to use the term "I-mind."

In the Surangama Sutra, the Buddha demonstrates the problems that arise when we depend solely on I-mind for understanding. To help Ananda realize the fundamental nature of True Mind, Buddha raises his golden-hued arm, makes a fist, and sends forth brilliant light. He then asks Ananda what he takes to be the mind that is dazzled by the light. Ananda replies his mind is that which has the capability of seeing, that which makes distinctions between light and dark, and that which determines "Bright! Dazzling! Buddha-fist!"

To which Buddha replies,

> *Ananda! That is not your mind!*[13] [my italics]
> . . . It is merely your mental processes that assign false and illusory attributes to the world of perceived objects . . .

> these processes delude you about your true nature . . . [and cause you] to lose touch with your own original, everlasting mind.[14]

OMIND

I-mind draws distinctions depending on whether things are self or perceived object, existent or nonexistent, the same or different. Once there is a fork in the mind's road, suffering marks each path. Beginning here and continuing for the next several sections of the Surangama Sutra, the Buddha teaches how liberation is available via the original, everlasting mind—the mind that cannot be boxed into "same as" or "different from," the mind that greets all being and nonbeing with equal love.

When we don't confuse mind with the objects of mind, we are freed from the illusion of perceptive selves that exist apart from that which they perceive; the seer and the seen arise together as beings, not as things. Here and now, mind is not a thing, not a "that," but the play of interbeing: "just this," the mind of equanimity, the mind of liberation that sees each in all and all in each.

The mind of liberation is neither grasping nor graspable; it is even free from discriminating "all" separate from "some." Eihei Dogen alludes to this mind when he says, "The Buddha Way is, basically, leaping clear of the many and the one."[15] Let's coin the term "OMind" for this Original Mind that, free from discriminative thinking, finds its home "far beyond form and emptiness." Whereas I-mind functions via concepts (both conscious ideas and webs of neurological associations that may or may not be conscious), OMind is *inconceivable*. This doesn't imply OMind need be esoteric or mystical. There are many phenomena we can label but can't nail down to something graspable: for example, twelve-dimensional space, infinity, *sunyata* (empty emptiness), and Lewis Carroll's Boojum Snark. OMind consists of and encompasses ordinary mind. Taoists speak of OMind when they say, "*Just natural!*"[16]

I hope OMind can evoke what the late Zen teacher Robert Aitken calls "the mind of clover."[17] Perhaps it can also echo the sound of the ubiquitous chants of OM MANI PADME HUM that continually thrum from Buddhist temples and villages in the high mountains of the Himalayas. OMind can help us cultivate an awareness of the space in mind, the vast container that encompasses all life and death. This is the mind conveyed intimately when one person plucks a flower and another person smiles; the words of I-mind give way to thunderous silence, a gasp, or a shout: "Oh!Mmmmm-i-n-d."

Here I am having fun with OMind, but in naming it, I need to be careful not to delude myself, or you, into thinking we can grasp it. Names seduce us with images, tempting us to turn intangibles into things. We relate to our minds through our bodies, and while words can point to vastness, we tend to think of "vastness" through the lens of a physical universe we can have and hold. Trying to seize OMind, we separate ourselves from it and turn both "I" and "OMind" into objects. We also introduce an artificial division between I-mind and OMind, but they are not two separate "entities." OMind includes I-mind; I-mind depends on OMind. In Zen parlance, we'd call them not-two, not-one: "although not one, not different; although not different, not the same."[18]

In Zen, we sometimes try to convey OMind through the simile of the ocean. We are fish swimming in the seas of Mind; our thoughts are bubbles, our bodies dependent on a briny world that, because it is our element, we take for granted. We are subject to its currents and tides, but being immersed in water, we cannot perceive its wetness.

In this simile, the ocean manifests itself through waves: no waves without water, no water without waves. My teacher used to say Zen practice is learning to navigate the surface waves while keeping our feet on the seabed. Even when we manage to do this, though, we're likely not aware of the far-off coastlines that contain our homes, the atmosphere above that grants us oxygen to breathe, the river of stars that surround us unseen.

OMind is vast beyond physical space-time, utterly without defining characteristics. In the Surangama Sutra, it's sometimes described as the Matrix of the Thus-Come-One. In *The Transmission of the Lamp*, Keizan Jokin—a fourteenth-century Zen master in Dogen's lineage—describes OMind like this:

> *There is a knowing apart from passionate thought and discrimination . . .*
> *It makes one raise one's eyebrows and blink.*
> *It makes one walk, stand, sit, and lie down,*
> *be confused, get into trouble,*
> *die here and be born there,*
> *eat when hungry and sleep when tired. . . .*
> *Is That One who appears magnificently . . .*
> *it is revealed in everything,*
> *including the croaking of bullfrogs*
> *and the sounds of earthworms.*[19]

How could it not include you?

4

The Nature of Visual Awareness

Seeing and Believing

Our I-mind is wedded to discriminative analysis and a sense of self, so it insists on separation. Holding itself apart, it fails to see itself in OMind. When we mistake our mind as "the part of *me* that distinguishes objects of perception, operates on information, and differentiates light from dark," we make the mistake of believing "*I* see things as they are."

Buddhist teachers sometimes offer the metaphor of an eternally pure mirror that reflects whatever comes.[1] This metaphor is evocative, but we need to recognize its limitations. During everyday life, when we look in a mirror, it shows a warped version of ourselves. It flattens us, reverses right and left, and is easily biased by our fears and hopes. It doesn't show our distorted sense of who we are, nor does it necessarily convey how others see us.

All our visual images are constricted by the limitations of our visual apparatus as well as colored by our concepts and desires. To take the image as the reality is to be corrupted in the same way Ananda was (almost) corrupted by the vision of loveliness he encountered in the Matanga courtesan. Shakyamuni warns Ananda,

> All that you can now see—the mountains, the rivers, the many lands, and the various forms of life—are the result of a disease that has existed in your visual awareness since time without beginning.[2]

We all succumb to the disease that deceives us into believing our senses are an accurate bridge between our I-mind "inside" us and the world "outside" us. Even in this age of Photoshop, we still say, "Seeing is believing." The page of words you see at this moment appears as your present reality, but it hides the ink and phosphors, the earth elements, the straight lines and curves that constitute it. You do not see the human sweat that molded it, and your sight cannot point to the ideas emerging from it.

In the previous chapter, we began exploring how our thoughts are really unreal. The remainder of the Surangama Sutra extends this to apply to all our sense-impressions, starting in this section with a lengthy discourse on the nature of visual awareness. To give you a feel for its complexity and detail, here's a list of this section's chapter headings:

- It Is the Mind That Sees
- Visual Awareness Does Not Move
- Visual Awareness Does Not Perish
- The True Nature of Visual Awareness Is Not Lost
- Visual Awareness Is Not Dependent upon Conditions
- Visual Awareness Is Not a Perceived Object
- Visual Awareness Has Neither Shape nor Extension
- Visual Awareness Is Both Separate and Not Separate from Objects

- Visual Awareness Arises Neither on Its Own nor from Causes
- True Visual Awareness
- Distortions in Visual Awareness Based on Karma
- Visual Awareness Exists Neither through Inhering nor in Conjoining

I won't attempt to cover all the issues this section brings up, but I hope to convey the main thrust of how the Buddha deconstructs visual delusions to help us see differently, perceive new perspectives on meditation, and glimpse wider realms of practice.

VICISSITUDES OF VISION

Shakyamuni begins by reminding us that it is the mind that sees, not the eyes. This is no surprise to anyone with a basic knowledge of the neurophysiology of vision. Light reflects off objects and passes through the lens of the eye to the rods and cones of the retina, where the light energy is converted into nerve impulses that crisscross on their way to the lateral geniculate nucleus and superior colliculus of the midbrain. From there the information is passed to the brain's occipital lobe, where the visual cortex assembles it into a conscious image. We assume the result (what we see) is a reasonably accurate representation "in" our minds of the objects around us. Unless we're disturbed by some anomaly, we usually take visual perception for granted, evincing a trusting belief in the reality of our perceptions. This is a shame, because it keeps us from fully appreciating the wondrous nature of vision—and its limitations.

For example, the Buddha points out how visual awareness does not move. When we're in a room and turn our heads from right to left to scan our surroundings, our visual awareness shows us a stationary room; we can tell it is our head moving, not the room. This takes quite a bit of brain processing, because different images of the room are moving across the retinas. The brain takes the series of moving images that arise and, with some help from the vestibular system, deduces that the lamp at the other end of the room is standing still. It presents this deduction as a stationary image.

Conversely, when a series of still images moves rapidly across our retinas in a movie theater, the brain fuses the still images into the appearance of movement. The film metaphor, though, is potentially misleading. The visual system is not a camera; it does not mechanically transfer light onto a retinal sensor and record it on a flash drive in the brain. We create what we see.

The lens of the eye bends the light passing through it so that the image projected on the retina is upside-down. The brain learns to reinvert the image so that we see the world "right-side up," but this is an ongoing, malleable process. In some classical experiments, volunteers wore goggles with prisms that bent the incoming light rays before they reached the lenses of the eyes: now the (doubly inverted) image projected on the volunteers' eyes was a right-side-up one conforming to objects' "true" orientation in the world.[3] The world looked upside down to the volunteers, disorienting them; they stumbled and fumbled. After six days of continuously wearing goggles, the subjects adapted and the world again looked right-side up—but if subjects took the goggles off and looked with their "real" eyes, everything they saw looked upside-down. (After a short while, they readapted to "normal" visual perception.)

The visual system does not function in isolation from the rest of the body. In the experiment, when goggled subjects traced seemingly upside-down objects with their hands, their vision adapted more rapidly. Their tactile touch of the world guided what their eyes perceived. When I trekked in the Himalayas, I noticed that visitors walking through the steep, uneven terrain relied mostly on their eyes: they'd look down at the ground and pick their way along the trail, stumbling frequently. In stark contrast, Nepali Sherpas and porters did not look down but ahead; walking long distances barefoot since childhood, their feet had learned to reliably "see" the ground immediately below. They rarely stumbled and almost never fell. I learned to imitate them and gradually acquired some ability to use my feet for trail vision, but—not having practiced it since childhood—it took so much concentration that after about fifteen minutes, I'd tire and need to resume relying on my eyes.

Our visual awareness arises through the entire body's interactions with the world. In order to see, we must act. The images we see are not mere projections of static icons; the images depict relationships and experiences.

VISUAL IDEAS

Given the physiological complexity of the seeing process, it's more accurate to say that our subjective visual images display *ideas* about the world, not the world itself. The Buddha points out that visual awareness has neither shape nor extension. It is the analytical I-mind that assigns the ideas of size and form to objects in the visual field, but these are a function of context.

Judging size and distance in the mountains is notoriously difficult, even for experienced travelers. When I stand on the Renjo

La pass in Nepal, the image of Mount Everest that appears on my retina is less than an inch tall, but the image that arises in my visual perception has no size or shape. The image does not span my occipital lobe like a projection on a movie screen. Cutting open my brain will not reveal a mini-Everest; the size arises as an idea computed from I-mind's comparisons and distinctions. Similar to our discussion in the previous chapter regarding thoughts, the visual images arising in our I-minds have no discrete, graspable location or physical form. All visual images are only as large as the attention we give them.

When we treat our visual awareness as an object, we confusedly mistake it for the object itself and make it seem like a fixed thing. Thus, the Buddha says to Ananda, "Visual awareness is not a perceived object . . . if visual awareness were a perceived object, then would you not be able to see my visual awareness as an object?" This leads the Buddha to propose a famous metaphor:

> Suppose someone is pointing to the moon to show it to another person. That other person, guided by the pointing finger, should now look at the moon. But if he looks instead at the finger, taking it to be the moon, not only does he fail to see the moon, but he is mistaken, too, about the finger.[4]

We often allude to this metaphor in Zen practice, but we need to be careful. When Shakyamuni says not to confuse the finger, with which someone is pointing to the moon, with the moon, which is being pointed to, he is not warning against mistaking one object for another object. The finger in the metaphor is visual awareness, and visual awareness *is not an object*.[5]

The key point here is that the nature of mind and objects is not dualistic: visual awareness (along with all other sense-awareness) arises together with, not separate from, objects. The Buddha gives an example: "If trees were separate from my awareness, how could I be seeing them? But if the trees were identical to my awareness, how could they still be trees? . . . Our visual awareness does not have a nature of its own that is distinct from the myriad things. Thus, your awareness is not something you can point out [and grasp]."

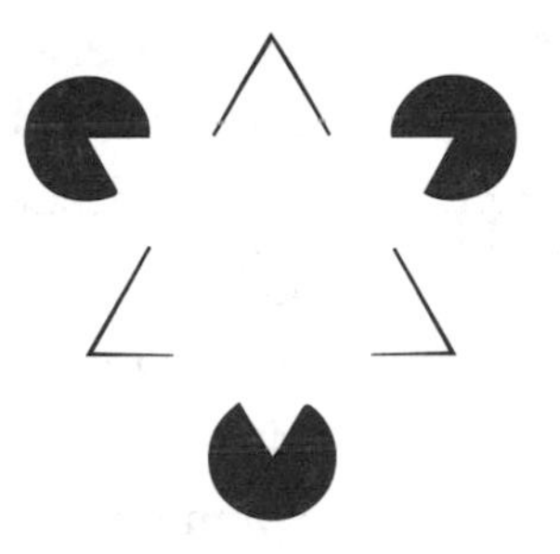

Let's use some examples from perceptual psychology to clarify this. When you look at the figure above, you can probably see the downward-pointing white triangle in the center, despite the fact that there is nothing there. The appearance of the triangle depends on the three black pie shapes and the placement of three carats (V-shaped lines). Without those shapes, there is no white triangle; but without our visual perception "filling in" the implications, there also would be no white triangle. We cannot grasp the white triangle itself, even though our visual perception brings its appearance to us.

The white triangle arises automatically to our conditioned minds. It cannot be grasped, but we can modify our awareness of it. With some effort we can override the conditioned perceptual processing and, by focusing directly on the pies and carats, "erase" the white triangle to see only the separate elements.

12
ABC
14

This is a little easier to experience with another example (above). Here our visual perception of the center of the figure shifts back and forth between appearing as the letter *B* and as the number 13. With some effort of visual awareness, we can "unsee" both *B* and 13 and instead see simply a straight line to the left of two arcs. Being aware of how our visual *perception* is both separate and not separate from things, our visual *awareness* can both see and not-see the letter *B* and the number 13.

In everyday life, sometimes we see things that aren't there. Perhaps you've been in a crowded airport terminal and, passing by a gate, were surprised to see a friend's face. You paused to say hello and realized you'd mistaken a stranger for your friend. Conversely, in everyday life, we sometimes *don't* see things that *are* there. Perhaps you've mislaid your keys, search all over for them, then eventually discover them where you first started looking. You had stared right at them—they were physically present—but you somehow failed to see them.

MODULATING (VISUAL) AWARENESS

How do the Surangama Sutra's teachings on visual perception help liberate us from suffering? It's helpful to remember the context: the Buddha is reminding Ananda not just to refrain from being tempted by alluring sensations but how the impermanent, illusory basis of sense-perceptions gives rise to desire, aversion, and suffering.

I've found that understanding the mutability of our visual processing, and learning how to modulate it, has practical value in everyday life. For example, children know how to exploit seeing not-seeing. When an adult is scolding a child, every child knows how to gaze up at them with wide-eyed innocence and look right through them. Adults seem to forget how to use this skill, but psychotherapy clients who become anxious during tense interpersonal confrontations can relearn how to make use of it.

Socially anxious clients often feel that when they're with other people, their only options are to cast their eyes downward (and imply passive submission) or risk escalating the conflict by glaring at the other person eye-to-eye (which can be interpreted as an aggressive challenge). Their difficulties with eye-gaze are exacerbated when they're in conflict situations. Many clients benefit from learning that other possibilities exist and can be called upon: softening one's eyes can soften one's emotions; moving one's gaze to a different focal point (the hairline or the chin of the other person) provides choices, increasing their sense of personal agency; interposing another image between oneself and the difficult person can provide a protective filter for a trauma. Intentionally altering one's visual "beam" so it can be narrow or wide, moving or still, can come in handy at boring lectures and stressful work meetings, as well as for actors gripped by stage fright.

More to our practice purposes, modulating *how* we see is an important aspect of meditation, since it allows us to realize that our relationship to the world need not be held to a fixed focus. If we only know how to meditate with our eyes closed, we'll have difficulties practicing meditation as we go about our daily activities. When we practice seated meditation, it's good to sometimes keep our eyes open, sometimes closed, sometimes half-open or half-closed.

Sometimes half-closing or closing the eyes can make it easier to deal with distractions. Sometimes, though, with the eyes closed, meditation slides into reveries leading to sluggishness or, alternatively, distressing replays of old traumatic memories. In such situations, opening the eyes wide can help ground and alert the student.

Because eye-consciousness and mind-consciousness affect each other, it's important not to be restricted to a single eye condition. Most often when I meditate, I like invoking the same instructions we teach for beginning Wild Goose qigong practice:[6] "Eyes open, but soft," or "Eyes open, seeing nothing," or "Eyes open, seeing far," or "Eyes open, looking within." Ultimately, though, cultivating equanimity requires us to learn to look at a situation with whatever eyes best meet the needs of the occasion. These can include the "inner eye" of wisdom, the eyes in the soles of our feet (e.g., for walking meditation), and the eyes of Avalokiteshvara in the palms of the hands to help us hold whatever comes with compassion.

AWARENESS ABIDES

Such exercises help us begin to realize an important point in this chapter of the sutra: our visual awareness abides even while our visual perception of objects is continually changing. Consider how visual awareness persists whether our eyes are open or closed.

When our eyes are closed, we are *aware* we are not-seeing; if we are driving a car and our eyes close from fatigue, we realize our peril and open them. When our eyes close while we sleep, our visual awareness brings us images we call "dreams." When we are awake, our visual awareness brings us the (dream?) images we call "the world."

Objects come and go, but visual awareness is not lost and does not perish. This has implications for our sense of ourselves. Looking in a mirror, we see different images of ourselves, depending on how we're dressed and how many years we're wearing. Visual awareness, though, does not age.

The Buddha illustrates this when, in this section, he reminds King Prasenajit that although the king may have seen the river Ganges when he was three years old and returned to see it again now that he is sixty-two, "Your Majesty, your face is wrinkled, but the essential nature of your visual awareness itself has not wrinkled." We might object: the king's eyesight probably is not as good as it was. Perhaps he has cataracts; perhaps he has gone blind. In either case, his visual perception of the river will be different than it was. His visual *awareness*, however, does not wrinkle.

If the king's eyes have gotten dim, he will be aware of blurriness; if he has gone blind, he will be aware of being blind. The Buddha gives examples of how an eye disease can cause us to see colored haloes around bright objects like a lamp; sometimes an atmospheric miasma will cause us to see colored rings around the moon. The distortion is not in the moon or the lamp, nor is the distortion in our awareness, since we know our vision is altered. An important aspect of our basic enlightened nature is that we are able to be aware of how we are deluded.

LIBERATIVE SEEING, NOT-SEEING

Visual awareness is not a thing but a form of being. It is not a reflection of the world, not a duplication of it, and certainly not a graspable box in the brain filled with the objects of awareness. The nature of visual awareness is akin to the nature of ourselves. We need not identify the seemingly external stimuli of awareness as "the world," and we need not identify the seemingly internal contents of awareness as "ourselves." We're not who we think we are; we're not who we see ourselves being.

The Buddha warns us, "From time without beginning, all beings have mistakenly identified themselves with what they are aware of. Controlled by their experience of perceived objects, they lose track of their fundamental minds. . . . The essence of visual awareness and what it is aware of cause what seem to be external phenomena to appear."

He then has an interchange with Manjusri, the Bodhisattva of Perfect Wisdom:

> The Buddha:
>
> Visual awareness and visible objects, and objects of mind as well, are like elaborate mirages that appear in space. They have no real existence of their own. Fundamentally, visual awareness and all its conditioned objects are the pure, wondrously understanding enlightenment itself. In enlightenment, how could there be identity or a lack of it?
>
> Mañjuśrī, I now ask you: you are Mañjuśrī . . . —is there a Mañjuśrī about whom one can say, "That is Mañjuśrī? Or is there no such Mañjuśrī?"

> Mañjuśrī:
> Neither, World-Honored One. *I am simply Mañjuśrī.*
> There is no one about whom one can say, "That is Mañjuśrī." Why? If there were, there would be two Mañjuśrīs. Nor is it the case that there is no such Mañjuśrī. In fact, neither the affirmation nor the denial of the statement "That is Mañjuśrī" is true.[7]

The Buddha teaches the nature of visual awareness to help us not be taken in by how we see ourselves (or by how we see the world, which is always a reflection of ourselves). We mistake seeing for understanding and don't realize that adding our ideas and perceptions introduces distortion. When we have a vision of ourselves as objects of awareness, we get lost in mirages. When we have a vision of the world as an object of awareness separate from ourselves, we get lost in (false) certainties of sensation. The Buddha says,

> Once we add another layer of understanding to our enlightenment, our awareness and what it is aware of become defective.[8]
> While the awareness that is added to enlightenment is defective, however, the awareness that is the fundamental, enlightened, understanding awareness is not defective.[9]

The more we delude ourselves into thinking we know what something is, the less we truly see it. In our quest for clear vision, we add measures, meanings, and names to our immediate experience, but this can come with a cost—the loss of our childlike sense of wonder.

There is so much we do not, cannot, will not see. We cannot even see ourselves clearly—how could we see anything else? While there's certainly nothing wrong with trying to understand ourselves, ultimately, we need to be able to say, like Manjusri, "I am no-thing. *I am simply myself.*"

We people of limited vision need to be compassionate toward each other. In the introduction, I mentioned that I first came across the Surangama Sutra as it appeared in the eighty-eighth koan of the *Book of Serenity*. To paraphrase the koan,

> *When I don't see, you cannot see my not-seeing.*
> *If you* could *see my not-seeing, it wouldn't have the taste of (my) not-seeing.*
> *So when you don't see my not-seeing, your not-seeing awareness is not a thing*
> *—just like you, just like me.*

The next time you sit down to meditate, don't try to see the truth. Don't observe, straining to force your eye to see itself. To avoid piling delusion on top of delusion, refrain from adding anything or subtracting anything. Follow Manjusri's example by simply being yourself, OMind moving and still, no picking or choosing. That's all. That's it. It's you.

5

The Matrix of the Thus-Come-One

The Matrix

Having deconstructed visual awareness in the previous section of the Surangama Sutra, we've begun to get a glimpse of why Buddhist sages often teach that our every thought, feeling, and sensation is a dream within a dream. This aspect of Buddhism sometimes goes unexplored when practitioners focus on the psychological benefits of meditation. As a neuropsychologist, I'm bemused by how meditators are willing to acknowledge that thoughts are often misleading but continue to believe that sense-perceptions are "really real." Our sense-perceptions, like our thoughts, are self-centered.

Our familiar I-mind is self-centered—that is its nature. I-mind, though, is one of the ways that OMind appears and also is a gateway to our fundamentally enlightened nature. Mind and nature form a necessary unity,[1] so human beings are not nature's creators but another of her members. Recognizing our delusions, we wake up to realize our true selves are neither gods nor demons but just natural—buddhas through and through.

In this section of the sutra, the Buddha further dispels our delusory self-centered dreams. Shakyamuni demonstrates how we pile up thoughts, sensations, and all the factors of body-and-mind into heaps, creating the oneiric illusion that there is a world separate from our selves. In each case, the Buddha shows how the myriad things add up to no *thing* whatsoever. Every aggregate is an illusion. Buddha addresses each of the various components of being:

- Five aggregates (form, sense-perception, cognition, mental formations, and consciousness)
- Six faculties (eyes, ears, nose, tongue, body, and cognition)
- Twelve sites (the faculties and their perceived objects, i.e., eye-faculty and visible objects; ear-faculty and sounds; nose-faculty and odors; tongue-faculty and flavors; body-faculty and objects of touch; cognitive faculty and objects of cognition)
- Eighteen constituents (the faculties; their perceived objects; and the six consciousnesses, i.e., eye-consciousness, ear-consciousness, nose-consciousness, tongue-consciousness, body-consciousness, mind-consciousness)
- Seven primary elements (earth, fire, water, wind, space, awareness, and consciousness)

The Buddha then shows how each "does not come into being from causes and conditions, nor does it come into being on its own." He employs a series of logical arguments to demonstrate that while the objects we experience are *dependent* on causes and conditions, they do not *arise* from causes and conditions. This distinction is subtle but important; it helps resolve what many find to be a seeming contradiction in Mahayana doctrine. If all is fundamentally empty of any essence, and birth and death are illusions, how can karma give birth to consequences in chains of reincarnations? (We'll discuss karma in more detail later in the sutra, in chapter 11.)

In one of the examples the Buddha offers while discussing the aggregate of form, he asks Ananda to imagine the following:

> [A] clear-sighted person looks up at a clear sky, where nothing but empty space is to be seen. Suppose that, for no particular reason, this person happens to stare, without moving his eyes, until they are stressed to the point that he sees in the empty air a disordered display of flowers, along with various other images that are disordered and chaotic and lack any real attributes. You should know that the aggregate of form can be described in similar terms.
>
> Now, this disordered display of flowers, Ānanda, does not come into being from space, nor does it come into being from the person's eyes. . . .
>
> Therefore you should know that the aggregate of forms is an illusion.
>
> It does not come into being from causes and conditions, nor does it come into being on its own.[2]

Today's readers might observe that the Buddha did not have our understanding of how visual hallucinations arise from disordered brain processes. In fact, many different conditions can lead to visual hallucinations: diseases of the retina, the optic nerve, the visual cortex, and the eye muscles; various sorts of dementia; chemical changes via multiple neurotransmitters and a wide assortment of drugs. The line between "hallucination" and "illusion" is rather fuzzy: sensory deprivation, op art, and meditation can lead to nonpathological visual hallucinations, as can grief (it's common for a recently bereaved person to see their deceased loved one appear in an otherwise empty room). When we watch a movie, it's a kind of hallucination: we're "really" seeing a rapid succession of still images that the mind fuses into the illusion of movement. The inspirations that come to artists in creative visions are not easily classified. When a sculptor looks at a piece of marble and envisages the statue it holds in promise, is it "unreal" or true vision?

We can identify conditions that are associated with hallucinations and illusions, but association is not causality. Human psychology tends to see causality in the presence of association. This can cause suffering. Therapists often see couples where one person complains about the other person's too-frequent withdrawal, while the other spouse explains they withdraw because their accuser complains too much. The therapist sees an ongoing vicious circle where each person's actions are associated with their mutual unhappiness, but each individual identifies a line of cause and effect, punctuating the cycle by ascribing the cause to the other person.

THE MATRIX: WAVES AND WATER

In another example, the Buddha uses a stretch of rapids as an example of the aggregate of mental formations:

> The waves follow one upon another, and those that are behind never overtake those that are ahead . . . the rapids

> are not brought about by space, nor are they brought about by the water itself. They are not identical to the water, but though they are not themselves the water, they are at the same time not separate from the water. Nor are they separate from space.[3]

In Zen, there is this saying: "no water without waves, no waves without water." This is interdependent co-arising, a dynamic, ongoing process where each provides the conditions for the appearance of the other with no fixed beginning or end. Our usual habits of thinking, though, tend to see one (independent) thing acting on another (separate thing) in a causal sequence, one after another. The Buddha teaches that this is an illusion.

We know waves transmit energy through the medium of water, but how do waves arise? Some of the factors include temperature and atmospheric pressure differentials that generate winds. The tides are also a factor, and everyone "knows" the tides are caused by the moon. It turns out that's a gross oversimplification. Other factors affecting tides are the rotation of the earth, the alignment of the sun and moon, the phases and amplitudes of waves, the shape of the coastline and near-shore depth variations—the National Oceanographic and Atmospheric Association lists thirty-two tidal constituents in the matrix table on its website.[4] The multifarious conditions of the tides are associated with each other; we can use these to make approximate predictions for what the average height of a tide will be at a particular time and place. To find the cause of a particular tide, though, we'd have to go back to its origin: the conditions of the day before, which arose from the conditions of the day before that, and so on until we got back to the origins of the moon, the sun, and the water itself.

Waters and waves are a meeting of matter and energy, a matrix of being. So are bodies and minds. Associations coalesce, which causes cascades, outpourings at each moment of time, every point of space.

We usually presume "if X, then Y" implies a linear temporal sequence where the cause comes before the effect, though even this is not always true.[5] All the factors intersect with each other, not in straight lines with a single origin but in a complex network. The Avatamsaka Sutra uses the image of Indra's Net to allude to this vast interconnectedness. When I imagine the vast sets of intersections that meet at infinite nodes yet also somehow come together as a unit, another image I find useful is that of a matrix.

In the Surangama Sutra, the Buddha is depicted as the Matrix of the Thus-Come-One. At each unique point, multiple threads meet. At each node of the net, at each cell of the matrix, strands are interacting with each other while simultaneously resonating to vibrations humming through the entire net. Every point of "just this" expresses itself along with the net as a whole, dependent on both the twining cords and the spaces between them.

OWNERSHIP AND THE BODY-MIND MATRIX

In this section of the sutra, the Buddha demonstrates how all the heaps—the aggregates, faculties, sites, constituents, and elements—and their seeming components are inherent in the Matrix of the Thus-Come-One, the field of enlightened nature far beyond form and emptiness. This

> true, wondrous, luminously understanding Mind contains the body and everything outside the body—mountains, rivers, sky, the entire world. . . .[6]

> Our enlightened nature can be involved with things throughout all ten directions, and yet it remains clear and still. It is eternally present. It neither comes into being nor ceases to be.[7]

This may seem wildly solipsistic or, at best, idealistic. We may intellectually acknowledge that we exist embedded in the world, but we feel there is a world "out there" separate from our world "in here," that material bodies are tangibly real, unlike thoughts. Our bodies and minds are not "eternally present": I was born, and I will die.

Perhaps not. When we delve more deeply into the neuropsychology of body-mind phenomena, we're in for some surprises.

Where does "my" body begin and end? Most cells in the body don't have human DNA in them: they are bacteria, or the microbiome, which we rely on to live. Some of us walk around with organs transplanted from other people; some of us have artificial hips, knees, or limbs. Many of us can't see unless we're wearing glasses or contacts. Gregory Bateson was fond of the example of the blind man whose eyes can be found in the hand probing with his cane.

Yes, we are enclosed in skin-bags, but every breath we take brings in stuff from the "outside" air and incorporates the oxygen into our cells (along with pollutants); every meal we eat takes in stuff from the "outside" world and converts it into muscles, organs, and energy. Sunlight strikes our skin, and our cells manufacture vitamin D. Sounds penetrate our bodies; it's not only the stirrups of our ears that move—our very bones resonate to infrasonic sounds. The human nervous system cringes to intense bombardments of high frequencies, and the fetus floating in the womb responds to the mother's music. Walk into a cool room, and you raise its temperature. Survive a virus, and you contribute to the evolution of new strains.

We are open to our environment, involved in a continual exchange with everything around and within. If this weren't so, we would die at once. Our bodies are the world, and the world is our bodies.

The sense we have of this skin-bag being "my" body is not a fact but a belief; one more mental phenomenon often disturbed when the nervous system goes awry. Some brain-injured patients experience asomatognosia, a syndrome where they do not recognize parts of their bodies as their own. The affected body part isn't paralyzed or insensate, but it becomes alien.

I had a brief taste of this after I had a cerebrovascular accident (CVA). It was an uncommon type of stroke, a cerebral venous thrombosis that produced intermittent symptoms, mostly problems with mental slowing, leg weakness, and imbalance. One day while working at the computer, I needed to use the mouse in my right hand to move the cursor to the menu bar. I gave the mental command to my hand, but then . . . *nothing happened.* This was a surprise, because I didn't have any sensory or motor problems in my hand: I could grip the mouse, I could move my hand (and the mouse) any which way. But when I told my hand to move the mouse to the menu bar, the hand simply didn't respond. I looked at my hand, puzzled. Wasn't this my hand? How could it be my hand if I could feel it, move it, but it didn't do the simple movement I wanted it to do?

Neuropsychology calls this experience an *agnosia*—the "lower" nervous system sensations and movements are intact but disconnected from the "higher" nervous systems of recognition and intention. I was relieved when, after several hours, my agnosia disappeared. It gave me a greater appreciation for patients who deal with more severe forms of this neurological disorder and also for the depersonalization and derealization that occur in some psychiatric disorders.

A related phenomenon occurs in reverse: a person experiences their body in places where it isn't. After a limb amputation, patients experience pain in the missing limb. The pain can persist for the rest of the person's life; it can be quite excruciating and usually doesn't respond well to pain medications.[8]

We think of these as disorders or illusions. From a Buddhist standpoint, though, they illustrate how our sense of "my" body is *always* illusory. Being illusory doesn't mean it is unreal, but it is incomplete: it is a brain image, a representation rather than a fact. Our culture tends to separate body from mind, and to treat somatic phenomena as somehow more real than psychological ones. The error of this ideology is evident in medical clinics where every day we see how thoughts and feelings are intimately entwined with flesh and healing. Instead of treating body and mind as connected, we'd do better by approaching them as two sides of one coin.

In modern economics, coins are not defined by their intrinsic metallic content but by how they function in currency exchanges; however many coins you have in your possession, ownership is meaningless unless they enable relationship transactions. The same holds true for body and mind. The sense that "my" body-and-mind belongs to "me" is a culturally reinforced delusion regarded as "normal" by our individualistic society, but this doesn't reflect its interdependent nature. In our current era, organ transplants, cell harvesting, and location sharing all raise the issue of "our bodies, not ourselves."[9] Historically, in times of war, your body belonged to the State and could be drafted into the army whether you wanted it to be or not. In patriarchal societies, the legal system explicitly treated (alas, in many places, still treats) the bodies of women and children as belonging to their husbands and fathers.

What if our culture has it backward? The Buddha teaches that our usual notion of "I have a body, which I occasionally share or aggregate with others" is false because it obscures how fundamentally all being—including "my" being—is interbeing. Perhaps the sense of "my" body is merely a bothersome addition to our collective "being" body. Perhaps each of us is one point on the Matrix of the Thus-Come-One. Perhaps the sense of "my" body is an extra layer that gets in our way as much as it protects and serves us. If each node on Indra's Net insisted on having its own way, it could strain the fabric.

Letting go of "my" body need not be pathological; it can scrape away the belief of personal ownership and allow us access to luminous experiences of nonseparation. Hopefully you've had experiences of this sort, where you've been so immersed in an activity that "you" vanish. Perhaps, singing or dancing, you've felt the music doing the crooning, the dance itself capering through your limbs. In qigong, tai chi, yoga, it's quite wonderful when instead of "us" doing "it," we feel the practice is performing the form through us.

Shunryu Suzuki used to say, "It is a big mistake to think *you* are doing the meditation."[10] When we sit down to meditate, it's important to get out of the way and let the meditation meditate. Becoming intimate with this process gives us greater access to ease in our everyday lives. If you are a carpenter, working with the grain of the wood, using the balance and weight of a hammer to secure a nail, is easier than pounding your will into the objects in your hands. A psychotherapist who eases off controlling sessions finds that when clients and clinicians seek each other in genuine meetings, the therapy arises naturally. When you garden, instead of pulling weeds out, reach down through the roots into the soil, draw on the whole earth and whole sky. Allowing the plant-in-the-wrong-place to find a new place in the light, it emerges effortlessly.[11]

SPACE IN MIND

In discussing the body-faculty, the Buddha gives an example of a person who joins their hands together when one hand is cold and the other is warm: with the exchange of warmth and cold, the person becomes aware of contact. This awareness of contact is inextricable from, and depends on, a sense of separation. However, separation-and-contact are two sides of one coin; neither can exist without the other. Thus, the dualism of separation-and-contact is illusory.[12]

Even when hands are seemingly separate—when they are not touching each other directly—they are continuously connected with each other through the rest of the body, the nervous system, and the environment. Because of this, acupuncturists often need to treat an injured hand by putting needles in the uninjured hand as well. When self-managing pain, if you move attention from the place that hurts to another part of the body that doesn't hurt, often the original ache subsides and feels better even when you bring your awareness back to the site of the hurt.

Conversely, when your hands are resting on each other, which hand is touching and which hand is being touched? Jointly experiencing this recursive contact, are the hands separate or apart? The philosopher Maurice Merleau-Ponty suggested we come to know ourselves by touching ourselves touching. I would add, "and through being touched by others." When we make love, we can sometimes let go of our sense of self until it's no longer clear which person is "having" a feeling. The sensations at such times often can transcend being sorted into a dualism of clearly pleasurable or clearly painful.

This sense of merging is usually transitory, and we're back into the strains involved in reaching out and shrinking back. The Buddha explains that when we discriminate contact-and-separation as pleasant, unpleasant, or neutral, it imposes a strain and distorts perception. Buddha also asserts this tactile body awareness has no ultimate basis!

How can this be? What is the nature of the distortion? It seems obvious that in contact-and-separation, touching ourselves or being touched by others, we close a spatial gap. Here the Buddha's analysis of what constitutes "space" comes into play.

We all are certain we know what space is: it's the physical thing that provides room for us to be ourselves and also the chasm that isolates us from the intimate wholeness we yearn for. We experience space as a mental phenomenon as well. Meditators attend to the space between thoughts, to the "space in mind," the infinite "room" in which consciousness seems to arise. On closer examination, though, space—whether physical or mental—is quite mysterious. The Buddha says to Ananda,

> Ānanda, consider the example of a person who takes up an empty pitcher and plugs up its two spouts so that it seems he has confined some space in the pitcher. Believing that he is carrying this pitcherful of space, he travels a thousand miles to another country with the intention of making a

> present of it. You should know that the aggregate of consciousness can be described in similar terms.
>
> The space that is in the pitcher, Ānanda, does not in fact come from the place where the person began his journey, nor is it transported to the country he travels to. It is like this, Ānanda: if the space had been transported from the first country by being confined in the pitcher, there must have been a loss of space at the place where the pitcher had come from. Moreover, if the space had been brought to the second country, then if the spouts were unplugged and the pitcher turned upside-down, the space within it would be seen to pour out.
>
> In this way you should know that the aggregate of consciousness is an illusion. It does not come into being from causes and conditions, nor does it come into being on its own.[13]

We're continually plugging up our consciousness with thoughts and feelings, urges and sensations. I-mind is constantly making its pitch, with shows of self-esteem and self-humiliation funded by commercials for things that, if we acquire or remove them, promise to improve us. Meditation helps us empty our pitcher of consciousness. This is quite a relief. But even when we quiet the skandhas of forms, feelings, perceptions, and formations, the beguiling skandha of consciousness has no more graspable essence than does physical space.

Buddha explains that space, in whatever amount, can never be accumulated. It's easy to fall into the illusion that if we accumulate mental space, it will expand into enlightenment. But in that case, enlightenment could come into being—which would imply enlightenment is subject to birth and death.

To counter this, the Buddha provides us the physical metaphor of digging a well. The Buddha points out that if you dig out soil to one foot, space is discernible to one foot; when you dig a well to ten feet, space is discernible to ten feet. But,

> . . . does the space in the well come into being out of the soil? Does it come into being because of the digging? Or does it come into being on its own? . . .
>
> The soil that is removed is solid matter, while the space is insubstantial, so they cannot function together. They cannot be aggregated or combined with each other. . . .
>
> Given that the fundamental nature of space is all-pervasive and does not move, you should know that the real nature . . . [of space, and the other elements] is one with the Matrix of the Thus-Come-One, neither coming into being nor ceasing to be.[14]

If this seems confusing, you may take comfort from the fact that space confuses physicists as well—they cannot agree on the fundamental nature of space.[15] When Isaac Newton was formulating his laws of motion, he was very aware that he left unexamined what might be the nature of the space "in" which motion occurs. When Einstein moved from the special theory of relativity (where he showed that *time* was not invariable) to the general theory, he demonstrated that *space* is not invariable.

Just as time dilates and contracts, space bends and straightens. Space curves around objects with mass (though we don't know whether the overall "shape" of space is flat or curved, negative or positive). Physicists cannot even agree on whether or not space is a thing. They agree matter cannot exist without space but cannot agree as to whether space can exist without matter. If space can exist without matter, space is a thing (in which case, physicists disagree on whether space is composed of small bits or an unbroken, smooth field). However, it's entirely plausible space is "only" a relationship—that space is defined by where matter isn't but has no qualities in and of itself.

One hundred years ago, experiments failed to find the ether that was supposed to "fill" space and provide the medium conveying the electromagnetic energy of the sun to the earth. So instead of a physical medium, physicists talk about—and can compute—the effects of energy fields. "Empty" space is "filled" with fields, but while physicists can compute the effects that fields have on matter, they cannot say what fields are in themselves. As one physicist notes, we've replaced the ether with the field, but the field is "the tension in the membrane, but without the membrane."[16] These are fields far beyond form and emptiness.[17]

Space, "the final frontier," is not a matter of inside-out or outside-in. Every atom in every object consists primarily of space: the appearance of solidity arises because nuclear spaces aren't very "squishable." It's the space in our lungs that lets us breathe; it's the spaces in between—the synapses—that allow nerve impulses to flow so we can sense and feel. As for our mental space, where are its boundaries?

BOUNDLESS

At this point in the sutra, the Buddha has dissolved our delusions of mind being inside, outside, in between, or nowhere; dissolved our delusions that the sense-objects we perceive exist separately from ourselves; dissolved our delusions that we are our bodies.

Having dissolved all the appearances of material objects, Buddha has dissolved any space in which they may appear. No wonder, then, that the disciples hearing this sutra were initially stunned.

What's left? Not even nothing (we tend to conceive of "nothing" as something that has qualities such as darkness or absence). We're facing the Matrix of the Thus-Come-One: a lattice with uncountable intersections, all the spaces between, each dimensionless point a field far beyond form and emptiness, each and all free yet mysteriously united.

I hope this has confused and unsettled you. That's the point. As Master Hua says in one commentary to the Surangama Sutra, "Reading this, you should feel terror."

At some point during meditation practice, we may begin to feel that we, ourselves—my precious "me"—are about to dissolve. Perhaps we yearn ardently for this but simultaneously feel terrified. Some of my friends have told me that when they reached this point, they spent several years holding on tightly, frightened that if they let go, they'd disappear. (Hint to anyone facing similar anxieties: when these people finally let go, they didn't disappear. Neither will you.)

Meditation practice sometimes becomes commercialized, complacent, content to restrict itself to providing a form of relaxation, a coping mechanism. Those are fine palliatives, and I welcome any lessening of suffering. However, I'm concerned that meditation loses some of its radical potential for liberation when it does not deepen to deconstruct our delusive sense of privileged separateness. Our self-centered delusions eat away at our interbeing, destroying species, insulating us from each other, and raising our temperatures to fever levels.

To experience true liberation, we need to drop all our assumptions and conditioned habits of "me" and "mine." We need to take refuge by recognizing, respecting, and taking responsibility for our co-arising with all beings. When we feel crowded by others, when we feel "I need my space," instead of thinking of space as a thing, we can find space as the Matrix: every-where-and-when free of obstructions. In Buddhism, these are sometimes called the heavenly abodes: compassion, loving-kindness, equanimity, and joy.

We don't need to create space *for* compassion: it's all around/within/free-from-obstructions-or-locations. Compassion-space, joy-space, loving-kindness-space, equanimity-space—they are free of obstructions, limitless, all-inclusive. Here is the place; here the Way unfolds. Here we are free to join with Ananda and the rest of the assembly who, at the end of this section of the teaching,

> felt that their bodies and minds were emptied and hardly seemed to exist. . . . That their minds pervaded the ten directions . . . that all things in all worlds are the wondrous, fundamental, enlightened, luminous mind that understands, and that this mind, pure, all-pervading, and perfect, contains the entire universe.[18]

Freed from hindrances, Ananda exclaims,

> *No need to wait forever to attain the Dharma-body.*
>
> *I vow to reach enlightenment, and . . .*
> *Return to rescue beings countless as the Ganges' sands.*[19]

When we glimpse freedom from illusion, we naturally are inspired, like Ananda, to find a way to express our part in this vast connectedness. Each of us manifests a unique node in the Matrix in concert with our community. When we sit with others in meditation, each body finds its shape, a variation on a common theme. When we merge our voice with others' chanting ancient texts in unison, we also need to express the Matrix in our own individual words. I attempt to echo Ananda's vow through my personal version of Zen's four great vows:

Beings are not numbers;
my vow is touching all in each.
Delusions are my self but bent;
my vow is unfolding.
Dharma gates are just this point;
my vow is turning.
Buddha's Way is ungraspable;
my vow is flowing, still.

6

The Coming into Being of the World of Illusion (I)

Let's Pretend

The Buddha has stripped away our pretensions to understanding. Shakyamuni has shown us how whenever we say "[*I* am] → [seeing/hearing/tasting/touching/thinking] → *that*]," we draw imaginary lines that cut off an illusory self from an illusory world. When we do this, we objectify the world, flattening it into an earth that revolves around us, alienates us from ourselves, and causes suffering.

At this point in the sutra the Buddha's disciples, having had all their perceptions uprooted, are assailed by doubt. We can empathize with their complaint, which I'll paraphrase: "We don't understand! The Buddha says the Matrix of the Thus-Come-One is fundamentally pure, empty of any thing that comes into being or ceases to exist. In that case, how do all the material things (including you and me) arise?" Even the very wise Purnamaitrayaniputra laments,

> . . . as I have been listening to the Thus-Come-One's voice as he has been setting forth such subtle and wonderful Dharma, I might as well be a deaf man trying to hear a mosquito from

> a distance of more than a hundred paces. Such a man could not even see the mosquito, let alone hear it.
>
> . . . having just now heard the Buddha explain this Dharma, I find that I am assailed by doubts. World-Honored One, if in fact the aggregates, the faculties, the various perceived objects, and the consciousnesses are all the Matrix of the Thus-Come-One, which is itself fundamentally pure, then how is it that suddenly there came into being the mountains, the rivers, and all else on this earth that exists subject to conditions? And why are all these subject to a succession of changes, ending and then beginning again?[1]

I'll paraphrase Buddha's response. He sighs, then says, "Ah, Purna! Still trying to understand. Still making conceptual distinctions. Still trying to sort the world into categories. Still trying to reconcile the many and the one, delusion and enlightenment." He explains,

> Because the category of what is differentiated and the category of what is uniform have been established, the category of what is neither uniform nor differentiated is further established.
>
> The turmoil of this . . . gives rise to mental strain, and as the mental strain is prolonged, grasping at objects of mind begins. . . .
>
> [this] creates a turbidity of mind, out of which the afflictions are generated.[2]

Does that clarify the matter for you? Or is your mind currently feeling turbid and muddy?

PRETENDING UNDERSTANDING, PRETENDING TO BE

Let's not disturb the clear flow of our minds by pretending to understand. When teaching meditation, Thich Nhat Hanh sometimes uses the metaphor of a glass of muddy water to represent the mind full of thoughts. If you try to calm the mind by picking out all the little pieces of dirt, you'll only stir things up and maintain the turbidity. If instead you just settle down and do nothing, the mud will gradually subside, and the glass of water will naturally become clear.

Meditators can strain themselves trying to control their minds, grasping and rejecting mucky mind-objects. However, the metaphor can be misleading. It can give the impression that the bits of dirt really exist, and the muddy water is really unclear. This, too, is delusion.

According to the Surangama Sutra, muddy water manifests as an illusion in the Matrix of the Thus-Come-One. Actually, the muddy glass of water is eternally clear throughout all time and space. Clarity appears, for this moment, as a muddy glass of water.

Our self-centered I-mind makes distinctions: muddy, clear. Then we get confused, and we have troubles understanding OMind, even though the Matrix of the Thus-Come-One is itself wondrous understanding. The Buddha encourages us to wake up to how—just like Shakyamuni—we all are, were, and will be fundamentally enlightened.

We mistakenly believe that we must gain some additional understanding in order to become enlightened. But that would mean our fundamental enlightenment is somehow incomplete, that it needs something extra—that *we* need something extra. When we try to add (I-mind's) understanding to (OMind's) wondrous enlightened understanding, we trip over our own feet and fall into the illusion of our (unenlightened) selves:

> An enlightenment to which an understanding is added cannot be a true enlightenment . . . an enlightenment that lacks understanding cannot be the true intrinsic enlightenment that is inherently pure. . . .
>
> *Once the category of "something understood" is mistakenly established in the mind, the category "that which understands" is mistakenly established as well.*[3]

When you or I try to understand something, we separate ourselves from what we wish to understand, creating an illusion of "self" and "objects" that alienates us from the world of interbeing. We are caught in a self-centered dream where "everyone dreams what they are, but nobody understands it."[4] In this dream of life-and-death, we run the risk of pretending to understand ourselves. Do you feel you understand yourself fully? If that's not the case, how can you ever hope to fully understand anybody else or judge them for their actions?

No matter how much we know, we are making things up as we go along, laying down a path by walking. The inevitable missteps and uncertainties often lead to us feeling insecure about ourselves. Sometimes we deal with this by *pretending* to be who we are instead of embracing the incomprehensible mystery of manifesting ourselves, together with all beings, in the Matrix of the Thus-Come-One. It's often easier to inhabit a role rather than acknowledge that we don't know what we're doing. This can give rise to our suffering "impostor syndrome"—feeling we're faking it, anxious that others will find out we are "really" phonies.

Children can play at pretending wholeheartedly. My three-year-old grandson Lucas idolizes his nine-year-old cousin Esteban. Recently Lucas has started playing games by announcing, "I'm Esteban! I'm really good at this!" While we are growing up, it's natural to stretch the seemings of our selves. We pretend to be circus fire-eaters or city firefighters, rookie NBA forwards or rock stars, heroes (boring?) or villains (exciting but risky?). We try on images of ourselves to see how they fit. When we age and act out roles with more elaborate scripts, though, our make-believe often turns into badges of identity. Then we risk imprisoning ourselves with our impersonations.

There's a well-researched psychological phenomenon called the illusory truth effect: the more often we see or hear or do something, the more we believe in it and, believing in it, begin to identify with it.[5] This proclivity is beloved by advertising executives and used in the repeated proclamations of politicians, television gurus, and internet influencers. It leads to political problems when, after the nth retelling and a few thousand "likes," lies masquerade as common knowledge.

When we pretend the same thing again and again, we can wind up convincing ourselves we have to conform to the roles we've adopted. Then our functions begin to feel like straitjackets constraining our character. After a few years of parenting children, working at a job, living in a monastery, or being homeless, we begin to believe our masks of being mothers and fathers, workers, holy seekers, or bums are all we are.

Some people are uncomfortable in their roles as workers or parents. They fulfill all their duties but feel like they are only pretending to a competence they don't really have (a competence nobody *really* has). They often feel they're just going through the motions, missing out on "real life." Conversely, some people take so much pride in their work and family roles that when they retire or their children grow up, they feel they no longer know who they are.

Buddhists sometimes like to pretend they're Buddhists. There are people who pretend to be enlightened, ensnaring religious communities in scandals of power, sex, and money. Most of us pretend we are *not* enlightened. This is very sad.

CLEARLY NOT UNDERSTANDING

When we stop pretending, we're able to see a little more clearly: to know what we know, know what we don't know, and cultivate wonder at the vastness of what we don't know we don't know. This is particularly important for realizing our enlightenment.

In Buddhism, all beings are fundamentally enlightened, but most do not know they have an inherent "knowing apart from passionate thought and discrimination"[6] and therefore have difficulties awakening to it. We assume "I" must wake up in order to become enlightened, just as we assume "I" wake up, and "I" go to sleep. However, while we're dozing, the brain stays active, and the heart continues to beat; in our enlightenment, delusions come and go. To think you are "out of it" when asleep (unenlightened) and "with it" when awake (enlightened) is an illusion.

My eight-year-old daughter once posed a riddle: "Why did the girl close her eyes when she looked in the mirror?" The answer: "To see herself asleep." Whenever we look at ourselves with I-mind, we are looking in the mirror with our eyes closed; we are asleep thinking we're awake. This is what happens when we pretend to ourselves that we're enlightened.

As a neuropsychologist, I find it remarkable to contemplate how little we know about what happens during sleep. We know sleep is essential: sleep is ubiquitous in mammals, birds, some fish, and, in somewhat different form, in reptiles, amphibians, insects, and some worms. Basically, any organism that has a brain has to sleep, or it will die. We don't really know why; medical research shows that for humans, sleep problems can alter the immune system and raise the risk for multiple diseases; even a small sleep deficit impairs cognitive functioning.

Still, we're unclear about how sleep restores us. We don't know what functions dreams fulfill (here, also, theories abound, none of them conclusive); there is no agreement on how much awareness people have in comas, seizures, sleepwalking, traumatic dissociation, delirium, or dementia. Most people have had experiences of vividly dreaming they are awake; most people have had experiences of getting out of bed but not feeling fully awake. Sometimes we "pinch ourselves to make sure we're not dreaming." Have you ever, at the end of a meditation period, been uncertain whether you'd been awake or asleep?

To counter my tendency to take sleep for granted, sometimes when I go to bed, I say to myself, "Time for dream-self to wake up." I try to remember to dedicate my sleep time to the welfare of all beings. Often, when I get up in the morning, the first thing I say to myself is, "How did that (waking up) happen?"

Thirty years ago, a friend asked me to teach a session of his graduate school psychology class. After I agreed, he told me the scheduled topic was dreams in psychotherapy. This posed me with a dilemma. I'd trained in therapeutic modalities with various methods to approach dreams as rich sources of unconscious meaning. However, as a neuropsychologist I saw dreams as physiological neuronal discharges with no inherent psychological significance beyond what therapist and client constructed and assigned to them retroactively during therapy sessions.[7] I couldn't decide which understanding to present to the students. Then, the night before I was scheduled to teach the class, I dreamed that dreams had meaning.

My waking mind goes back and forth trying to understand this; what happens when we're asleep seems to be out of the purview of I-mind. Yet often if, needing to get up earlier than usual the next morning to catch a plane or make an appointment, we set the alarm on our clock accordingly, we find ourselves waking up before the alarm goes off. If just before I go to bed, I'm stuck on a crossword puzzle and leave it unfinished, when I get up in the morning the answer appears clearly. We can walk, jump, even drive an automobile without thinking much about what we're doing. The mind that takes care of us while we're asleep or unaware—could this be close kin to the OMind the Surangama describes as "enlightened wondrous understanding"?

Psychotherapy often functions by helping a client gain access to what they know but don't know they know. This can apply to painful experiences that have previously been shunted out of conscious consideration, but also to a client's skills and resources that, distracted by distress, they haven't looked to. If I'm seeing a person suffering from chronic pain who used to be an avid bicyclist, I might ask them how a bicyclist on the road deals with sharp curves and steep climbs. After they explain this to me, I ask them, "So when a pain flare throws you a curve, how do you lean into it? When the rehab process is an uphill slog, how do you switch gears?" Usually clients are surprised to rediscover what they didn't know they knew and enjoy applying the reclaimed skills to their difficulties.

The same applies to spiritual practice, where we often don't know how to proceed. When we don't understand, it helps to trust in the wondrous understanding OMind that doesn't rely on concepts, that knows enlightenment, even when we're in the dark. This is why, in

Zen, we find our practice in our everyday activities: how we open the hand of thought as we unfold a napkin, how we pick up a glass of water and set it down to let the myriad things rest.

UNDERNEATH UNDERSTANDING

A little girl closes her eyes and looks into a mirror to see herself asleep. This is the good practice of understanding our not-understanding—it helps us acknowledge our delusions and prevents us from thinking, "I'm enlightened."

Conversely, it's important to acknowledge our enlightened nature, so we can wake up to it. Sometimes we look in the mirror with our eyes open but have trouble seeing we're awake. Perhaps you've heard an audio recording of your voice and thought, "Do I really sound like that?" Sometimes we look in the mirror and cannot believe what we see. I remember putting on a three-piece suit for a job interview, looking at my image in the mirror, and thinking, "Is this really me?" So long as we look in the mirror with open eyes, knowing all mirrors are mere reflections, we are awake even if we can't credit it. So long as we recognize that material forms, feelings, perceptions, formations, and thoughts are mere reflections, we are enlightened—even though we do not recognize this in ourselves.

Enlightenment is not a personal possession; it does not come and go. When our inner eye is not open, we make false discriminations between asleep/awake, enlightenment/delusion. We don't realize we are always fully ourselves wherever, whenever, however we are, asleep or awake, or all the various states between. To think otherwise is like thinking the sun is "gone" when it sets at night and "here" when it rises in the morning.

The sun is always here; we just turn away from it for a while every twenty-four hours. The stars are always here; we just are too dazzled sometimes to see them. Enlightenment is like the sun; it is not a lamp that needs to be plugged in, an appliance that turns on and off. Enlightenment is like the dark that reveals the stars. Nothing is extinguished or snuffed out.

When we open the eyes of OMind and let go of our attachment to narrow understanding, we have access to the horizons of wonder—wonder that can open what is locked.[8] Understanding has its practical uses, but thinking we know what's what can diminish our awe at the ever-ungraspable. Understanding can be a form of fruitless grasping and cause us major problems. As Shakyamuni says,

> [Once understanding arises] there arises a firm attachment to that understanding, and this firm attachment is categorized as solidity.
>
> . . . A point of light is seen to appear. When the light is seen clearly, deluded thoughts arise—both hatred in response to incompatible points of view and love in response to compatible ways of thinking.[9]

Light is wonderful, but it also pollutes: most urban areas are so well lit at night now that we cannot see the stars. Similarly, in the light of knowledge, we become attached to our dualistic distinctions. We identify with our limited ideas of who (me-not-you) and what (this-not-that). From these illusions come desire and aversion, which bring suffering.

All our understanding is partial, constrained by the limits of our experience, the demarcations of our reasoning, and the limits of our imagination. Perhaps this is why one of the Lojong guidelines for cultivating compassion is "Don't try to figure things out." When I first read that, I was shocked. I *like* figuring things out.

Then I remembered how frustrated my loved ones and friends get when they want me to just listen to them, but I start analyzing and problem-solving instead. Trying to figure things out can get in the way of empathizing and being fully present.

As soon as we start to figure things out, we identify causes and conditions. We try to fix it or try to find reasons to blame someone or something for our difficulties. When we encounter suffering without trying to analyze it, we respond naturally with loving-kindness. If I'm attending my daughter's middle-school concert and start dissecting the performance, I can cavil about ragged entrances, wince at wrong notes, and grimace when pitches wander out of tune. If I let go of critical analysis, I can find, deeper down, how to listen with nothing but love. Then, when my daughter comes up to me after the concert and asks how I liked it, I can respond sincerely that it was *wonderful* and we can dance together, celebrating with sympathetic joy.

UNDERSTANDING AND INSIGHT

Understanding is not insight. Insight turns us back to the fundamentals, looking for the teachings within all of us, our *in*tuition. Insight resonates in ways that do not always require words. In contrast, our need to articulate intellectual understanding sometimes comes from pride ("I am only as good as what I understand") or fear ("If I don't understand what's going on, I'll lose all control of the situation").

There's nothing shameful about not understanding. Incomprehension often is the spark we need to bring out previously unthought-of perspectives. Sometimes after a Dharma talk, my students will ask me about something by beginning with, "This is a stupid question, but . . ." Usually what follows is a great question;

it's often about something I've taken for granted. When I begin to answer but encounter difficulty expressing myself, I become aware that my understanding is inchoate; the student's inquiry challenges me to probe further.

My teacher, Sojun, sometimes would say, "If you want to realize enlightenment, you have to be willing to be a little bit stupid." This is very true—though I was so attached to being insightful and accomplished that it took me a while to understand it.

"A little bit stupid," though, is not the same as ignorant. Ignorance is the breeding ground for delusion. If we grasp at understanding, we aggressively break the universe apart into small bits. This violates the universe. However, if we settle for *not* understanding, we miss out on the wonders of the universe. This dishonors the universe.

Practice is not a matter of understanding or not-understanding, not a matter of illusion and reality, muddy and clear. All these do is perpetuate dualistic distinctions. Whenever we separate delusion from clarity, we tend to treat clarity as better, as more "real." We tend to treat delusion as if, being false, it were also "unreal"—perhaps even evil. A successful illusion is completely real in its deceptiveness. It can be really destructive or really beneficial. The myth of weapons of mass destruction in Iraq justified a war; the placebo "illusion" has very real curative effects.

Clarity is ungraspable and transparently invisible, so how can you call it "real?" That which does not exist is very real in its nonexistence. As the *Tao Te Ching* says, "That which is *not* penetrates every crack." If that which does not exist were unreal, where would there be room for all that exists?

Trying too hard to understand false and real can give you a headache. Before pinning our hopes on understanding false and real, right and wrong, enlightenment and delusion, let us appreciate the limits of our understanding. There will always be more of what we do not understand than what we do. To paraphrase Ivan in Dostoevsky's *Brothers Karamazov*, we have three-dimensional brains, so how can we hope to understand a universe that has ten dimensions (or more, according to scientists and mathematicians).

Do we even understand what understanding is? School systems have problems measuring it; philosophers have trouble defining it. Zen insists words cannot describe our understanding, even though we are continually demonstrating our understanding by how we live. Dogen advised, "Brilliance is not primary, understanding is not primary, conscious endeavor, memory, imagination and introspection are not primary. Without resorting to any of these, harmonize body-and-mind and enter the Buddha Way."[10]

Luminous, wondrous, enlightened understanding is not a cognitive operation (though it includes, and is not separate from, cognition). We realize our enlightened understanding by how we stand here and face now. Eihei Dogen called this the *Genjo Koan*[11]—actualizing the fundamental point. Intimacy with "just this" is always in good standing; it underlies all.

What is under *standing?*
The Great Earth.
What is under The Great Earth?
The center.
What is the center of the center?
A dimensionless point.

My teacher, Sojun, once said at the end of one of his Dharma talks to our sangha, "I could explain it to you, but it would be doing you a disservice."

7

The Coming into Being of the World of Illusion (II)

Beyond Is and Is Not

Our practice actualizes the fundamental point; we find the dimensionless pole of emptiness, arriving where we already are. The *Tao Te Ching* puts it this way:

Reach the pole of emptiness; abide, still, in the center.
Constant things co-arising; see them turn and re-turn.
Return to the root;
At the root to be still
In stillness recover, revive, and endure.

This practice, in its simplicity, can be confusing and frustrating. We may reach, but can never grasp, the pole of emptiness. Attempting to settle the self on the self, we stir the waters that we are trying to clarify and may fail to notice we're all wet. Bewildered by mirages of this and that, ignorance and realization, we can get lost on the very path our feet are laying down by walking.

In this section of the sutra, one of the Buddha's listeners (the sage Purna) asks Shakyamuni, "If we're all fundamentally enlightened, why do we suffer from delusion?" The Buddha responds with the parable of Yajnadatta, who looks into a mirror and, seeing a face with perfectly clear features, becomes enraptured—but then goes mad, fearing he has lost his own head. Buddha reassures Purna that Yajnadatta's madness was an illusion with no basis in reality; he had never truly lost his head. Similarly, our feeling that we're not enlightened is merely delusion. Yajnadatta isn't aware that he is mad; we aren't aware that our confusion is based only on confusion.

Many Buddhist teachers urge their students, "Put your whole being into your practice." When students misinterpret this to mean "Try hard," they bang their heads against a wall in futile efforts to cure their headaches—until they realize they cannot help but bring their whole being to every moment of their lives. Many Buddhist teachers urge their students to "let go completely." When students misinterpret this to mean "Throw everything out," the more they shovel the snow in front of them, the more it piles up behind—until they realize there is nothing to let go of. I had years of head-banging and snow shoveling—sometimes simultaneously (!). Sometimes our terrors need to blow themselves out.

Perhaps instead of saying, "Put your whole being into practice," we should say, "Be whole." Instead of saying "Let go," advise, "Let be." I doubt, though, that any words are sufficient to help us get over ourselves without going through ourselves and dealing with the difficulties that result.

In this regard, there's a nice story about Layman P'ang and his family.[1] P'ang was studying a sutra—perhaps the Surangama!—when one day he sighed.

> "Difficult, difficult, difficult!" P'ang said. "Like storing ten bushels of sesame seeds in the top of a tree."

His wife overheard him and responded: "Easy, easy, easy! Like touching your feet to the floor when you get out of bed."

Their daughter Lingzhao chimed in: "Neither difficult nor easy! Like dewdrops sparkling on the tips of ten thousand grasses."

I would comment, "Both difficult *and* easy! As Ching Ch'ing says, 'It's easy to express oneself; to say the whole thing is difficult.'"[2]

Everyone has had the experience of trying to do something that looks easy but turns out to be difficult. Everyone also has experiences of braving something difficult that turns out to be easy. Difficult and easy complete each other as surely as sickness and health, delusion and enlightenment; bewilderment and "aha!" are kissing cousins. The problem lies not in the ache and strain, the comfort or ease of our efforts at understanding. The snare lies in how our minds leap to dualistic opposites, sorting everything into "is" and "is not."

BEYOND "IS" AND "IS NOT"

In this section of the sutra, the Buddha crystallizes the issue: "The inherent luminous mind that understands is apart from 'is' and 'is not' and yet both is and is not." Master Hua echoes this in his commentary: "If you can understand that within the Buddha's Dharma there is no 'is' and no 'is not,' you can become enlightened."

Increasingly we live in an either-or culture. You're either for me or against me, progressive or conservative, kind or cruel. Political parties' spokespersons give diametrically opposed versions of reality. It reminds me of the shouts of grade school arguments on the playground—"Is so!" "Is not!" "Is!" Is not!"—that devolve into wrestling on the ground, ear-pulling, and tearful finger-pointing: "He started it!"

The easy/difficult parable of the P'angs demonstrates a way out of the sufferings born of dualistic either-or. It illustrates the four sides of the *tetralemma*, an Indian Buddhist logic developed by Nagarjuna around 200 C.E. The tetralemma asserts that all phenomena always manifest in four ways: is, is-not, both-is-and-is-not, and neither-is-nor-is-not. In formal logic, it's written as presented in the following chart.

The Tetralemma

A	Enlightenment	Difficult
~A	Delusion	Easy
Both A and ~A	Enlightenment ↔ Delusion	Both difficult and easy
Neither A nor ~A	~~Enlightenment ↔ Delusion~~	~~Neither difficult nor easy~~

Everything *simultaneously* manifests each and all of the four possibilities, despite them seeming mutually exclusive. At this and every moment, you (and I, and everyone) are alive, dead, alive-and-dead, neither-alive-nor-dead.

This may seem like a head-scratcher to the thinking of our analytical I-mind. It becomes a little easier to feel a sense of the tetralemma by approaching it with our heart-mind's intuition. The heart, with its four chambers, has room for all the blood it pumps through the body, whether that blood is old or young, depleted or newly oxidized. At this moment, as you breathe, perhaps you can be aware of how the following are true:

- Breathing is very simple, continuing whether we're aware of it or not.
- Breathing is very complicated, many different muscles coming into play to produce many different kinds of breath: shallow or deep, inhaling or exhaling, chest or belly.
- Breathing is simultaneously simple and complicated, subject to volitional control yet operating in its own fashion even when it is shaped with our awareness.
- Breathing is neither simple nor complicated; it manifests in its own way, impossible to capture in words. "The breath" is the ins and outs of how life manifests in breathing.

The phases of the breath are as natural as the ebb and flow of the tides and their intricate codependence with the phases of the moon and movements of the heavenly bodies. Earlier in the sutra, when Buddha and Manjusri discussed the moon and the finger pointing at the moon, the Buddha said,

> Actually, Mañjuśrī, there is really only one moon. We can neither affirm nor deny the statement, "That is the moon." . . . all your various interpretations of visual awareness and visible objects are nothing but delusion, and in the midst of delusion one cannot avoid thinking "That is" and "That is not."
>
> Only from within the true, essential, wondrously understanding, awakened mind can one escape the error of trying to point to what "is" and what "is not."[3]

I-mind is continuously comparing everything we encounter, sorting things into "same" or "different," classifying them as familiar/unfamiliar, friendly/threatening, is/isn't. Our heart-mind (OMind) continually graces us with an intuitive sense that there's more to experience than "is" or "is not."

If you've ever been intimate with someone, you know there are times when you love them to pieces unreservedly, even while some quirk of theirs is annoyingly getting under your skin. Furthermore, that very quirk often makes you smile and fills you with tenderness. Meanwhile, loving or abhorring is irrelevant to which of you is washing the dishes and which of you is drying them in the kitchen. (Of course, we can recruit our feelings to justify judgments about who should and shouldn't be doing the dishes, and how good a job each is doing—but that way brings surplus suffering.)

The tetralemma also frequently appears in our relationship to ourselves. When someone says, "I'm not myself today," which self is speaking from which of the four quadrants' realms?

Nevertheless, when we think about our mixed feelings and try to sort them out, we often allow I-mind's analysis to convince us that the alternatives are really mutually exclusive. We tell ourselves that if we love someone, we "can't" hate them; when they die, we "shouldn't" feel sad and soothed; we may get upset at feeling numb (numbness is a very common initial reaction to death). We create suffering if we start worrying that feeling neither sad nor soothed means we never truly cared about the deceased.

Our problem of holding mutually exclusive possibilities owes a lot to Western thinking's adoption from ancient Greek philosophy of the rule of the excluded middle, the rule of logic that says something cannot be simultaneously both A and ~A (not A).

This seems to be common sense: something either "is" or "is not." You're alive or dead; you can't be half-pregnant. The cruelty of that last statement is evident to anyone who has carried a not-quite-a-fetus-but-still-a-spark-of-life through a tenuous fertility treatment, a miscarriage, an abortion, or a stillbirth.

We seek to escape or soften the tyranny of the excluded middle with in-betweens: the Greeks favored the Golden Mean, a middle between two extremes. We employ "kinda," "sorta," and "-ish" to qualify our statements. These fudge the excluded middle with in-between shadings but still confine us within a misleading territory, a line with "is" and "is not" at either end. Describing temperature as hot, medium, or cold doesn't adequately capture what it's like to be twelve thousand feet up on a glacier under a cloudless sky: the temperature may be a "pleasant" 70°F, but the sun burns your skin, while the wind blowing from the ice feels freezingly cold. Poorly insulated by the thin air, your body leaches heat, while your exertion makes you sweat. Your average temperature does not convey how you are hot *and* cold while also being neither-hot-nor-cold *nor in between.*

Halfway points and bland compromises are not the hallmark of the Middle Way. The different images of our left eye and our right eye do not combine into a flat compromise, but instead merge sameness/difference to reveal a depth dimension. Similarly, the Middle Way of the tetralemma reveals previously unimagined dimensions of experience.

THE DARK LIGHT OF SCIENTIFIC REASON

The logic of the excluded middle serves as a useful tool for breaking down phenomena into their component parts, making it easier to grasp the bits and pieces, but it can also obscure how biological organisms function as emergent wholes. As an example, although we know tadpoles develop into frogs, it seems the two mutually exclude each other: How can an animal be both? Craig Holdrege, in his book *Seeing the Animal Whole*, points out that if you'd only ever seen tadpoles, you wouldn't be able to imagine frogs; if you'd only ever seen frogs, you wouldn't be able to imagine tadpoles.[4] Neither is a compromise version of the other. Tadpoles have gills; frogs have lungs. The tadpole does not have anything that can be identified as the precursor to a lung; the frog does not have anything that can be identified as the residue of a gill. When the tadpole transforms, it doesn't expand its gill into a lung; rather, many of the tadpole's tissues and organs dissolve into a formless goop whose cells are repurposed to shape entirely new organs. Holdrege argues that a tadpole does not turn into a frog: each is a complete "being-at-work," and each has a distinct way of interacting with the world.

Similarly, firewood does not turn into ash, nor does a newborn baby turn into an elder on his deathbed.[5] A little girl is not a half-grown woman; we'd err if we related to the child in the same way we related to the adult. It's like when we tell a story or write a poem; once the first chapters or stanzas are set down, they advise their authors what developments will be available or impossible. To approach spiritual practice as a journey from delusion to enlightenment misses the wondrous reality of how beings are always "communing with the source and communing with the process" manifesting as the Matrix of the Thus-Come-One.[6]

Nature's realities don't abide by our simplifications to follow the rule of the excluded middle. Science shows that light is both a wave and a particle, but most people don't fully realize how—according to is/isn't thinking—this is fundamentally *impossible.* Particles are material substances; when one particle encounters another, they bounce off each other. Waves are energy flows that affect solid matter but are not themselves material; when one wave encounters another, they merge and meld to produce interference patterns. Light is/isn't a wave (A) and is/isn't a particle (~A), is both light and particle (A and ~A), and is neither A (light) nor particle (~A).

Psychological and somatic phenomena also resist being parsed into an is, an isn't, and an in-between. When you are watching a movie, so absorbed in the film that you do not hear somebody call your name, are you in the room with the other person or in the film with the characters you identify with? It's possible to induce some people into a deep hypnotic trance in which they can answer questions but not feel a knife cutting into their flesh. At such times, is the person "all there" or not?

When you meditate, if you try to hold still and not move at all, your muscles will become rigid and your body will tremble. If instead you relax, your muscles will make subtle adjustments on their own to let you settle into stillness. Meanwhile your lungs continue to expand and collapse, and your heart beats. Meditation is movement-in-stillness, stillness-in-movement, leaping clear of "is" and "is not."

You might object: "That is all very well, but if I'm driving and someone crosses the street in front of me, that person is either there or not. If I run them over, they will either be alive and uninjured, alive and injured, or dead." In reply, let's turn to a quote from the Buddha in this section:

> [T]he effortless path to enlightenment is the ending of both arising and perishing.
>
> [but] . . . This is a teaching that must be left behind, and the leaving behind, too, must be left behind. [This is] the Dharma that transcends idle speculation.[7]

Drive carefully! All of the Buddha's teachings are skillful means. They do not destroy or oppose our ordinary ways of thinking and being; they fold and unfold these ways to reveal further dimensions to our being. I-mind and OMind depend on each other.

WIDENING THE FIELD

The rule of the excluded middle's either-or creates a linear field in a two-dimensional plane. This can be a good field for meditation. For example, one form of mindfulness meditation cultivates the awareness of experiences as varying along a line of pleasant—neutral—unpleasant. Here we can contrast delusion with enlightenment, discriminate black from white, and gain an appreciation of the vastness of all the shades of gray between.

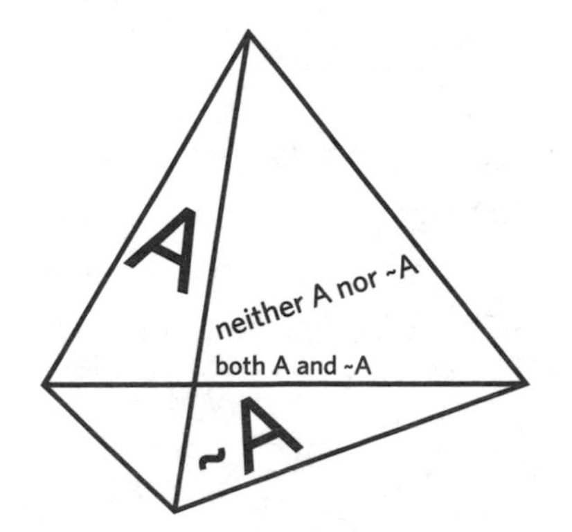

The tetralemma expands our possibilities by implying a three-dimensional object, a tetrahedron with the four faces of A, ~A, A and ~A, and neither A nor ~A (as shown in the diagram). These multiple planes are more in keeping with our embodied being in the world, where experiences can be simultaneously pleasant and unpleasant and neither pleasant nor unpleasant.

The center of all four planes is a pivot point. This center is not neutral, if by "neutral" we mean "static or dull." The center is a dynamic balancing we (inadequately) label "equanimity." The center is a pole of emptiness, a node, a meeting point whose space, with its zero dimensions, accepts all the forces that come to bear on it while maintaining freedom from any particular push or pull. From this center, we can rotate the tetrahedron to meet our immediate experience in whatever way fits the moment—sometimes with one face, sometimes with another, sometimes with all four.

These explorations of "is" and "is not" may seem overly abstract, but they are central to the liberation from suffering that is at the heart of the Surangama Sutra. On this path, our hindrances are the gateless gate; our delusions of perception are our vehicles for realization.

NAVIGATING TURBID WATERS

During Zen meditation retreats, we end our meals chanting, "May we exist in muddy water with purity like the lotus." It's a nice image, but it doesn't quite convey the concrete reality.

Growing up in New York, I'd never seen a lotus pond, so I was very excited the first time I went to visit one. It was a hot, humid summer in Tokyo. I was dismayed to see how poorly tended the pond was, its turbid waters clogged with muck, the lotus flowers drooping in the heat and begrimed by the soot of the city. More recently, I took some photos of lotus flowers at a well-tended garden in San Francisco, but when I got home and examined the pictures, every blossom and leaf had some speck, a minute tear, or a discoloration. It was tempting to Photoshop them into more ideal images.

I was disappointed that the lotuses of Tokyo and San Francisco did not conform to my ideal image of them—nor does any lotus in any pond. To appreciate the messy reality of actual blossoms, I need to drop my illusory flowers and enjoy lotuses as gloriously, ineluctably themselves.

When we get caught in dualisms of clean and dirty, ideal and real, delusion and enlightenment, we may be tempted to edit ourselves and to prettify false images of practice. We need to cultivate "dis-illusionment" along with enlightenment. Unless we're sufficiently aware and appreciative of our garbage, we can't compost it so that it fertilizes our practice.

Since we practice in muddy waters, it behooves us to learn ways of navigating the turbidities that arise in the mind. This section of the sutra describes five turbidities that arise when awareness, mind-consciousness, sense-consciousness, space, primary elements, and karma become entangled with each other:

- The turbidity of *time*: We get confused by how we seem to go from a past to a future. (At the lotus pond, most flowers can seem to either not have reached peak beauty or to have already begun to fade.)
- The turbidity of *perception*: We get confused by how our

representations of the world seem real. (The mental picture of a perfect lotus interferes with the perception of the lotus as it is, beyond name or image, even when it's right in front of us.)

- The turbidity of *afflictions*: We get confused by how hurts seem to hinder and stain us. (The glare of the sun on the pond water hurts the eye and spoils the photo. Feeling disappointed when experience doesn't conform to expectations is one of the most common manifestations of suffering.)
- The turbidity of *individual beings*: We get confused by how we seem to exist apart from everything and everyone. (Each lotus has some aspects of the ideal, but no lotus embodies all aspects perfectly. A flower's petals may be mostly pristine but have one petal with a brown spot; another lotus has beautiful petals but insect-eaten leaves.)
- The turbidity of *life spans*: We get confused by how we seem to appear at birth and vanish at death. (The lotus appears differently as seed pod, bud, and bloom; it droops when plucked or, left alone, loses its petals, decays, and disappears into the pond.)

Feelings of hurt, feeling there's never enough time, feeling caught in the afflictions of an individual mortal person with compelling sensations and perceptions—these cloud our minds and hearts. Clouds, though, do not block the vast sky of our being. The turbidities may seem to be impossible barriers to liberation, stagnant swamps and fearsome rapids that prevent us from crossing to the other shore. In truth, when we can find our place on this shore, we're already on the other side.[8] Every moment, we are navigating this river-and-shore of easy impossibility and impossible ease. In Zen, we call this practice-enlightenment. Take heart! Your wondrous enlightened understanding knows the lotus does *not* bloom in the mud. Instead, let me suggest that

> the lotus continuously blooms *through* the mud,
>
> and
>
> the mud continuously blooms *through* the lotus.

PART TWO

Heart

Then the World-Honored One took pity on all the Hearers of the Teaching and on the Solitary Sages in the assembly who did not yet abide effortlessly in the fully awakened mind. . . . He revealed the wondrous path of practice in accord with the Supreme Vehicle.

. . . [you must] examine the resolve that is the basis of your practice that leads to enlightenment. Is this resolve identical to the awakening that will be the result of your practice, or is it not?[1]

. . . You must decisively let go of everything that has conditioned attributes. Carefully examine the source of your afflictions, which since time without beginning have created your karma and nurtured its growth. Who is it that creates this karma and undergoes retribution?[2]

8

Instructions for Practice

Musics of the Mind

The ten sections of the Surangama Sutra are not divided into two parts, but at this point there is a distinct shift in the material. The first part sets the stage for the discourse and alerts us to the error of confusing mental objects and the skandhas with reality: "That is not your mind." It then introduces the original, everlasting True Mind, the Matrix of the Thus-Come-One.

The second part is less abstract; beginning with the section "Instructions for Practice," it goes to the heart of our intentions and actions. Faced with his followers' perplexity, the Buddha offers specific practices to untie the knots of attachment and delusion. He invites twenty-five sages to describe their paths to enlightenment, emphasizes the importance of proper conduct, and explains how to establish a place of awakening. He provides a powerful protective mantra, then goes into detail about the kinds of consequences that arise from deluded acts. He also warns against dangers that can arise with advanced practice and gives advice for practicing safely for the benefit of all beings.

The Buddha concludes, as is customary, by describing the merits of studying and practicing the sutra.

❂

Attempting to clarify understanding by drawing lines between easy and hard, lotus and mud, can make things murkier. Although it sometimes seems that Buddhism has never met a list it didn't like, cataloging our confusions into the turbidities of perceptions, afflictions, individual beings, time, and life spans can cloud our consciousness as well as sharpen it.

We overvalue consciousness, as if it were somehow superior to its companion skandhas (form, feelings, perceptions, formations) as a basis for practice. Later in the sutra, Manjusri, the Bodhisattva of Wisdom, says,

> *Consider contemplating consciousness: this consciousness is intermittent.*
> *Its existence in the mind, as well, is only an illusion.*
> *How then could this consciousness guide beings toward a breakthrough to enlightenment?*[1]

The Buddha asks Ananda, "How can these consciousnesses, which will ultimately perish, be the basis for practice as one strives for the Thus-Come-One's everlasting realization?"

We often realize something without being conscious of it. During the California summer when wildfires rage, sometimes I am only consciously aware that the sky overhead is brilliantly blue and looks clear. I am unaware of my lungs reacting to invisible smoke-born particles in the contaminated atmosphere until I realize them through coughing.

The basis of our practice relies on unawareness as well as awareness, absence as well as presence. We can take a cue from the famous Sherlock Holmes story about a stolen racehorse. Inspector Gregory and Holmes have the following exchange:

> GREGORY: Is there any point to which you would wish to draw my attention?
> HOLMES: To the curious incident of the dog in the night-time.
> GREGORY: The dog did nothing in the night-time.
> HOLMES: That was the curious incident.[2]

The key that clarifies a mystery sometimes lies in the dog's bark, sometimes in the silence. Similarly, sometimes it's important to attend to what we do not see, hear, touch, smell, taste, or think.

In this section of the Surangama Sutra, the Buddha offers us instruction for practice that meld the sensible with the insensible, seeing and not-seeing, thinking and not-thinking. The very faculties that give rise to illusion (eyes, ears, nose, tongue, body, and mind) are also the paths to enlightenment. The Buddha introduces us to this method of practice by encouraging us to hear the music of the mind.

ENLIGHTENED HEARING

The Buddha tells Ananda that the six sense-faculties are twists to our pure awareness: perceiver and perceived are twining vines.

When we add conditioned "understanding" to true enlightened understanding, we don't notice how the six faculties entangle us in illusion, binding us, tightening us in knots. If we cannot see the knots, we won't discover how to untie them.

The Buddha encourages Ananda: choose just one of your faculties and let go of all its conditioned attributes. Practicing this way will liberate all six faculties. He gives Ananda a key to this practice (italics are mine):

> *Extricate one faculty by detaching it from its objects, and redirect that faculty inward* so that it can return to what is original and true. Then it will radiate the light of the original understanding. This brilliant light will shine forth and extricate the other five faculties until they are completely free.[3]

Ananda objects: If the six faculties are such unreliable guides, how can they lead us to enlightenment? Seeing and hearing, tasting, touching, and smelling arise and fall; they come into being and cease to exist. Doesn't this also hold true for the sixth faculty, the mind-consciousness?

> The mind-consciousness must cease to exist when it is apart from its own objects [of awareness] . . . No matter how much I look here and look there, going about in circles in an exhaustive search, I can find nothing that fundamentally is my mind or my mind's objects.
>
> On what then can I base my quest for supreme enlightenment?
>
> . . . It seems to be mere speculation![4]

We may empathize with Ananda, but Shakyamuni seems to almost sigh. He has attempted multiple times to convey to Ananda the mind that grasps at objects of awareness—*that is not your mind!*

Here Buddha replies to Ananda's question by saying [my paraphrase]: "You just don't get it. I know you're sincere, but you don't seem to be able to trust what I'm saying. So let me try again, using an everyday situation to get it across to you." Then Shakyamuni offers the assembly a pivot point for practice.

> The Buddha instructs Rāhula to strike the bell once. Rāhula does so, the bell resounds, and Buddha asks everyone in the assembly: "Do you hear?" Ānanda and everyone else responds: "We hear."
>
> Buddha waits until the sound of the bell dies away, and asks: "Now do you hear?"
>
> Ānanda and everyone responds: "We do not."
>
> Buddha does this three times, asking the same questions each time. Each time he receives the same responses.
>
> After the third time the Buddha asks: "Why have you given such muddled answers?"[5]

The listeners protest, "What do you mean, muddled? When the bell was ringing, we heard it. When the bell wasn't ringing, we didn't hear it."

I'll paraphrase the Buddha's reply: *You did not clearly distinguish between hearing and sound.* You thought you heard the bell when it was ringing and didn't hear it when it wasn't. In that case, how could you know the sound had ceased? *You had to be able to hear the sound's absence.*

> Your true, unconditioned hearing-awareness includes both sound and silence; it is more fundamental than sound and silence.

At this moment, do you hear the words you are reading? As you read this, are you listening to your voice, or mine, or the sounds of your surroundings? When you say to someone "I hear you," are you referring to the squawks and buzzes made by their vocal cords, lips, and tongue shaping air into insubstantial words? Or is your heart responding to theirs?

Throughout our day, we rely on hearing what is "unsounded." We habitually glance both ways before crossing the street, but our vision often is blocked by other people, tall trucks, and flashing billboards; we continue only so long as we hear the absence of brakes squealing and no crescendo of a revving engine's approach. When we interact with other people, our emotions are often reactions to what they *don't* say. If someone bumps into us without an apologetic "excuse me," we may bristle at perceived rudeness. If we tell someone we love them and they don't reply, our hearts sink.

On the other hand, when we listen closely to someone we care about, what they leave unsaid often speaks eloquently of their fears and hopes. In music, the spaces between the notes let the music breathe; in breathing, the silent pivot point between inhalation and exhalation offers a fermata to the importunities of thought.

Our most fundamental sounds often go unheard. When the composer John Cage sought silence in an anechoic chamber, shielded from any outside sonic vibrations, he was surprised to hear an ongoing, faint high pitch along with a continuous low throb. The sound shielding of the room was supposed to provide silence; instead, it revealed the keening of his nervous system accompanied by the drumbeat of his heart.[6]

Every place is always sounding itself. I was in my college's music library when I put on headphones and listened to a piece by the twentieth-century composer Alvin Lucier. It began with his voice saying, "I am sitting in a room, different from the room you are in, now." Lucier described how he was then going to replay the recording of his voice over the speakers in his room and re-record it. Doing this repeatedly reinforced the ambient frequencies of the room in which he was recording. By the third or fourth repetition, buzzes, squeaks, and rumblings began to emerge. After more iterations, all semblance to his original voice was destroyed. By performing this process, Lucier brought the sound of his place, the sound of the room itself, to the sound of me in my place.

When you replay yourself to yourself, what kind of sounds do you make? Too often we don't really listen to ourselves. Too often we don't listen to what we're not-hearing.

The unheard sounds of our settings enfold us. The cascades of our unheard thoughts propel us. Mindfulness practice can help us be more attentive to our thoughts, but until we become aware of their tonal colors, their tempos and rhythms, we will remain deaf to their music.

Does the rush of your inner dialogue sound like white water or white noise? Does your internal dialogue speak kindly to you, or does it command you with an edge to its voice? Do you listen to the still, small voice within that whispers wisdom or override it with willfulness? If you want to be intimate with the compassion of your inquiring mind's fundamental constitution, you need to hear how your grievances chant threnodies, your desires croon love songs, and you fall into step with the military marches of anger.

When we hear these unheard sounds more clearly, we're less likely to get stuck by what we've set our sights on. When we learn how to turn *toward* rather than away from what we usually avoid, we can catch glimpses of the selves we'd rather leave unseen. We begin to allow our thoughts and feelings to express themselves without becoming engulfed by them. Like a waterfall, their roar warns us of their power but also reminds us they are flows, not facts, connecting us to the sea in continuous cycles of departures and returns.[7]

The starting point of this sutra—and also its ending point and its heart—is the ocean of liberation. Shakyamuni urges us to turn the six consciousnesses back onto themselves. Return to the root: turning the mind-body-sense-consciousnesses back on themselves settles the self on itself, freeing us from the outflows[8] of desire and ignorance.

Freeing yourself from outflows doesn't mean isolating yourself from the world by retreating into yourself. It simply means don't get caught by the objects of perception.

OFF AND ON: MERGING OBJECTS AND AWARENESS

Modern life is busy, busy, busy, demanding us to be always "on" at work, at home, even at play. This can be exhausting. We go on and on until we collapse and turn "off." This misses how "off" and "on" depend on each other and how the separation is unhealthy: it doesn't allow "on" to relax in effortless effort, and it doesn't credit how "off" is vibrant and restorative. If we think offline and online oppose one another, we dam a flowing stream.

There's a risk of this happening with Dharma practice. I've heard many students complain that they are able to practice in the zendo but "lose it" when they leave the grounds for the so-called real world. Many students feel meditation means sitting in some special position while practicing a technique such as breath-counting, koan inquiry, or shikantaza. This is a mistake, one Zen Master Joshu corrected in this encounter:

> A student asked Joshu, "What is meditation?"
> Joshu replied, "It is not meditation."
> The student asked, "What do you mean, 'it is not meditation'?"
> Joshu replied: "*It's alive!*"[9]

In reality, there are no ins and outs to practice, no nows and thens. It may look like we need to go from a world inside to a world outside, there and back again. This is the illusion of a journey *from* delusion *to* enlightenment, when in reality practice-enlightenment is *round*.

OMind rounds all our dualities—practice/realization, sound/silence, self/other—in undivided activity, tracing them along the folds of a Möbius strip uniting two and one.[10] Delusion and realization, practice and enlightenment, sound and silence are like this.

Sometimes students complain to me after a meditation session marked by a neighbor using a chainsaw, the siren of an ambulance speeding to an emergency, or a family member playing music in a nearby room: "I couldn't meditate because of all the distractions." In reality, there are no distractions, only things as they are or, as Shunryu Suzuki liked to say, "things as It is." When we feel distracted by a sound, it's a good cue for us, when hearing, to go to the enlightened basis of hearing. When we feel swept away by emotions, thoughts, sensations, or impulses, it's a good reminder: go to the enlightened basis of feeling, thinking, sensing, desiring.

Meditating with hearing is good practice for this. I've included some detailed instructions for three hearing meditations in appendix I. The fundamental principle is straightforward: begin by tuning in to sounds you can hear easily; as you quiet down and become more receptive, notice how the sound-field expands. From there, cultivate an awareness of all you are not-hearing—the sounds *and* the silence. Settled in stillness, rest in the openness of OMind. When it feels natural to do so, shine your light inward and listen to yourself. Allow listening to the silent sounds of thoughts and the tender touch of breath and flowing course of blood to merge subtly and insensibly with the enlightened basis of hearing itself, adding nothing extra, taking nothing away.

In this meditation, we become aware of how the marvelous OMind responds without picking and choosing. We rely on silence to perceive each individual sound along with the entire soundscape as a whole. We naturally steer clear of the many and the one.[11] This is the functioning of ordinary mind.

Listen to a string trio. Free from turbid mental and emotional processes, free from aversion and attachment, you can pick out the violin, the viola, and the cello while enjoying how their individual voices—each pursuing its horizontal line—blend into chords at every vertical musical moment. Each instrument sounds itself merging with the others. So do we.

Your Dharma-eye is clear and bright. As the Buddha says, "How then could you fail to go on to realize a supreme understanding and awakening?"

We are not separate from the music of the mind. In the sound of the bell and in its silence, each and all of us resonate with the Buddha's voice:

> When objects are not perceived as separate from awareness, that itself is nirvana. . . . Why would you allow anything else to be added to it?[12]

9

Twenty-Five Sages Speak of Enlightenment

Untying the Knots

Earlier in the sutra, the Buddha showed Ananda that he'd nearly violated his vows because he had not recognized the illusory nature of his sense-perceptions. The Buddha told his listeners that turbidity arises because their "pure, perfect, wondrous enlightened mind that understands is divided into the functions of seeing, listening, touching, and cognition. Objects you perceive and your mind-consciousness become entangled with each other, [and] the mind becomes turbid with afflictions."

Now the Buddha, using the example of the bell's sound, urges his disciples to choose one faculty and, by going to its enlightened basis, liberate all six. He seems to say the functions of seeing, listening, touching, and cognition provide a path to liberation and the vanishing of all illusions. Once again, the Buddha's listeners complain that they are perplexed. How can the functions be the cause of afflictions and also the means of liberation?

(One of the reasons I'm fond of the Surangama Sutra is the refreshing honesty with which it depicts the Buddha's students frequently confessing they are flummoxed. This reassures me that there's no shame in being bewildered by the Dharma if sages like Purna and family members like Ananda can be similarly stumped. I remember taking comfort from hearing my teacher Sojun, in one of his lectures on a mind-boggling passage, pause and say, "Each time I study this and give a talk on it, I seem to understand it, and as soon as I put it aside, all my understanding dissolves. The next time I encounter it, I have to start over again.")

Here Ananda speaks for the assembly (and for us) by confessing he doesn't understand; he feels all tied up in knots. Ananda begs Buddha to explain how we can disentangle ourselves, saying, "[S]omeone trying to untie a knot must understand how the knot was tied in the first place . . . otherwise he will not be able to untie it."

The Buddha replies,

> Well done, Ānanda! You want to understand the ignorance that you were born with. The source of the knot—what causes you to be bound to the cycle of death and rebirth—is your six faculties of perception, nothing more.
>
> Also, since you wish to understand the supreme enlightenment, you should understand that it is through those same six faculties that you can quickly gain bliss, liberation, and stillness, wondrous and everlasting.
>
> . . . The faculties and their objects [i.e., I-mind and the sense-objects of consciousness] come from the same source. *What binds and what unbinds are one and the same.* [my italics]
>
> . . . Neither the objects nor perceptions of them have an essential nature; they are dependent on each other, like intertwining reeds.
>
> . . . In our true nature, all conditioned things are seen
> as empty . . .

In the perceiver and perceived, there's nothing that is real;
They are like vines that only stand by twisting
round each other.[1]

To illustrate these twists and turns, Buddha picks up a *kata* (ceremonial scarf) and ties a knot in it. He asks his listeners, "What is this?" They reply, "It is a knot." Buddha then ties another five knots on the same scarf.

If we came upon this twisted jumble on a shelf, we might not recognize it as a kata; if the knots were tight enough, we might even take it to be a solid object. Nonetheless, the scarf remains unbroken; when we unravel the tangles, all the knots disappear to reveal the kata.

Buddha picks up the scarf, pulls it from one end, and asks, "Is this the way to untie the knot?" The answer, of course, is no. Buddha pulls the scarf from the other end, from both ends, and is unable to untie the knots. He asks Ananda how to untie them. Ananda responds, "World-Honored One, you must pull on the scarf from within each knot. Then they will come undone."

Have you ever unraveled a tangled string? It can seem hopelessly snarled, but as we keep at it, seeking the original snag, sometimes there's a point where the whole mess suddenly loosens and falls apart. Other times, we go step by step until finally we come to one last knot, which seems too small to have occasioned such a large mess. Sudden or gradual, when we come to the center of a knot, we find that it's empty.

UNRAVELING

We all hit snags during the course of our spiritual practice. Sometimes choices hook us on the difficulties of deciding; sometimes choices twist us through our difficulty of living with the consequences of a decision. Attachment and aversion trap us with an infinite number of ways we can tie ourselves in knots. When we are seized in snarls, we have a tendency to struggle and tug hard at any strand we can grasp. This usually tightens them further.

I experienced this when, after a decade or so of practice, I became enmeshed in a two-year struggle with myself. During this time, the more I meditated, the deeper I spiraled into depression and anxiety. I responded by meditating "harder" and more often, but since meditation neither soothed nor enlightened, I'd become more depressed and anxious. I'd enter sesshins with a pit in my stomach, fearing what the days would be like while ardently hoping they'd bring a breakthrough. I pushed myself to let go of my expectations, but this ricocheted: trying to let go I'd stiffen up, feel like a failure, and redouble my efforts. My root teacher encouraged me to persevere, but I got more and more stuck.

One day I had practice discussion with a friend, a kindly senior practitioner, Maylie Scott.[2] I described my difficulties and distress to Maylie and asked her for suggestions to modify my meditative technique. Maylie was silent for a while and then simply said, "Maybe it would be better if you didn't meditate so much for a while."

Doh! Hearing this, the hard lump of *trying* suddenly dissolved and was replaced by a sense of spaciousness. Permission to open an exit hatch revealed an entrance portal, reminding me of what I'd lost sight of: practice is always about liberation.[3] Once I felt able to meditate or not, I realized I had been confusing compulsion with devotion.

Our culture often substitutes commerce for devotion and compulsion for contentment; the economy stokes consumption by overvaluing the latest, shiniest, newest-and-most-improved versions of software, clothing, memes, meditations—even lovers. Throw out anything outmoded; replace, don't repair. "Be all you can be!" challenges the ads for the US Army. Athletes are urged to peak performance all the time—a contradiction in terms with a steep price. (As I write this, champion athletes are beginning to come forward with stories of the harms they've suffered in the drive to excel.)

We sometimes become lost in the minutiae of mastery; we can get so skilled at a profession we forget why we got into it in the first place. Then we burn out. We can develop such skill in our meditation and other forms of practice that we become adept at modulating our breath without ever touching our hearts.

To be able to decide when to let go and when to persevere, we first need to learn freedom from more and less. Finding the pivot point requires not titration but truth. The Surangama Sutra shows us how easily our perceptions divert us from the truth of our lives: our discriminating I-minds braid aversion and attachment into blindfolds.

We cannot untie the knots that secure our blindfolds by tugging on them. This narrows our vision just when we need to loosen our thoughts and feelings in order to cultivate a sense of spaciousness where creativity can flourish. When faced with painful personal dilemmas or important decisions, though, we're liable to tighten up.

At such times, it's helpful to remember that all our knots are, at their center, empty. The options facing us, along with our decisions, are mental objects and perceptions. Like all conditioned things, these are sandcastles by the sea, lacking any essential nature. It's good to be aware of our thoughts and feelings, but it's the spaces between them where we find our pivot point. As the eleventh verse of the *Tao Te Ching* teaches,

Thirty spokes converge on one hub;
the center is empty,
so the wheel can turn.

As a psychotherapist, I often saw people faced with pressing life decisions who got tangled up in the specific details and potential consequences. When I was a novice therapist, I endeavored to help them reach a decision by exploring their fears and desires. As I became more experienced, I learned that their difficulties usually lay not so much in *what* to decide but in having no sense of *how* to decide.

How we practice is often more important than what we practice. Many of us don't think much about the "how" of our decision processes. We often seem to assume that if we just keep batting our heads against a problem, we'll figure out the right answer. This can happen in spiritual practice, where dogged determination sometimes substitutes for flexible discernment.

In spiritual practice, as in life, there are no clear right answers. Both have their hazards, but unlike in the game show *Jeopardy*, we often can't even be sure we're asking the right questions.

Since we cannot make clear choices based on certain knowledge, we can only make our best guess and deal with whatever comes up. Given this existential uncertainty, it's helpful to have a variety of ways of coming to decisions and a variety of practice methods to draw on to fit our changing circumstances.

For my psychotherapy clients, the decision process could involve taking a long walk or talking with a few friends to see where opinions converged. Some clients benefitted from mental imagery; others needed to sleep on it, meditate, pray, experiment with a trial run, consult an oracle, or rely on a coin flip. Once we figured out a process that fit them, the decision usually became less stressful; a loosening of "shoulds" broadened the spread of possibilities. I have heard too many meditation practitioners bemoan being "bad" practitioners because they feel they are not practicing as they "should"; their focus on how they're not doing "enough" often confuses quantity with quality, hindering them from exploring ways to modulate their practice and find the proper attunement.

COMPLICATIONS OF CHOICE

For us to be in tune with our practice, we need to be playing an instrument that fits us. Finding a good match can be difficult, because the fit between path and practitioner needs to be mutual. I loved playing *shakuhachi* (Japanese bamboo flute), but although I could sound the notes, the music never truly flowed; it took me ten years to admit that the bamboo flute favors an embouchure formed by thick lips, and my own lips are thin. Similar issues arise with spiritual paths, regardless of whether or not they involve meditation, Buddhism, or other forms of devotion and realization.

We are fortunate to have many practice paths readily available to us, easily accessible over the internet even when they're not conveniently nearby. We can sample many different flavors of Christianity, Judaism, Buddhism, Islam, Hinduism, and Taoism. There are many others to explore: indigenous practices (to the extent these have survived erasure by cultural colonialism) such as sweat lodges, spirit quests, shamanism; suppressed ancient practices of European traditions such as Wicca and Druidism; lesser-known paths like Bahá'í and Zoroastrianism. When approaching non-Western practices or traditions, those of us from European heritage especially need to beware of deracination and disrespectful cultural misappropriation.

On top of the list of traditional practices, our modern culture has given rise to all sorts of New Age offerings and Scientology seminars, not to mention self-help books, mindfulness-based stress reduction, neurofeedback, and psychotherapy. The list goes on and on.

This rich smorgasbord of practice offerings reminds me of the pleasures and perils of a restaurant in New York, The Stockholm, which my family would sometimes visit for a special treat. One price gained us admission to an all-you-could-eat buffet table heaped high with mounds of deliciously enticing food. My family *loved* (still loves) to eat, so The Stockholm was our nirvana. We'd start by taking little samples on our plates to find out what we liked, then go back for the serious eating while attempting to leave room for dessert. Two of my aunts so enjoyed the process that they sometimes gave in to FOMO (fear of missing out); after eating their fill, they'd head to the restroom and vomit on purpose to empty their stomachs so they could go back to the buffet and enjoy eating more.

Although I think my aunts' behavior was indicative of their zeal for food rather than an eating disorder, our society's strange mixture of overindulgence and judgmental condemnation has led many people into such disorders. Likewise, overconsuming self-help can lead to suffering in devotional binges and purges and/or spiritual anorexias. Eagerness to sample every flavor of exotic spiritual comestible can get in the way of committing oneself to an ordinary, wholesome diet of steady practice. If we stuff ourselves full of self-righteousness, we risk nauseating others; if we gulp down the words of gurus without digesting them, we can give ourselves spiritual stomachaches. Conversely, overly devout immersion in spiritual zealotry is sometimes followed by a loss of appetite for faith.

To be faced with too many possibilities can be paralyzing. When I began learning meditation, my first teacher taught to focus on the breath by counting. Subsequent teachers taught to prolong the breath intentionally by expanding and contracting the diaphragm, while others taught to let go, relax, and follow the breath regardless of whether it is shallow or deep. Some of my teachers encouraged focusing on a koan; some taught thinking non-thinking. Some taught labeling thoughts and feelings. At one point I was so confused I stopped visiting teachers and instead spent a year of meditation gazing at a piece of red Jurassic rock I'd picked up while hiking on nearby Mount Diablo. (This was very helpful for grounding me. Forty years later, I can still visualize, and take refuge in, that rock.) It took me many more years to trust the process, let the meditation do the meditating, and allow it to teach me how to practice.

Beyond the problem of selecting a spiritual method, in our consumerist society, the difficulty of committing to *any* focused spiritual practice is compounded by our habit of comparing products based on their cost-benefits. When we choose a spiritual practice on the basis of what personal benefits it will offer us at the expense of effort, we can tie ourselves in knots. I sometimes am perplexed, facing the plethora of offerings of toothpaste, how to choose not only between different brands but between multiple flavors and a multitude of options—maximum fluoride, extra-whitening, tartar control, breath control. Our modern era's spiritual supermarkets can feel similar, with so many avenues to explore—each offering its own brand of Supreme Special Ingredient—that when we want to choose a spiritual path, we can come to a bewildered halt. Even when we've narrowed down the acreage to Buddhism and the field to Zen, many of us struggle to figure out what to practice, let alone how to practice.

During a public question-and-answer session at Berkeley Zen Center, a student who was perplexed about this asked our abbot, Sojun,

> "I've been reading about Zen students of the past. Some of them devoted themselves to studying thirty years under one teacher. Others wandered from teacher to teacher. Whichever they did, some of them became enlightened and some of them struggled for a long time. I can't figure out what I should do. Which way is better?"
>
> Sojun thought for a long time, then replied, "All told, maybe better to stick to the poison you already have."

I liked Sojun's response, though I don't think it applies to everyone. Ultimately, each person needs to decide this issue for themselves. People often continue doing something when they should stop—and often stop just when they should continue. I've seen friends practice Zen faithfully and rigorously for twenty years and never "get it." I've seen friends start a meditation practice but give it up when they come up against difficulties; hopping from one path to another, they never fully taste the fruit of doing one practice completely.

This section of the Surangama Sutra offers us a choice of practice methods. The Buddha asks twenty-five sages to describe the practices they used to break through to enlightenment. (A list of these methods appears in appendix III.) They vary according to the object of meditation, the perceptual faculty employed, the mode of consciousness cultivated, and which primary element was involved. One can meditate on the sound of a metal bell or a wooden block, the mantra of flowing water, the winds of change, the silences between thoughts. One can meditate with awareness wide or focused, scanning or still; on the flame of a candle, the intricacies of a mandala, the curiosities of a koan or the wisdom of devotion; by dropping everything or picking up anything.

Perhaps, if you examine the sages' twenty-five methods, you will find one that particularly appeals. The question remains: Should you choose that method on the basis of it's being appealing? If we limit ourselves to doing only the practices we like, we can get boxed in our by our preferences. Taking up a practice that doesn't initially fit us can help us break free of our conditioned habits. Either way, by choosing consciously we can be misled by our biases. But tumbling around indecisively, we're just spinning our wheels. We can choose to gamble on whatever comes up randomly—but is this abrogating personal responsibility? Do you have faith that the universe, or the Buddha, will somehow guide your spin so you'll come up a spiritual winner?

There are no winners and losers in spiritual practice—but that evades the issue. There is a Buddhist saying: "Sometimes we turn the Wheel of the Dharma, sometimes we are turned by the Wheel," but that doesn't offer any more guidance than "think not-thinking."

CHOOSING

How do we decide? In the last chapter of this section, the Buddha rather mischievously says to Manjusri,

> Consider now what has been said by these twenty-five sages . . . they all said that theirs was the best method for breaking through to enlightenment. In fact, none of the

> methods employed by these sages can be ranked as superior or inferior to the others. But now it is Ānanda whom I wish to teach how to become enlightened. Which then of these twenty-five methods of practice is most suitable for beings at Ānanda's level? And which one, after my nirvana, will lead beings of this world to practice in accord with the Vehicle of the Bodhisattvas and to follow the path to supreme enlightenment? Which of these methods will lead them most easily to success?[4]

I think the Buddha is being mischievous here because the whole issue of choice requires making the kinds of discrimination that are the hallmark of illusion ("in fact, none of these methods . . . can be ranked as superior or inferior"). But which is the best? Choice also presumes there is "someone" doing the choosing, which is a bit tricky in the context of the Buddha's fundamental doctrine of *anatman* ("no-self," "no-essence").

Using discriminating I-mind to determine the means for realizing nondiscriminative OMind seems contrary to Chan Teacher Sengcan's advice in the *Hsin-Hsin Ming*: "The Great Way is without difficulty, save that it avoids picking and choosing."[5] Every time we discriminate "this" from "that," we tie a knot in the fabric of "just this." Nonetheless, our everyday activity isn't possible without making discriminations; we're continually selecting one course over another. Every night when we go to bed, do we have a choice about whether to wake up the next day? Every morning when we wake up, we need to choose which side of the bed we'll get out of (or whether to get out of bed at all!). The koan of choice, free will, devotion, self-realization, and selflessness can be disconcerting.

Meditating on nondiscriminating mind during one meditation

sesshin, I got off my cushion for walking meditation and became discombobulated. For a few moments, I couldn't take a step: Weren't we discriminating by having everyone walk in one direction? Why shouldn't each person walk their own path (as is done in some traditions)? Perhaps I should express my liberated nature and shake up the sangha by walking counterclockwise: For that matter, why not walk sideways like a crab or backward?

I joined the group walking meditation in the usual fashion, but when it was my turn to have *dokusan* (practice discussion) with Sojun, I asked him, "How can I decide anything without falling into discriminations?" His answer was pithy: "Discriminate from the standpoint of nondiscrimination."

Very Zen but not, perhaps, all that clear about how to operationalize it—especially when we're feeling anxious in unmarked territory, unsure which direction will lead us to our destination.

When I'm hiking in the mountains and lose my way, the first thing I do is stop. I find myself where I am, look all around me, and orient to my center to compose myself. I let my self-imposed fears and previously formulated goals unravel and calm down. This helps me see many possibilities besides going straight ahead or retracing my steps. Our ideas, our preferences, and our aversions sometimes interfere with our route-finding—especially when we want to be certain that our efforts will take us where we want to go.

I learned an important rule of thumb for decision-making when I was in college and took a yoga class taught by a genial dean of students, Henry Littlefield. A broad-shouldered former Marine, a history teacher, and completely bald, he looked a lot like Mr. Clean. After a year or so studying with him, I saw an advertisement for a workshop by an Indian yoga teacher. I was tempted to enroll, but it was expensive, and my cash resources were tight. I asked Mr. Littlefield whether he knew the yoga teacher and thought it would be worth spending my money. I never forgot his reply: "I don't know that teacher, so I can't comment on what he offers. But I do know that if you take his workshop wondering whether it's worth it, then it won't be."

Measuring potential gains and losses is a good way to get mired in the bogs of our desires. Our attempts to gain clarity by making finer and finer discriminations and evaluations will ultimately confuse us. Looking ahead fills us with fears and hopes; looking back fills us with regrets and congratulations.

Better, I think, to throw ourselves into whatever we do completely, with no holding back. Perhaps this is what Dogen means in his meditation instructions when he tells us to "drop body-and-mind" to enter the gate of ease: to engage fully in all our activities irrespective of whether or not they work out the way we want them to. Better, when we love, to love wholeheartedly.

Faced with decisions about our spiritual practice, if we ask ourselves, "What use is it to me? Is it worth it?" we risk confusing ourselves by getting in our way. The verse from the *Tao Te Ching*, quoted earlier in this chapter—"thirty spokes project from one hub; the center is empty so the wheel can turn"—gives us a better alternative with its next couplet:

A pot is made from clay;
the center is empty,
so the vessel can be used.

I once asked Sojun, "After you have died, if someone asks me what was your teaching, what shall I say?"

He thought for a while then replied, "When I forget myself, I find myself."

If instead of asking, "What good is this path to me?" we ask, "How can I be a vessel of the Way?" we forget ourselves and find ourselves at the empty center. The fact is that all practices are fundamentally empty, including the Dharma. Because of this, any practice—prayer or meditation, drawing sand mandalas or sewing Buddhist robes, mindfulness of the breath, concentrating on a koan, thinking not-thinking—any of these can be done kindly or fiercely, compassionately or competitively. When we practice from a self-centered perspective, we're full of attachments and aversions that bias our compass readings. It's easier to orient when we practice from the empty center, together with all beings.

CENTERING

When I first began practicing, I wanted to center myself but had no idea how. For many years, I groped clumsily, failing to find a point where I could rest. I focused on a mudra, I practiced yoga, I read books about centering, I consulted with teachers—all to no avail. I felt ashamed of my "failure" and became so frustrated I'd get angry if I read a book about centering, tried its recommendations, and found they didn't work for me. Getting angry, of course, only made me feel worse. I only found a way to practice centering when I wasn't looking for it.

A friend suggested I might experience some relief from chronic pain by learning Dayan (Wild Goose) qigong. Within a few months of practice, I began to discover some intuitive direction that complemented zazen sitting meditation. Because my gratitude for this is immense, I want to share some of it with you, so I've included a qigong centering meditation in appendix II.

Perhaps this is a mistake; in a chapter describing twenty-five sages' paths, another possible meditation might only confuse you. I remember the frustration I felt when books offered instructions that didn't work for me, and should that happen to you, please accept my apologies. However, since this meditation is not well known outside the practice of Dayan qigong, I thought I'd make it available in the hope that some of you might find it helpful. Details are in the appendix but basically, it consists of physically gathering yourself to yourself. Let gravity do the work; feel your feet on the ground, the top of your head in the sky, and somewhere on the line that connects them, notice where your body finds it balance. Let your mind find that pivot point and, when your attention wanders away, return again and again to the empty hub.

Whatever paths we choose, we'll come upon many side trails and forks in the road. We can try to plan our routes by poring over a GPS topo, but once we're walking the actual territory, it will look different from the map. In the time since the map was drawn, floods may have washed away some markers; landslides may have blocked some paths while creating other openings. Climbing steep terrain and scrabbling down loose scree, on firm level ground and shifting soft sands, we continuously find our balance, lose it, and rediscover it. When we fall down, we use the earth to get back up.

On this continuously spinning globe, rotating around a star hurtling through a galaxy, we establish our balance where we are. Just this is enough. As Dogen says in *Genjo Koan*, "When you find your place where you are, practice occurs, actualizing the fundamental point."[6]

10

The Bodhisattva Who Hears the Cries of the World

Hearing the Cries of the World

The Wheel of the Dharma turns without pause. It centers on an empty, dimensionless point that is vast beyond measure. We live our lives, though, on three-dimensional surfaces, bumping along where the rims meet the road, occasionally pierced by sharp spokes—whirlpools of desire whose centripetal pulls suck us in, centrifugal pushes of aversion that spit us out.

Recently we took my two-year-old grandson, Lucas, to his first experience of a merry-go-round. While we waited our turn at the ride's entrance gate, Lucas watched wide-eyed, transfixed by the carousel ponies circling and pumping up and down to the honky-tonk music. He was fascinated but trepidatious: the brash noise and bright colors were almost more intense than his young mind could handle. When the carousel started moving, Lucas felt overwhelmed; he started crying, and struggled to get off. His father hugged him, and his sobbing receded, but he barely tolerated the experience. Then, when the carousel stopped moving and his father picked him up to leave, Lucas screamed, struggled to escape from his father's arms, and cried out. "*Again!*" he demanded. He wanted to get back on.

Welcome to the merry-go-round of suffering. Have you ever, like Lucas, had an experience you found stimulating but unpleasant that, once it was over, you wanted to try again? Have you ever tried one solution to a problem that didn't work or that backfired, then tried the same thing again, sure that this time it would work? When your car is stuck in the snow, putting your foot on the accelerator spins the wheels and digs you in deeper. Wanting what we don't have, having what we don't want, we're prone to singing the "if-you-love-me-I-will-leave-you, if-you-leave-me-I-will-love-you" blues.

THE CRIES OF THE WORLD

Ambivalence causes suffering; so does certainty. Much of society these days is polarized into factions that blame each other. In politics, those on the left and those on the right refuse to grant their opponents the possibility of having goodwill; they point fingers at each other and cry "Evil!" When one side's political candidate wins, the other side despairs and cries out, "Unfair!"

Avalokiteshvara (the Bodhisattva of Compassion) hears the cries of the world. In our partisan self-righteousness, we forget that Avalokiteshvara hears all cries equally—our opponents' along with our own, those of impoverished children crying from hunger pains, and those of wealthy adults crying from stomachaches due to overconsumption.

When thinking of Avalokiteshvara hearing the cries of the world, we tend to imagine the keening of mourners and the wails of people in agony. This mistakes the practice of hearing with the sounds that are heard, as we learned in chapter 8. The enlightened hearing of compassion is equally receptive to all cries, whether they are of dark pleasure or blindingly bright pain. Every being is continuously crying out the First Noble Truth: the suffering of existence itself.

After the sun sets, when midnight's darkness cools the air and stills the noises of the preceding day, you can hear the building creak. Relieved of its burden of expanding to meet daylight's demands, the house cries out as it settles itself on itself. An owl hoots, breezes rustle the leaves. These, too, are the cries of the world. A car engine revs, a cat screeches briefly; the bedsprings protest in response to your body shifting position or the throes of love. These are the cries of the world. Just as you're about to fall asleep, the voice of your three-year-old child calls out, "Mommy, get me a glass of water! I'm thirsty, Daddy!" You cry silently, "I'm exhausted!" Sweet and sour, the cries of the world.

The cries of the world are just as they are. Whether we hear them as pleasing or harsh is a condition of the ears that hear them. When I visit friends in Australia, I am thrilled by the harsh squawks of cockatoos telling me I am in an exotic place below the equator. My friends hear the irritating caw of an annoying pest raiding their wheelie bins.

Perhaps the most powerful cry impelling us around the carousel of life and death is "I love you." Expressed or repressed, voiced in words, glances adoring or beseeching, touches caressing or clenching, "I love you" is sought after and feared, a balm and a binding, a cry of the world continuously calling on compassion.

In the previous chapter, the Buddha asked twenty-five sages to share their paths to enlightenment. Avalokiteshvara was the last one to share her story. When the Buddha asked Manjusri to judge the paths, Manjusri chose Avalokiteshvara's as the best. I suggested this to be rather mischievous on Buddha's part, but Manjusri's choice of Avalokiteshvara was inevitable. Manjusri and Avalokiteshvara, being the embodiments of wisdom and compassion, form an inseparable pair. Compassion without wisdom easily falls into idiocy; wisdom without compassion easily hardens into heartlessness.

Avalokiteshvara describes her practice:

> Because I did not listen to sounds and instead contemplated the listener within, my mind became like a great flawless mirror that reflected the emptiness of the Matrix of the Thus-Come-One.[1]
>
> I can now hear the cries of suffering beings throughout the ten directions, and I can bring about their liberation.[2]

Be careful. If you think you know what crying sounds like, you will not hear the suffering in every empty boast, the fear in every empty threat, the anguish in every empty evasion. You then risk limiting your compassion to only those you think deserve it or those you think are "really" suffering.

At the end of the practice period where I served as *shuso* (head student), during a public question-and-answer ceremony, my twenty-something daughter asked me, speaking from her yearning for social justice, "Are some sufferings worse than others?" I had to answer, "No."

Many people object to this answer. It doesn't seem to take into account systems of power and oppression that operate unjustly in society. It could even be a form of spiritual bypassing. However, my daughter's question was not "Are some sufferings more unjust than others?" or "Can we identify causes for suffering, assign responsibility, and take action to remedy the situation?" I share my daughter's outrage at injustice and her commitment to being socially engaged. However, she was attending a Zen temple ceremony when she asked, "Are some sufferings *worse* than others?" From a practice perspective, making comparisons and moral judgments can get in the way of our commitment to respond to the suffering of all beings.[3]

The simple fact is that hurt hurts. As soon as we start discriminating degrees of suffering, we slip into triage mode, dispensing limited quantities of compassion according to urgency or need. This is appropriate for the practical necessities of a hospital's emergency room, but even there it can be misused. In my work with patients who suffer from chronic pain, almost all of them relate experiences where they've had an acute flare of pain, gone to see their doctor, and been told they "shouldn't" be experiencing so much pain and should just tough it out. This usually reflects the ignorance of the provider rather than deliberate cruelty, but it is terribly invalidating for the patient and increases their suffering.[4]

When a person feels pain, they feel pain. In the same way, when beings suffer, they suffer. "Should" and "shouldn't," "fair" or "unfair," are beside the point. If we say, "His suffering is more than hers," we are in danger of overlooking the deeper reality we share with all beings, the First Noble Truth: life *is* suffering.

Because life is always moving, it is always life-and-death, beginnings-and-endings tumbling over and replacing each other. Every moment we are burning ourselves up to maintain our warm mammalian bodies; we need to constantly make adjustments to deal with ever-changing conditions. This roiling and rolling being continuous, suffering is boundless. If compassion is to liberate us from suffering, compassion also must be limitless. For this reason, true compassion is founded in nondiscriminating, nondual deep wisdom: prajnaparamita.

The cries of the world are the voice of the Dharma. The voice of the Dharma is proclaimed by every sentient being, by insentient tiles and pebbles, by ungraspable starlight and the dark maw of fathomless caverns. Even supposedly mute rocks speak; when water erodes their edges, rocks roar under waterfalls and whisper beneath streams' trickles. When the temperature drops and water freezes and expands, stones shout when they split apart. *Crack!* The sound of enlightenment.

COMPASSION'S RESPONSE TO SUFFERING

Every newspaper headline, social media post, radio and television announcement broadcasts the crying of the world. Even laughter can be tinged with sorrow, a momentary release from the yearnings of impermanence. Byron once said, "And if I laugh at any mortal thing, 'tis that I may not weep."

Byron, with his Romantic attachment to the dark glamor of suffering, takes it too far. As the Third Noble Truth teaches, there is release from suffering. The silent movies of Charlie Chaplin and Buster Keaton elicit genuine laughter, though they also touch our tender hearts. To experience liberation, we need to be receptive to joy, and joy needs space to breathe—which only comes when we're also open to hurt. Compassion does not deny or minimize pain:

rather, compassion responds to affliction by opening its arms and offering an embrace that widens the world.

Around ten or fifteen years ago, psychotherapists began discussing the uses of compassion. I felt happy when workshops on compassion for psychotherapists started cropping up, but I was a little leery of how psychotherapy, in its search for useful fixes, sometimes limits itself to intervention techniques. Just as it's possible to fall into spiritual bypasses that avoid grappling with social and psychological issues, it's possible to fall into psychological fallacies that avoid exploring existential and spiritual issues. Nonetheless, when I was asked to teach a workshop on compassion to graduate students in psychotherapy, I readily agreed, confident that my experiences as a therapist and meditation practitioner qualified me. As I began planning the workshop, I had an unpleasant realization: I didn't have words to communicate compassion's true nature. Dictionary definitions don't convey compassion's generous reach, but although I had an intuitive sense for the feel of compassion, I couldn't articulate it.

I was clear about a few things. Compassion isn't the same as empathy or sympathy. Compassion is not just wanting to help people. Being well-intentioned is insufficient by itself; too many terrible things have been done by people who later protest, "I only wanted to help."

I couldn't say what compassion was, but I was fortunate to have an experiential reference point. Years earlier I'd had a stroke during a high-altitude trek in the Himalayas. My companion left me to summon help. I lay alone, propped up against some rocks, and silently cried out to the surrounding mountains, "I'm having a stroke! I might die, here, now, any minute, alone!"

The mountains responded with deep quiet and soaring calm: "Welcome to the club! Everything dies. We mountains die too." The compassionate voice of earth-meeting-sky enfolded me, warming the thin Himalayan air.

I began to meditate in shikantaza (just sitting), but I was surprised to find myself turning instead to metta (loving-kindness) meditation, extending compassion to everyone I loved, everyone in my life, every being. I practiced metta until help arrived.

Later I felt bothered by how I'd turned to loving-kindness meditation rather than shikantaza; I'd always assumed that, if given the opportunity to face death with full awareness, I'd do so via the latter. I asked my Zen teacher Sojun about this: Since shikantaza is the foundation of our Soto Zen practice, why didn't it provide a refuge when I felt in extremis? Why had I turned to metta meditation when I felt I faced death?

"Well, that sounds natural," he replied.

Compassion is just natural.

When I began preparing materials for the workshop on compassion but couldn't find words to express it conceptually, I thought back on this experience. Every morning before the start of my daily meditation, I summoned the intuition of compassion and asked, "What is this?" before settling down into shikantaza. During the day I carried compassion as a koan, a thread to follow while driving my car back and forth to work, seeing clients, parenting my daughters, cooking dinner, brushing my teeth.

After several months, the first line of the Heart Sutra responded to my question: "Avalokiteshvara Bodhisattva, when practicing deeply the prajna paramita, perceived all five skandhas in their own-being are empty, and was saved from all suffering."

Compassion, practicing deep wisdom, realizes no *thing* exists but flows. Every seeming thing is a ball tossed on rushing water: moment to moment, nonstop flow.[5] Realizing this, Avalokiteshvara is able to compassionately respond to suffering not with a pained grimace but with a gentle, loving smile.

EMPTINESS AND COMPASSION

The words of the Heart Sutra seem to be about emptiness: "No eyes, no ears, no nose, no tongue, no body, no mind." The Heart Sutra, though, flows together with all being, continuously singing compassion. It flows through words into an ungraspable mantra sounding the bell's ringing, sounding the bell's silence: GYA TE GYA TE.

Compassion relies on and rests in an emptiness that is itself empty. Compassion is boundless, free of characteristics, the Matrix of the Thus-Come-One released from suffering not by fixing it, not by denying it, but through embracing it. Through this embrace, compassion realizes how suffering in its own-being is empty. Realizing that suffering is ungraspable, we are liberated from suffering's grip.

The Surangama Sutra turns on the pivot point of emptiness. Describing her path to enlightenment, Avalokiteshvara reported that she began by turning hearing toward its source, where

> external sounds disappeared . . . t[hen] with sounds stilled, both sounds and silence ceased . . . awareness and the objects of my awareness were emptied . . . then even that emptying and what had been emptied vanished. . . . The ultimate stillness was revealed. . . . everything in the ten directions was fully illuminated.[6]

Realizing the emptiness of emptiness put Avalokiteshvara in touch with the roots of compassion:

> First, my mind ascended to unite with the fundamental, wondrous, enlightened mind of all Buddhas in all ten directions, and my power of compassion became the same as theirs.
>
> Second, my mind descended to unite with all beings of the six destinies in all ten directions such that I felt their sorrows and their prayerful yearnings as my own.
>
> My power of compassion became the same as the Buddhas'. I was then able to go to all lands and appear in thirty-two forms that respond to what beings require.[7]

Be careful: don't be misled by words. The words with which Avalokiteshvara conveys her story seem to imply a before and after, as if emptiness is some *thing* that we must first achieve, so that later we can be compassionate. Our fundamental, ancestral compassion, though, is beginningless and endless. Emptiness, free of any defining characteristics, cannot be near or far, past or future. Emptiness—even "here" and "now"—being ungraspable enables compassion to be boundless.

Compassion is not a feeling we create, an emotion that comes and goes. Compassion is our heritage. The time of compassion is ever with us; the place of compassion is ever at this very point. There's nothing mystical about it; in the words of verse 15 of the *Tao Te Ching*, compassion sounds "the mysteries of the unfathomable Way, deeply ordinary, profoundly unremarkable."

Because compassion underlies our being, we can draw on it by reaching beyond ourselves.[8] Compassion reaches to us through everyday experience while we reach for it, whether or not we are aware of it. I like to use the analogy of the cable cars of San Francisco, which seem to use their own power to navigate the ups and downs of the city's steep hills. In reality there is a cable underground that cycles in a continual orbit. The cable car operator only needs to reach down and engage the cable.

Whether you are aware of it or not, you are reaching for compassion at this moment, through your mind searching to understand; through your ears listening to your thoughts (and perhaps mine); through your hands holding a book or e-reader, your eyes scanning shapes. Compassion expresses itself reaching to you via trees and minerals offering themselves to provide the substances that form your book or tablet. Compassion reaches to you through the people who labored to fashion these devices, through these fingers of mine typing words. The *reaching* is key.

A Zen koan addresses this reaching.[9] Two friends are questioning each other: Why does the Goddess of Compassion (Avalokiteshvara) have a thousand hands and eyes? One of them says, "It's like groping for the pillow at night."

Compassion, like the pillow at night, is always available, but often we're half-asleep, have difficulties finding it, and can only reach for it. Sometimes we reach for it and find it easily, even in our sleep; sometimes, though fully awake, we grope for it and miss.

WHEN SUFFERING RISES, BUT COMPASSION IS HARD TO FIND

As I get older, I've found—as many people do in the process of aging—that several chronic medical problems have gotten worse. I have not had a pain-free day for several years; sometimes

I'll have periods of pain flares where the pain becomes severe enough that I'm unable to perform my usual coping activities (qigong, sitting meditation), and when I reach out for physical relief (anti-inflammatory medication, physical therapy, acupuncture, and so forth), I don't receive much benefit. I've learned, at such times, that I can find relief from suffering by reaching within to the empty center.[10]

When pain that cannot sleep rouses me from my bed at 3 A.M., I make my way to the place my sweetheart has helped me prepare beforehand.[11] In its compassionate arrangement of blankets, pillows, and props, it serves as my ally, offering me a place where I can lie more comfortably. Sometimes, though, I'll continue to wince involuntarily in reaction to sharp nerve spikes or muscle spasms, automatically bracing myself against the next onslaught.

I've learned that, in such situations, I cannot change the pain in my spine, back muscles, buttocks, and legs. I can, however, change my *relationship* to the pain by cultivating awareness of another area of the body.

I usually begin with my lips. If I'm clenching my mouth muscles, I remind myself these can function independently of the pain in the other parts of my body. I soften my lips while placing the tip of my tongue so it lightly touches the upper palate, as in meditation. This doesn't touch the pain, but it makes it easier to smile gently, allows my facial muscles to relax and enlarges the space in mind in which I can grope for compassion.

This helps me explore where the center of the pain is. Often this is difficult to locate; the center seems to be first at one spot, then another. So whenever my attention lights on a spot, I pause and explore that spot further: What is at the center of just this spot? By continuing this, the pain usually settles into a general area.

I then look for the center of that area and, once there, continue toward the center of the center. There I rediscover what, from experience, I know I'll find: the center of the center being an infinitesimal point, it has zero dimensions. Communing with this commodious emptiness, often, for a few moments, the pain disappears completely.

When this happens, it would be a false hope to expect the pain won't return; it will. Knowing it will come and go, I'm able to cease resisting the pain when it reappears. Then my suffering eases, giving me room to summon compassion for myself and all beings. By engaging with this again and again, eventually the pain and suffering lightens.

I've taught many clients this method and found it often works even for people who don't meditate—but it is easier to access for people who practice meditation and cultivate compassion and loving-kindness.

NOT ALONE

Reaching comes from compassion and returns to compassion. Compassion calls to us; our fundamental nature responds, drawn by the compassion that supports us by returning us to ourselves. We rest in a hammock of compassion—our fundamental connectedness, Indra's Net, the Matrix of the Thus-Come-One. Here we are never alone. Pain eases in companionship.

When I can't find a word, when I cannot explain something, my friends help me out, their minds leaping to fill in the gaps. This is happening at this moment while I sit writing and you sit reading—our words, thoughts, feelings, and fellowship arise compassionately together. Our groping for each other is usually hit-and-miss; problems arise, we miscommunicate; we get upset as we struggle to express ourselves, to understand each other. "Just this" is our practice merry-go-round.

Suffering is lonely. Compassion reminds us we are not alone. We *cannot* be alone. As surely as the enlightened basis of hearing manifests through sounds that depend on silence, we always exist as interbeing. Our miseries of alienation and separation arise from the illusory split between a perceiver and the objects of perception. In the Surangama Sutra, we hear how, to heal this split, Avalokiteshvara offers herself to every being in the form they need—namely, in their own form.

Avalokiteshvara describes how, once she had "realized the wondrousness within the wonder at the heart of my hearing," she was able to "appear to them as they are and will instruct them in the Dharma . . . by displaying kindness, by inspiring awe, and by manifesting samādhi and wisdom, I can rescue and shelter beings, allowing them to attain great mastery and ease." To dragons, she appears as a wish-fulfilling dragon; to kings, she appears as a king; to ordinary people, she appears as an ordinary person. She reflects their suffering while instructing them in the Dharma, like a mirror that reflects everything without being stained by it. Compassion greets all life with equal love.

Compassion is not a feeling. Compassion is not a skill we can acquire by following an instruction manual, not a thing, not a chemical humor we can manufacture. If it were, we would risk running out of it and be subject to compassion fatigue. We only get "compassion fatigue" when we think *we* are the source of compassion. Compassion is bigger than us—it is the water we drink and the ocean in which we swim.

Whatever form compassion takes, it is never a one-way street; compassion is always an *inter*action, born of our inherent, wonderful interbeing. Our practice helps us learn how to reach for compassion at its source, so we can be vessels to convey it as necessary. Compassion arises in response to suffering with an instinctive impulse that, in its very reaching, knows what to do. Sometimes compassion acts through satisfying a wish or soothing a hurt, sometimes by frustrating a wish or bringing a hurt to light. Often it simply shows up via a willingness to be present and share someone's journey on the—merry-go-round?—of life-and-death.

HAPPY BIRTHDAY

Suffering is synonymous with birth-and-death; so is liberation. They arise with each other like Manjusri does with Avalokitshvara, wisdom and compassion's mutually supportive interbeing. Manjusri ends this section of the sutra with a series of verses summarizing all the prior teachings, then praises how turning hearing to touch its enlightened source enables us to listen to the cries of the world. Compassion brings us home to the cries of the world, sounding the double helix playing the music of birth-and-death.

My father died on a bed in my living room, after a long illness. My sister and I kept him company through his final coma, meditating as he drew his last breath. Afterward we sat silently with each other.

When the hospice worker started preparing his body to be taken away, my sister was startled by a realization. She turned to me and exclaimed, "It's your birthday!" She repeated herself, her voice filled with commiseration and sorrow, "Dad died on *your birthday*!"

I hadn't been aware of this until she said it. Once the words were out, I started to feel a little sorry for myself.

My sister turned toward the hospice worker and in a slightly louder voice informed her, "Our dad died on my brother's birthday!"

The hospice worker stopped what she was doing with our father's body. She paused. Then she turned to me, smiled radiantly, and said, "*How wonderful!*"

Her compassionate smile bridged a seeming sorrow, helping me connect birth-day with death-day to see the circle as unbroken. This liberated me to feel grateful in the midst of grief. After the storm, good weather. What could be more natural? After sorrow comes happiness.

We practice so that when we encounter suffering, we also have access to wonder and gratitude. Then our hearts break open, enabling us to smile gently, lovingly, even in the face of pain. When Ananda and all the assembly heard the teachings of compassion offered by Manjusri and Avalokiteshvara, kindness flowered like the lotus. The Matanga woman who had ensorcelled Ananda was present; having been rescued by the Surangama mantra, she'd become a nun and joined the Buddha's community. Hearing Manjusri's verses, she was transformed into an arhat. Hearing the teachings, Ananda and everyone present

> were like someone who have traveled far from home on matters of business: although the traveler has not yet been able to return, he knows the road that will lead him home.[12]

11

Four Clear and Definitive Instructions on Purity

Sex! Murder! Theft! Lies!

The Buddha's listeners—fellow travelers on the Surangama's heroic march—are untying the knots of suffering and delusion. In the process, they—and we—are reconnoitering the road that will lead us home. However, as the Buddha indicated earlier in the sutra, if we want to restore the whole cloth of our being, we need to untie the knots in sequence. We have a few more knots to attend to before we can proceed further.

In the Buddha's Eightfold Noble Path, right view, right intention, right speech, right conduct, right livelihood, and right effort all come before right mindfulness and right meditation (samadhi). Currently, many people in our society begin practice by learning meditation as a way of cultivating mindfulness for good health and emotional peace. This is almost a complete reversal of the traditional sequence. Notice the order of the elements in what the Buddha says to Ananda in this section of the Surangama Sutra (I've separated the elements with bullet points).

You have often heard me speak of the three essential elements of spiritual practice:

- precepts, which require us to guard and focus the mind;
- samādhi, which arises from following precepts; and
- wisdom, which appears out of samādhi.

The Eightfold Noble Path teaches us that first we need to become aware of suffering, its causes, and the possibility of relief from suffering. Until then, we're chasing mirages through the mazes of life-and-death. Once we become aware that we contribute to the creation of suffering for ourselves and others, and that this is not inevitable, we can begin to generate wholesome aspirations and strengthen our determination to realize them. On the bodhisattva path, we devote ourselves to the benefit of all beings (including ourselves).

The next step is to translate our awareness and intention into concrete forms. The Buddhist precepts help us shape our behaviors—how we speak, dedicate our work, interact with others, and focus our energies—so they serve our understanding and intention. What Norman Fischer calls "the awesome power of our actions"[1] prepares the soil and plants the seeds so that conditions become propitious for mindfulness and meditation to blossom.

IMPORTANCE OF PRECEPTS

Meditation is becoming increasingly common in our society. Mindfulness is often taught in medical centers, schools, psychotherapy clinics, and corporate offices; it is offered as a technique for stress reduction, for sharpening attention and increasing productivity. Surely it has introduced many people to a wider sense of awareness and alleviated much distress. However, when meditation (of any sort) or mindfulness (in particular[2]) is taught only as a technique, shorn of its spiritual dimensions, it cannot address the unquestioned assumptions and existential questions that underlie much of our current anguish—an anguish affecting not only humans but also, in the Anthropocene era, other species and the global environment. When meditation is taught as a technique, it become results-oriented, mirroring the pressures of a society that focuses on accomplishment more than insight and emphasizes doing over being.

When we turn meditation into a tool for mastering the mind, we not only condemn ourselves to an impossible task (since mind is ungraspable) but also diminish the possibility of allowing the heart of enlightened understanding to emerge. When we aim for meditative samadhi without first exploring our way via the precepts, we don't take advantage of the moral compasses that help orient us to find our place together with all beings.

The *Oxford English Dictionary* defines "precept" as "a general rule intended to regulate behavior or thought."[3] The word comes from the Latin *praeceptum* and *praecipere*, meaning to "warn, instruct," combining *prae* (before) and *capere* (take). So a precept is what arises before we take action; it offers us some instruction or at least some hints on which way to turn, what compass direction to orient toward. When we adopt precepts, they become our lenses on the world; they help us see the world in ways that open up some avenues of engagement while fencing off others. However, precepts are never absolute; they always arise in response to circumstances.

We may be healthily skeptical of moral absolutes. In the last few hundred years we have begun to realize how our values are bound by our cultural contexts, our individual and societal histories. Some people take refuge from these shifting sands in rigid dogmas, while others throw up their hands, proclaim "everything's relative," and find no vantage point where they can stand firm.

While truth may be relative, that doesn't mean it does not exist. As the Buddha pointed out earlier in the sutra, the truth of emptiness steers clear of the false dichotomy of "is" and "is not." Buddhist wisdom lets go of any fixed, timeless truths or ideal goals, but it does not succumb to random arbitrariness. "The fact that the ground we stand on—the planet Earth—is always rotating on its axis and orbiting around the sun does not mean that at any particular moment it is not precisely somewhere."[4]

Our individualist society encourages us to insist that nobody has the right to tell us what we should and shouldn't do. Perhaps we've become allergic to formulating moral principles after seeing too many sermons preached but not practiced. Some people have had childhoods warped by religious authorities wielding moral rules to mete out sin, guilt, and punishment. Ethics become distorted by power relationships when authoritarian leaders invoke adherence to unjust rules and mislabel obedience as morality.

THE NATURE OF BUDDHIST PRECEPTS

Buddhist precepts are not divine "shoulds" and "shouldn'ts" handed down on tablets carved on mountaintops, not a moral code dictated by a deity demanding obedience backed by threats of celestial wrath that will be meted out to transgressors. The Buddhist precepts are not commandments but forms of practice: they are gateways to enlightenment, ease, and joy.

Just as there's no one right way of practicing meditation, there's no one right way to practice a precept. Right practice isn't a virtue in the sense of "right" as the opposite of "wrong." The "right" in right practice is the kind you find when you're righting a ship or trueing a board. It's balancing, aligning so that you function harmoniously along with everything and everyone else. There's no "should" to mindfulness and no special honor to it; it's just that when we're not mindful, we are more constricted by our unexamined assumptions, mired in conditioned patterns of behavior that too often cause us to miss out on our lives.

The Surangama Sutra reflects its times by taking the precepts of the *vinaya* (the rules of conduct for monks and nuns) as a given. It neither explains the rationale for the rules nor delves into thorny ethical dilemmas. It reflects the assumptions of its historical and cultural setting. The sutra's story of Ananda being in peril in the presence of a courtesan takes as a given that having sex is inimical to realizing enlightenment. Just as matter-of-factly, another section of the sutra states with complete conviction that eating onions arouses sexual desire and anger, causing meditation practitioners to be reborn as demons and fall into Unrelenting Hell. Perhaps we all need to change our diets.

Historically, Buddhist precepts arose piecemeal in response to practical difficulties in the day-to-day life of ordinary human beings. Their ad hoc nature is evident in how, when the Buddha was dying, he told Ananda that if the members of the sangha wished to amend or modify some rules, they could do so.[5] The precepts are practical responses to how to live in the world. They help us discover a way of living that in the long run is the easiest and most balanced way of meeting the challenges we encounter.

This might not be obvious in this section of the Surangama Sutra, with its strict title "Four Clear and Definitive Instructions on Purity." In it, the Buddha warns that meditation will be fruitless if we don't abjure sexual activity, killing, stealing, and lying. Nevertheless, I detect a certain playfulness in its metaphors:

> . . . one who practices entering samādhi while practicing meditation in stillness without renouncing sexual activity is like one who cooks sand in the hope that it will turn into rice.[6]
>
> . . . one who enters samādhi while practicing meditation in stillness without renouncing all killing is like one who hopes that nobody will hear him shout if he stops up his own ears.[7]
>
> . . . one who enters samādhi while practicing meditation in stillness but who does not refrain from making false claims is like someone who molds a piece of excrement into the shape of a piece of sandalwood incense in the hope that it will then be fragrant.[8]
>
> One who enters samādhi while practicing meditation in stillness but who does not renounce stealing is like one who tries to fill a leaking cup with water.[9]

I can imagine myself having a good time playing on the beach with my grandchildren, pretending to cook sand. I definitely have been in situations so noisy I've covered my ears while shouting a request to turn down the volume. I can loosen my attachment to a noxious habit when I hear someone say, "Everyone thinks their own shit smells like perfume." And the older I get, the more leaks spring from this body-and-mind vessel of mine.

Still, judgmentalism and moralistic perfectionism can creep into any practice when it is reduced to a manualized set of instructions. When a religious practice is weighed down by an excessive emphasis on purity and correctness, it can become overly serious, even grim. A non-Buddhist friend of mine says she loves much about Zen but is repelled by what she experiences as its rigid, harsh superego. I wish she'd accompanied me to the lecture where I heard the Zen teacher Robert Aitken respond to an earnest question by pausing, breaking into a beautiful smile, then saying, "You don't understand: it is *play*. *Play*."

PLAYING WITH THE PRECEPTS

The precepts are not designed to be gateways to guilt but to liberation. The Surangama Sutra explores the chimeras of consciousnesses not to mire us in complexities but to free us from their twists and turns. It teaches us the straightforward mind is the place for awakening.

We need to have a sense of humor about our frailties, or we'll feel ashamed and unwilling to admit to them. If you are embarrassed by the fact that after many years of practice you still sometimes struggle with your temper, you'll be more likely to erupt in angry outbursts. I find it helpful to rely on others to keep me from becoming overly serious or self-righteous. I'm very grateful to my daughter who, for a year or so after I was shuso (head student) at Berkeley Zen Center, preceded any question she asked me with a sardonic "Oh, Wise One." She said this fondly but still with a sweet yank on the chains of my ego—good medicine to disabuse me of any claims to sage moral authority!

I'm attracted to Chinese Chan and Japanese Zen practice in part because, being influenced by Taoism, they usually were (and are) iconoclastic, leery of rigid rules and ritual purity. There is an unbroken thread between the ancient verse (38) from the *Tao Te Ching*:

High virtue isn't "virtuous"
thus it truly has virtue;
low virtue never frees itself from virtuousness,
therefore it has no true virtue.

and Aitken Roshi's contemporary *gatha*:

Preparing to enter the shower
I vow with all beings
to wash off the last residue
of thoughts about being pure.[10]

Chan and Zen Buddhism draw from a Taoist tradition that seeks to return us to our original nature. There is a phrase in the precepts ceremony we used at BZC: "Originally pure, don't defile. This is the great awareness." The "purity" in this phrase is not a spotless goodness; it is the purity of "just natural," of original nature empty of any abiding characteristics, unstained by either good or bad.

The precepts provide structure to support us, forms to pour ourselves into, means to strengthen our moral muscles so that our bones can take us where our intentions aim. They need to be actualized in concrete actions that fit specific situations. Most of us have a sense of ourselves as being reasonably moral, so we can be surprised to find how we don't always act according to our principles. As verse 53 of the *Tao Te Ching* says, "The Great Path is very smooth and straight, but all people are fond of bypaths."

For example, one of my students, when he began studying the precept of avoiding false speech, told me he thought it wouldn't be much of a challenge for him: he never lied. Then one evening, while he was doing the dishes after supper, his wife called out to him from another room: "You're not cleaning the nonstick pan with the scrub sponge, are you?" He found himself saying, "No, no," automatically—even as his hands were scouring the pan with steel wool.

Such surprises help us wake up to what we do—the title of Diane Rizzetto's book on an Ordinary Mind approach to the precepts.[11] I've found her approach very helpful in aiding students to explore the precepts prior to committing to them. We invite students to take one precept at a time, live with it at the forefront of all their actions, then—when a student has an anchored sense of how the precept applies to everyday life—we ask the student to write the precept in their own words, as a guideline for their continuous practice.[12] For example, two of my friends, when they got married, used the precepts as a scaffold for their wedding vows. They pledged to not take life or steal by saying, "I vow not to kill your joy. I vow not to take you for granted."

Most of the precepts are stated in the negative: I vow not to kill; I vow not to take what is not given; and so forth. Some people prefer to rephrase the precepts as positives; for example, the vow of not killing can be reworded to "I vow to take up the way of supporting all life," and the vow to not steal can be reframed as "I vow not to take what is not given and to give freely all I can." It's important for each person to formulate their vows in words they can live by and to balance the intention to do good with the intention of not causing harm.

Framing vows in the negative keeps to a Taoist perspective that is leery of doing too much. This is in keeping with the Jewish version of Christianity's Golden Rule, as stated by Hillel: Do *not* do to others what you would *not* have them do to you (my italics).

Sometimes our best intentions of doing good lead to harmful consequences. In Bangladesh, well-meaning government and aid groups urged villagers to stop drinking pond water; they built tube wells to tap into underground aquifers. Unfortunately, nobody tested the aquifers for arsenic. Twenty years later, health experts estimate as many as 20 million Bangladeshis are being slowly poisoned by the arsenic waters from such wells.[13]

As Albany says in Shakespeare's *King Lear*, "Striving to better, oft we mar what's well." If there is a single principle underlying ethical behavior, it might well be "first, do no harm"—or at least the minimum amount of harm required by a situation. There's a corollary: rather than being overeager to do good, often it's wiser to do *less*.

Too often we respond to a situation by wanting to immediately *do* something. Usually it's better to pause and see how the situation develops. Caught on the horns of an ethical dilemma, a moralistic stance makes us tighten up, fearful we may do the wrong thing. In contrast, the basic precept-before-precepts is simply what we teach children: before crossing a street, stop, look, and listen.

Sometimes situations resolve themselves; other times we need to respond but are unsure what course constitutes right action. Then we can rely on another basic principle: when in doubt, cooperate.

All our actions are interactions, so they have consequences. This is called "karma." We make a mistake if we think karma is solely an individual affair. Our actions' consequences rebound to us by generating reactions in the beings around us. What they do affects their karma, which affects ours. If the way we deal with a situation fosters a sense of mutuality, that's a sign we're acting in accordance with the precepts. When we create paths wide enough to make room for everyone, we're traipsing through the terrain of interbeing. The teaching of the Dharma is simple: we're all in this together.

SOME SPECIFICS ABOUT ZEN PRECEPTS

Zen Buddhist traditions vary in both their phrasings of the precepts and which precepts they include in the precepts ceremonies. Let's look at four precepts the Buddha raises in this chapter of the Surangama Sutra and see how they can inform our lives. I will list each precept phrased in two ways: the form we use at Berkeley Zen Center, which consists of the statement of the precept in the negative, along with its Soto Zen *eko* derived from Dogen, and the form used in many Ordinary Mind Zen (OMZ) sanghas, as expressed in Diane Rizzetto's excellent guide to the precepts, *Waking Up to What You Do.*

Stealing

BZC: I vow to not take what is not given.
The self and objects are such as they are. Two yet one. The gate of liberation stands open.
OMZ: I take up the way of taking only what is freely given and giving freely all I can.

There is nothing in our lives we've haven't taken from someplace else.

Usually we think, "My ideas and my feelings are my own." However, as a baby you took up words from all the people you encountered; you learned your emotions according to how you were (or weren't) fed, picked up and put to bed, how you were held and pushed away. By the time you could read, you were absorbing concepts from all your interactions with the environment; your brain deconstructed and reassembled these bits and pieces like mental Lego blocks.

How much of what we take is truly freely given?

How much of the food you eat was grown and harvested by people who freely gave of their labor? How many of the fibers that constitute our clothes were torn from animals and plants, extracted from petroleum reserves fracked and processed into synthetic fabrics? Did all the earth and the living beings involved surrender them willingly? We take DNA from our parents and the generations before them; we take all our energy from the sun—how do we repay our debt?

When we expand the field of illusory ownership beyond its usual dualistic opposition of "yours versus mine," we find an antidote to thievery in the paramita of generosity. If instead of holding on tightly to what we've taken from others, we move things along, we experience the pleasures of sharing. If instead of opposing life against death by forbidding all killing, we ally with the natural process of arising-and-passing-away, we realize our deaths are necessary for a healthy ecology. When older trees fall in a forest, they make an opening for the sunlight that gives life to new growth.

Even robbery can arise from generosity in the face of need, and good thieves live by a code, as related in the *Chuang Tzu*:

> One of Robber Chih's followers asked him, "Does the thief too have a Way?"
>
> Chih replied, "How could he get anywhere if he didn't have a Way? Making shrewd guesses as to how much booty

is stashed away in the room is sageliness; being the first one in is bravery; being the last one out is righteousness; knowing whether the job can be pulled off or not is wisdom; dividing up the loot fairly is benevolence. No one in the world ever succeeded in becoming a great thief if he didn't have all five!"[14]

Lying

BZC: I vow to refrain from false speech.

The Dharma Wheel turns from the beginning. There is neither surplus nor lack. The sweet dew saturates all and harvests the truth.

OMZ: I take up the way of speaking truthfully.

Before taking up the practice of "not lying," take time to examine the potential consequences. The next time someone asks for your opinion on an ugly painting they've done, a maudlin poem they've written, or an unappetizing meal they've cooked, how will you respond? (Hint: parents learn to say, of their children's efforts, "Wow, look at how blue you colored that sky!")

On a more intimate level, let's say yesterday you fell into an old habit and did something you were ashamed of. If today someone asks you, "What did you do yesterday?" are you prepared to answer truthfully? Of course, you can always say, "I don't want to talk about it," but that will pique your listener's interest. You can talk about yesterday while omitting the embarrassing incident—but is omission a form of lying? These are the sorts of things you'll need to decide in pursuing not-lying.

For myself, I've decided that whatever question a person asks me, I will answer truthfully. I may ask the questioner why they want to know or even tell them I don't think it will be helpful to talk about it. If they persist, though, so long as answering does not cause actual harm, I am willing to answer without adding or subtracting to what happened.

I find this kind of radical transparency helps me in tricky situations where I'm tempted to do something questionable. Then I say to myself, "If someone asks me about this, will I be able to own up to what I've done?" So long as the answer is yes, I can feel comfortable, knowing I'm living a life I'm not ashamed of. This turns any self-imposed limitations on my actions into sources of expanded freedom.

I've gradually learned the truth is my friend. I found it initially awkward to say, in response to an invitation to an unwanted event, "No, thank you. I'm not interested," rather than the white lie "I'm sorry. I'd love to, but I'm busy." It's easier to be straightforward rather than to pretend I'd like to go but have a (nonexistent) scheduling conflict. If I fail to be honest about my disinterest, the other person might invite me for another time, and it will be awkward to refuse.

I've discovered the truth does set us free, so long as we're willing to accept the consequences of how people respond. I sometimes catch myself, toward the end of a meeting or a conversation, saying, "I need to go now" when the truth is closer to "I want to go now." Even if I have another appointment, I don't *need* to go to it or to whatever is my next planned task. Yes, if I'm late or don't go to the next thing on my agenda, it may be inconvenient or rude. There may be unpleasant consequences: perhaps people will get mad at me; perhaps I'll miss out on some opportunity. However, if I don't do the next thing I've said I "need" to do, it's unlikely it will end in utter catastrophe.

A need implies something is a matter of life and death. "Need" removes the element of choice. In reality, there are very few things we truly need. We need to breathe, sleep, eat; at some point, each of us needs to die. Excusing myself from the current meeting or conversation, though, is purely a matter of preference. It might be impolite, unwise, frustrating, problematic, or silly to not follow that preference—but that doesn't make it a need.

Speaking truthfully doesn't mean blurting things out. It doesn't mean forgoing tact or ignoring how our words need to fit the circumstances. It might, though, require giving up the easy little fibs, along with avoiding the deceit of deliberate whoppers.

Initially I was a little anxious about replacing "I need to" with more truthful words; it seemed impolite and blunt to say, "I have another meeting I want to go to." I've rarely gotten any flack for it. When I stopped saying, "I need to . . . ," I felt less compelled by external circumstances and internal pressures. One more small step on the road of liberation.

Killing

BZC: I vow to not kill.

By not killing life, the buddha tree seed grows. Transmit the life of Buddha and do not kill.

OMZ: I vow to take up the way of supporting all life.

The precepts of not making false claims and not stealing have the potential to relieve us of the strain of pretending to be other than we are. Not killing sounds like more of an imperative, but first we need to stop pretending we can live without taking life.

Our immune system routinely kills off harmful bacteria so that we may live. Factory farms are cruel even if they produce milk from crowded cows rather than meat from slaughtered cattle. Even a strictly vegetarian diet feeds on the deaths of plants; organic farming needs to kill off invasive species in order to promote life. On the other hand, being overly scrupulous about the sources of your food when friends and family are hungry can starve them of necessary nutrition. Refusing to eat something that friends prepare for you can butcher a friendship.

It's not easy scraping out a living in the high villages of the Himalayas. One time I was trekking with my friend Joel through a remote, impoverished area, looking for the village where an American friend was living while doing a research project.[15] When we came to the village, our friend delayed meeting with us because a yak had broken its leg. The yak was in pain, and the villagers were hungry but, being Buddhist, would not kill the ox. Our friend had agreed to get his hands bloody; he put off meeting with us until he'd slit the yak's throat. The villagers then happily cut the yak into pieces and held a feast—offering us some of the highly prized meat. Should we have refused?

It's situations like these that lead the Buddha, in the Surangama Sutra, to find a work-around for people who want to practice sincerely but who may need to eat meat out of necessity: "I have compassion for those who wish to live purely but who live among humid marshlands or in hot deserts where grains and vegetables cannot be grown. Out of great kindness and by means of my spiritual power, I change the meat they eat so that it is without sentience. It is merely called meat and merely tastes like meat." Was this the original Impossible Burger?

The problem with killing is that once done, there's no way to make repairs or amends. If we execute a convicted criminal, there's no Undo command should we later discover that person was innocent. Whenever we murder in the name of justice, we kill off some part of our own kindness and goodwill. Something similar can happen in less dramatic situations. If we tell some children to stop their noisy play, but they keep at it until we yell at them angrily to the extent we murder their pleasure in play, being a killjoy harms everyone's hearts.

Misusing Sexuality

BZC: I vow to not misuse sexuality.
Let the three wheels of self, objects, and action be pure. With nothing to desire one goes along together with the buddhas.
OMZ: I take up the way of engaging in sexual intimacy respectfully and with an open heart.

Sexuality is perhaps the field where mutuality finds its fullest expression, but it is also an area where it's easy to fall into deceiving ourselves and others. Sex is sticky in more ways than one.

Desire is good at disguising itself, especially when spiritual communities shove it into the dark corners that foster masquerades. A reluctance to have open discussions about sex—ones where we acknowledge its powerful allure and our personal proclivities—has led to scandalous betrayals of trust in many religious communities. When sex is relegated to the dark while enlightenment is idealized as the climax of meditative absorption, practice can become something of a joke.

I know of one instance where a Buddhist monk and a nun lived in celibate practice centers, the two temples separated by a hill between them. The monk and nun met, fell in love, and took to climbing to the top of the hill for midnight trysts. After a particularly strenuous night of passionate sex, the monk returned to his monastery for early morning zazen, then fell into a deep sleep while sitting facing the wall in full lotus. When the head monk noticed him slumping, he hit him with the *keisaku* (wake-up stick) several times until—crack!—the keisaku broke. Afterward the monks were in awe and whispered, "Such deep samadhi (concentration)! Such deep kensho (enlightenment)! He was far beyond the sensory world of the stick." In their idealization of meditation, a more earthy explanation never occurred to them.

This would be an amusing story if it weren't for the many instances where overidealizing supposedly enlightened leaders enabled them to engage in harmful sexual relations with members of their communities. When these cases come to light, they're often followed by expressions of remorse. Other times, though, the perpetrators not only deny they've done anything wrong but even attempt to justify their actions as expressions of "divine love" or "complete perfect enlightenment." Such justifications are spiritual sophistry, bypassing a basic truth: when people in leadership roles have sex with people in subordinate positions, true mutuality is not possible.

Mutuality is a hallmark of the precepts. Sexuality that is intimate and genuinely mutual can open up selfless abodes of love, kindness, acceptance, and joy. Discrepancies in position and privilege in relationships, though, are often problematic. Power doesn't mix well with love; the resulting cocktail is intoxicating but leads to hangovers of shame and fury, depression and fear. Surrender is part of sex and can liberate us from our individual egos, but when sexuality is marred by coercion or false pretenses, surrender—even if it seems consensual—will cause psychological sepsis. This can poison not only the individuals involved but entire communities.

Sexuality is often experienced as a drive impelled by deep, powerful energies. Like any energy reservoir, these can be dissipated, suppressed, or tapped for work; sexual energy can be exploited by self-centeredness or lead to sublime intercourse where our concern for those we love helps us find ourselves by forgetting ourselves.

Two thousand years ago, the Taoist adept Chuang Tzu observed, "If you try to fulfill all your appetites and desires and indulge your likes and dislikes, then you bring affliction to the true form of your inborn nature and fate. And if you try to deny your appetites and desires and forcibly change your likes and dislikes, then you bring affliction to your ears and eyes." I think Robert Aitken Roshi offers us a beautiful middle way between these extremes when he writes in one of his gathas, "Embracing my lover in bed, I vow with all beings to bring patience and care and the joy of new life to our ancient dance."[16]

Most meditation practitioners these days are neither celibate nor monastic. The vinaya rule prohibiting sex is now usually rephrased as "I vow not to misuse sexuality." This is pretty vague; it's open to a wide range of interpretations that can easily become misinterpretations.

We need to carefully consider our personal decisions about practicing the precept of sexuality, and when we are in a sangha, we need to do so in harmony with the others in our community. There's a lot of disagreement on this topic in Buddhist communities. At Berkeley Zen Center, we had many spirited discussions about socializing and sexuality. We easily came to the consensus that in order to safeguard practice relationships, sex between guiding teachers and students was not allowed.

Other boundaries were not so clear. Where did senior students (long-time practitioners who gave Dharma talks and meditation instruction, and offered study groups and practice discussions) fit in? What about situations where two members mutually wanted to date each other? Some felt we should forbid any sexuality, dating, or intimate relationships; these people advocated for a safe place where everyone could concentrate on their Buddhist practice without having to fend off alluring invitations or worry about being hit on. In contrast, some members wanted a community where they could not only meet other people devoted to practice but have an opportunity to fall in love and join a partner in a lifelong journey—one that included sexuality.

Eventually we came to a compromise: during a person's first year in the community, to ensure they'd have a clear space for focused practice, newcomers are off-limits for intimate relationships, shielded from social or romantic involvements. After a year, they participate with the rest of the community in navigating the uncertain social territory, exploring how the Dharma manifests in relationships placid and passionate, romantic and platonic.

Sex is what it is—and what we make of it. Its power can cloud our consciousness or clarify it, ruin a relationship or ratify it. Formulating a precept governing sexuality for our nonmonastic Dharma communities is still very much a work in progress.

We are in the process of developing a modern Buddhist practice for the full expression of the Dharma by householders and the homeless, workers and those who retire from the world, spouses and single people. Equanimity is not disturbed when compassion and wisdom greet all beings with equal love: straight and LGBTQ+ folks, people who express their gender in binary or nonbinary ways. When we can approach the precept governing sexuality as a Dharma gate, it offers opportunities for putting interbeing into play, exploring paths of ease and joy.

Whether we choose to engage in sex or to remain celibate, let's find ways to celebrate the intercourse of all beings.

12

Establishing a Place for Awakening

Space in Mind

In the previous section of the sutra, the Buddha taught the importance of right behavior "so that your comportment may be as pure as the glistening frost. Then very naturally you will no more be able to commit the three errors of the mind and the four errors of speech than a tree is able to leaf out in freezing weather." However, recognizing many of us are not able to adhere to such a high standard, the Buddha offers some skillful means:

> As for people who cannot get rid of their stubborn habits, teach them to recite single-mindedly the mantra of supreme efficacy, which is called "Mahā-Sitātapatra"—the "Great White Canopy."[1]

We are almost ready to encounter the mantra named in the sutra's title, "the Surangama Mantra Spoken from Above the Crown of the Great Buddha's Head," the mantra the Buddha gave to Manjusri to free Ananda and the Matanga woman from ensorcellment. First, the Buddha tells the assembly to prepare for the Surangama mantra by establishing a place for awakening.

Before any important occasion, it's customary to get everything ready and arrange for circumstances to be favorable. If we're planning to welcome guests for a dinner party, it helps to tidy the house and set the table beforehand so we can pay full attention to our guests and enjoy meeting with them.

The precepts give us boundaries we can carry with us wherever we go. Establishing a place for awakening draws boundaries to define a place we can enter whenever we need a haven where we can recover, revive, and endure.[2]

BOUNDARIES ESTABLISH THE PLACE FOR AWAKENING

The Buddha advises that after finding a teacher and receiving the precepts, you take a bath, put on clean clothes, burn incense, recite a mantra, then set up a practice place and safeguard its boundaries as follows:

> Find a strong white ox living in the Himalayas, one that feeds on rich fragrant grasses and drinks only the pure waters of the mountain snows. The dung of such an ox will be of exceptional purity: mix this pure ox-dung with sandalwood incense and spread the mixture upon the ground.
>
> The dung of an ox that does not live in the Himalayas will be foul smelling and too unclean to be applied to the ground of a place for awakening.[3]

For most of us living in urban settings, this sounds a little far-off and unrealistic. Even in the Himalayas, the only oxen that drink pure water of mountain snows are yaks. Yaks, though, have adapted to high altitudes and normally cannot live below ten thousand feet. Even up high, where dung can be useful, their ordure isn't necessarily pleasant. When I joined the crowd of devotees, oxen, donkey, and horses on the pilgrimage to Kedarnath temple at 11,755 feet, the dusty fourteen-mile uphill track was inundated in dung: sometimes in heaps, sometimes as a thin film covering entire stretches of the path. Its foul smell permeated even through the clouds of incense.

Fortunately, the Buddha acknowledges the issue and offers a practical alternative: if Himalayan dung is not available, yellow loam can be substituted. Mix the loam with ground spices, spread the mixture in an octagon sixty-five feet across, and fashion a lotus to place in the center. The lotus can be made of gold or silver, of copper or wood.

When building a sanctuary, I use whatever is suitable and readily available. Two of my backpacker friends, when they set up their mountain campsites, fashion a little altar out of the pinecones, twigs, and stones from the immediate surroundings. When they pitch their tents—their sanctuaries from the weather—they are careful to site the tents properly to protect them from wind. Where necessary, they fashion a trench whose boundary provides adequate drainage. When they leave the site, they bow to their sanctuary and recite, "Thank you, camp! Good camp! Be well, camp!" When I join them in this, a little bashfully, we all smile.

The Surangama Sutra provides details for establishing the place of awakening appropriate to the customs of its time. Adorn it with flowers, protect it with flags, surround it with mirrors. The mirrors betoken how whatever place of awakening we create, it reflects our practice.

We cannot help but express ourselves every moment in everything we do. Understanding this is awakening itself.

CREATING YOUR MEDITATION SPACE

Whether you create a meditation space for yourself with a pillow in a corner nook or devote an entire room to a statue, *zabuton*, *zafu*, incense burner, ceremonial bell, and all the trimmings, it's important to do so in a manner that aligns with your practice. If you just meditate once in a while, a fancy *thanka* and an embroidered meditation cushion might conflate decoration with devotion. Conversely, if you meditate regularly but pay no heed to the implements and spaces that support you, perhaps you're holding back from acknowledging how important your practice is to you. Whatever the physical arrangements, and whether we are by ourselves or with others, it helps to gather all the elements and create some ritual to center ourselves.

Marking a boundary clarifies the terrain: we're in a place of awakening. At a zendo, we have specific forms for entering the meditation hall, walking to our places, and sitting down. I know some people feel Zen is excessive in its rituals. There's always some risk of becoming overly attached to rigid forms, but paying attention to the details of how we do things can help us focus and make it easier to align our efforts with our intentions. Most athletes and artists have a ritual they use to help them get "in the zone" when they step into the batter's box or set up to face a blank canvas. Meditation is both exercise and art, so I find it helpful to have a ritual that helps me enter the empty field.

I'll describe what I do each time I establish my meditation place, so you can consider whether you'd like to adopt any part of this ritual to support your personal practice.

FREEDOM FROM PHYSICAL STRAIN

I pause before entering the meditation area. If there's a door, I bow before I step into the room. Otherwise, I draw an imaginary threshold, pause there, and bow. As I walk to my meditation cushion, I align my posture and pay attention to how the sensations in the soles of my feet ground me.

When I reach the cushion, I stop, collect myself, and bow to the cushion. Then I turn around, face the world, and bow to everyone and everything. This helps me approach meditation not just as a time for my individual relaxation or growth but as a way of offering myself to the liberation of all beings (which, of course, includes me personally).

I'm surprised when I see others begin meditation immediately after sitting down. I need to take a little while to adjust my body to get comfortable and my mind to follow suit. For this reason, when I sit on the cushion, I make some time to center myself. I sway to the left, to the right, forward, back, then I let my body find its own way to settle into this place and time.

I invite all the pieces of this body-and-mind to cooperate with each other by doing the following: I place the tip of my tongue very lightly against the upper palate; position my hands in a mudra, being careful to let the fingers relax and the thumbs to touch as lightly as possible. I open my eyes, take one or two deep breaths, then let the breath come and go naturally.

I then usually let my eyes go soft—"looking far, looking inward, seeing nothing." Just as it's helpful to learn to meditate in a variety of positions—sitting, standing, walking, and lying down—I think it's helpful to learn to meditate with eyes focused, unfocused, open, half-open, and shut. We can establish places for awakening throughout our daily activities, but while you're driving an automobile it's unwise to meditate with your eyes closed. It helps to practice keeping our eyes and mind open to the world facing us while simultaneously to the world within.

FREEDOM FROM INVOLVEMENTS

Having prepared the practice place physically, I set up some protective psychological boundaries by reminding myself of Eihei Dogen's fundamental meditation instruction:

> Set aside all involvements, and let the myriad things rest.[4]

Setting aside all involvements and letting the myriad things rest means letting everything be. This is the foundation for any meditation, whether it be following the breath, concentrating on a koan, reciting a mantra, labeling thoughts, or thinking not-thinking.

It's not always easy to set aside all involvements. Pausing and bowing at the threshold of the meditation hall helps, but one usually needs a bit more assistance. When I used to meet friends for lunchtime runs to metabolize the morning's stresses, I'd pick a landmark a few hundred yards ahead and say to myself, "When I reach that spot, I'll leave everything else behind." Usually once I reached my chosen spot, I'd feel as if thick rubber tendrils anchored back at my office were still clinging to my body; I had to summon up a mental image of giant scissors to snip the threads before I could focus on the rhythms of my run and the fellowship of my friends.

I've recently found an easier way of reinforcing "set aside all involvements, and let the myriad things rest." I fill a glass with water, pick it up with both hands, and pause for a moment to center myself. Then—still using both hands—I gently place the glass down so it rests on the counter while keeping both my hands lightly touching the glass. I pause for another moment to focus and pay attention to what follows: how, as I let my hands relax and drop away from the glass, this body and mind intuitively know how to let go, without relying on words or effort. I tune in to this feeling in muscle-and-bone, to the relaxation and release that accompany the easing of a weight in the ordinary act of letting the glass be.

I do a miniversion of this exercise whenever I have a cup of tea or drink of water. It's soothing, and it helps me focus for a moment and memorize the physical feel of "letting go." This makes it easier for me to summon it mentally when I'm in the grip of painful emotions, or holding on tight to a cherished opinion, or otherwise taut with tension. When I'm getting caught by aversions or attachments, calling up "letting be" reminds me that the spaciousness of OMind is always right at hand.

FREEDOM FROM DISCRIMINATION

The Way is not difficult for those who have no preferences, but we usually come to meditation from the standpoint of discriminating minds.[5] To free ourselves from our usual mental habits, Dogen's meditation instructions tell us, "Do not think good or bad. Do not judge true or false, right or wrong. Give up the operations of mind, intellect, consciousness; stop measuring with thoughts, ideas, and views." Another helpful meditation instruction comes in Tilopa's "Six Words of Advice":

> Don't recall. Let go of what has passed.
> Don't imagine. Let go of what may come.
> Don't think. Let go of what is happening now.
> Don't examine. Don't try to figure anything out.
> Don't control. Don't try to make anything happen.
> Rest. Relax, right now, and rest.[6]

Basically, meditation involves releasing our hold, easing off our participation in everything we're usually enmeshed with. Being still ourselves allows everything to be itself, still.

To cultivate this stillness, we establish boundaries for our place of awakening: during meditation, we don't respond to interruptions. We don't need to block things out or push things away, but we also don't need to be pushed around by the things of the world. We modulate our responses according to what's truly called for.

We don't need a Himalayan cave or a soundproof room to meditate. I've heard people complain after a meditation session that they couldn't meditate because there were too many interruptions from noises, too many distractions from the room being too warm or cold, too many discomforts from insects buzzing or a meditation mat that was too soft or too hard. Certainly it's easier to meditate in quiet, comfortable, protected places; especially when beginning to learn meditation, it's best to make it easy on yourself. The heart of meditation, though, is welcoming each and all we encounter as our companions.

When we do this, how can there be any interruption? An interruption *is* the meditation. By remaining still, simultaneously self-contained and receptive, we cultivate an empty field. Making room for whatever appears, we assist the self-becoming of all beings—including this being called "my self" that is continually arising in response to conditions.

When I teach meditation, I've found it important to be explicit about handling frustrations and so-called interruptions, whether these come from insects or telephone calls. People like the idea of taking a time out for meditation but often balk when we get into specifics. I usually say something like, "Before beginning, figure out how much time you can make for your meditation. If necessary, let others know when you'll be unavailable and when you'll return. Once you've started, though, if your cell phone rings, don't pick it up. If someone knocks on the door, don't respond. If your children or other members of your household call out to you, don't answer them."

People often respond with, "I can't do *that*!"

PRACTICE BOUNDARIES ARE SEMIPERMEABLE

If a family member is dealing with a critical situation, I'll meditate with the phone nearby to answer if needed. Usually, though, I'll leave my phone behind or simply not answer the phone if it rings. Many people, though, become anxious at the idea of intentionally making themselves unavailable, even for a little while. Some feel it would be selfish not to respond promptly to peoples' needs. Others protest that their children, family members, employers, and friends won't respect a boundary or will feel neglected, hurt, or angry.

Indeed, this can and does happen. Setting boundaries usually invokes feelings in other people, so it's important to discuss and, if necessary, negotiate the terms. Making time and space for meditation often requires some practical problem-solving. Since we live with others, establishing our place inevitably brings up issues around limits, expectations, and responsibilities to others and to ourselves.

Negotiating these limits is not just practical: when we examine the anxiety that arises as we put aside our involvements, we learn something about our attachments, aversions, yearnings, and fears. We all have feelings about needing and being needed, taking care of others and being taken care of. If we're not at others' beck and call, will they love us? Does making a place for ourselves stimulate guilty feelings of being unworthy or egotistical?

We often catastrophize the consequences of what will happen if we put off responding for a little while. In our high-tech, always-connected world, we've come to expect instant responsiveness, but it's easy to mistake convenience for necessity, and desire for need. A sense of urgency often masks self-importance, impatience, or doubt. When we assume things will fall apart if we're not actively tending to them, we exaggerate our own importance. We also can, unwittingly, convey that we don't trust others to take care of themselves.

Without some trust in the unfolding of ourselves and our world, in the continual falling-apart-and-coming-together of life-and-death, it's difficult to follow Tilopa's meditation instructions to "relax, right now, and rest." We live in unsettled times. Parents fear their children will be abducted or abused; citizens fear their government officials will lie and conspire; workers and employers fear being taken advantage of. Young people who are coming of age fear their careers will become obsolete and that the very environment will turn unlivable. Spiritual practice is an expression of faith in mind: without some basis for trust, what can we rely on?

Young adults in particular face many difficulties trying to find their place in the world. When my two daughters were in their twenties, they sometimes telephoned me to talk about their life dilemmas and occasionally asked for advice. Initially, I made the mistake of offering what suggestions I could. Usually my daughters responded by telling me, "That won't work," or "That's not the way it is these days."

Gradually I learned they were right. Our society has changed so much in the fifty years since I was in their position, I cannot fully understand the situations they face. Instead of offering advice, I learned to say instead, "I don't know what you should do in this situation. But I trust you. I'm confident that whatever you decide, you'll deal with it. If you make a choice that turns out badly, you'll learn from it. If you make a choice that turns out well, you'll learn from that too. Either way, I trust that you'll figure things out as you go along."

REGULATING OUTFLOWS AND INFLOWS

We awaken to ourselves inseparably from our interactions with the world. For that reason, our place of awakening needs flexible boundaries that can titrate our outflows and inflows. We need boundaries to filter out the toxins of greed, hate, and delusion that we're exposed to in unhealthy environments. It's also a mistake to think that somehow our spiritual practice within those boundaries will suffice to make us immune to our surroundings when we emerge from our sanctuary.

Wholesome practices like qigong, yoga, tai chi, and meditation can help restore our balance, reinforce our health, and even create a buffer of healthy energy around us to protect against exogenic pathogens. However, it would be foolish to make a habit of doing our practice while facing a garbage dumpster a few inches away. Similarly, we need to establish boundaries that can handle the violence and psychological pathogens we're exposed to daily on the highways, at our workplaces, and in the photos and videos we're barraged with in newsprint, magazines, cell phones, televisions, and computer screens.

Last year I noticed myself becoming upset whenever I read the newspaper. I took this as a signal that I needed to establish some boundaries to make the newspaper a place for practice. Now before I read the news, I pause and recite my vows: beings are numberless, I vow to awaken with them, delusions are inexhaustible, and so on. This helps me view the newspaper as a Dharma gate. A friend of mine, Kenshin Catherine Cascade, has a simpler method: she told me that each time she opens the newspaper, she reminds herself, "Here's the next chapter of *The Iliad* and *The Odyssey*."

Instead of relying on a single sitting place for our meditation or restricting our place of awakening to a temple or Dharma center, we can reinforce our efforts by selecting some of our daily activities and framing them as opportunities for practice (for some examples, see the citations in the previous chapter: Robert Aitken's book of gathas, Norman Fischer's book for training in compassion, and Diane Rizzetto's book for waking up to what you do). For many people, saying grace before a meal is a time-honored way of setting off mealtime as a place for awakening. Even a single word can suffice (my sweetheart and I use the Japanese word *itadakimasu*). We also often like to recite the grace Kenshin Catherine Cascade uses before meals:

We bow in gratitude to the providers of this food:
Earth, air, water, fire;
People, tools, plants, animals;
Turned in the Wheel of living-and-dying.

Desiring the natural order of mind
Let us join our hearts with the one heart of the world
Realizing the compassionate way of awakening
with all beings.[7]

Saying grace before meals alters our inflows by joining us with all around us.

In the Surangama Sutra, the Buddha also teaches the importance of modulating our outflows. Altering our outflows doesn't require we withdraw from the world or avoid taking any initiative. When our thoughts and actions are no longer devoted to manipulating objects but turned toward the Dharma, they are no longer flowing "out"; rather, in assisting the self-becoming of all beings, they flow "throughout" the Matrix of the Thus-Come-One.

There's a difference between involvements and engagements. When we get *involved* in an activity, we become enmeshed in it, attached to our stake in how it turns out. When we are *engaged* in an activity, we give ourselves to it fully in a spirit of supporting it.

A good example is raising children. In our involvements with their schools, sports, and relationships, we can be coercive in our caring. When we pressure our children to perform and "succeed," when we criticize them for "failing," we subject them to our own agenda. The agenda might come from fear, or hope, or a concern for how our children's actions reflect on us. However well-meaning the agenda might be, it unwittingly treats the child as an object, a means for realizing a goal.

In contrast, we can engage with their schools, sports, and relationships by being appreciative, curious, and encouraging. If our agenda is to help them discover how to fully enjoy an activity, how to figure out whether something they're doing is a true fit for them, how to help them grow into themselves, then we offer them a supportive kind of caring. Then we're fully engaged with them as companions on the mysterious paths of self-becoming.

The same distinction between involvement and engagement applies to work, play, and all our relationships and activities. Involvements are with objects. Whenever we get involved with an object and draw up an agenda other than the Dharma, this constitutes an outflow. The way we turn around an outflow is to turn it in the direction of the Dharma, which is always engaging in interbeing.

When we interact with people based on our self-concern, we turn others into objects. When we interact to assist the self-becoming of others, we create a practice play for mutual discovery. When our consciousness is directed toward *objects* of sight, sound, touch, smell, taste, and thought, consciousness becomes obscured by our attachments and aversions. We get caught by dreams and delusions. When our consciousness is directed to the enlightened *source* of hearing, seeing, and so forth, consciousness turns away from objects and finds itself in the continuous, illuminating play of ungraspable being.

PLACES FOR AWAKENING ARE BLADES OF GRASS

There is no special place to practice. There is a lovely book by Jon Kabat-Zinn called *Wherever You Go, There You Are*. I would tweak the title slightly to say wherever you go, there *it* is—life-and-death itself, the truest teacher. The arches of heaven are found not only in the clouds above but even in the neon golden arches of fast-food joints. One time I mentioned to my teacher Sojun that going into a McDonald's made me shudder. Sojun shrugged, smiled, and replied, "McDonald's can be OK." (Note: McDonald's does make heavenly, tasty French fries).

The fourth koan of the *Book of Serenity* is titled "The World Honored One Points to the Ground":

Buddha was walking with his retinue, came to a pleasant area and commented: "This would be a good place to build a sanctuary."

The Hindu god Indra took a blade of grass, stuck it into the ground and said, "The sanctuary is built."

Buddha smiled.

The smile is the sanctuary. It's not always easy to smile when we hear the world crying through the stresses of living-and-dying, and especially difficult to smile in the face of pain and injustice.

To help ourselves and all beings, even though there's no special place to practice, we establish special practice places, refuges where we can refresh ourselves and remind ourselves of that which can never be lost. To do this, we need to pluck a blade of grass—nothing special, but a token that helps us feel held in the Matrix of the Thus-Come-One.

We suffer from an illusion: that things exist apart from the matrix of interbeing, that each of us is a separate, isolated island. In the thirty-seventh koan of the *Blue Cliff Record*, Panshan Baoji reminds us that in the Triple World, not a single thing exists.[8] Each blade of grass is an entire ecology, a dynamic organism, and every organism can "be itself differently"[9]—a photosynthesizer in soil, the cornerstone of a sanctuary in a smile.

The rigid lines by which we draw our charts catch the cartographers; they are idealizations that fail to take into account all the actual small inlets, the bays and bights, the curlicues of land. When we magnify these curves and look closely, we see each curve is itself composed of curves. It turns out that every coastline, every boundary needs infinite length to enclose a finite space.[10]

Our body-and-mind study of the Way is like this—similarly fractal, emptily fruitful. By establishing the boundary of the place of awakening, we discover it to be boundless. We let go of our involvements, let the myriad things be, and realize *here* is the time; *now* is the place. The Way unfolds at this very point, a singularity free from hindrance.

Without any hindrance, no fears exist: with a whole heart we pluck a blade of grass, place it just so, and establish the sanctuary. How could the Buddha not smile?

13

The Surangama Mantra

Communing with the Source

Then from the prominence at the crown of the World-Honored One's head there welled forth a magnificent light, radiant as hundreds of precious gems, and a magnificent thousand-petal lotus welled forth from within that light. The Thus-Come-One made appear a Buddha who was seated at the center of the magnificent flower, and from the crown of that Buddha's head, ten beams of light shone forth as if from hundreds of precious gems. Everywhere throughout space there appeared, from within those beams of light, ten times as many vajra-warriors as there are sand-grains in the River Ganges. Some of them held aloft a mountain, while others brandished a vajra-implement.

All in the great assembly gazed upward, overwhelmed by awe and wonder. Hoping to receive the Buddha's compassionate blessing, they listened intently as the Buddha who sat invisible to ordinary sight amidst a blaze of light at the crown of the Thus-Come-One's head proclaimed this spiritual mantra.[1]

Mantras express form as emptiness, emptiness as form. Through silent meditation, reverberant recitation, and rotating prayer wheels, they attune us to the Dharma, proclaiming the wisdom of the heart's sutra.

The Sanskrit word *mantra* is sometimes translated as "magic spell" or "charm." Some Indian interpreters describe mantras as "mind protectors" for how they liberate the mind from illusion's snares. The Chinese and Japanese words for mantra (*zhenyan* and *shingon*, respectively) portray mantras as "true words." Mantras can be recited to propitiate a deity, to invoke protection and healing. They can also be used as aids to any form of meditation, though they are especially associated with tantric methods.

The syllables of a mantra may or may not have semantic meaning; the sounds themselves invoke a spiritual resonance. Travel through the Himalayas and you'll feel the mantric impact of hearing "OM MANI PADME HUM" intoned continuously, a thrumming undertone recited by pious villagers, chanted in temples both Hindu and Buddhist, broadcast over loudspeakers in pop music.

MAGIC MOMENTS

My upbringing shaped me to be scientific and skeptical; I tend to shy away from practices and people that claim magic powers. Nonetheless, I enjoy "magic moments" that kindle my sense of mystery, wonder, and awe. I recognize there are many phenomena we can't explain; I've seen and experienced powerful forces exerting inexplicable effects. People with terminal diseases who "shouldn't" get well make sudden, "impossible" recoveries after prayers and healing touch. Deep in the Australian outback, standing face-to-face with the red sandstone formation of Uluru, bathed in its vermillion light, I felt as if the rock sensed me, *knew* me.[2] I shook off that eerie feeling, drove to nearby Kata Tjutu, hiked a ways into the outback, my heart lifted by inexplicable joy—then dusk found me walking deeper into a dangerous wilderness, lured toward its dark places, drawn almost against my will.

These phenomena are powerful; we need to respect them and employ them with care. Even adepts acknowledge that such powers are mysterious, untamed, and inconsistent. Shamans who claim precise control are shams; I'm more comfortable trusting *kahunas* who acknowledge that sometimes the magic works, sometimes it doesn't.

Repetition and rhythm have undeniable physiological and psychological effects. We make use of their soothing properties in lullabies and of their healing powers in medical hypnosis; we summon their beauty in musical movements and dance performances. Despots are often masters at using repetition and rhythm to command and control. Religious rituals channel puissant energies—both light and dark. Advertising executives employ repetitive jingles to beguile us into buying things; we easily absorb, and are influenced by, viral memes and rhyming ditties. In the 1950s, the slogan "I like Ike" won two elections; "Winston Tastes Good Like a Cigarette Should!" motivated people to become smokers through its malignant mantra. We get caught by catchphrases; their syllables can coalesce into habits benign, harmful, or both in their compulsiveness.

Children are especially impressionable. Childhood tapes etch themselves onto developing brains; subconsciously we follow their engraved paths as adults. When my sister and I were young, we loved listening to a recording of the Golden Book story "The Little Engine that Could." Its mantra of "I think I can, I think I can" propelled us through many a difficulty but also led us to push ourselves mercilessly through some unnecessary uphill battles. Our society loves maxims like "You can do anything you put your mind to"; these can provide encouragement when we need it but can also set us up for self-blame when they sometimes turn out not to be true.

When our mental murmurs are unwholesome, they eat at us and coerce us as fiercely as any external tyrant. Psychologists call these negative mental habits "automatic thoughts," "life-scripts," or "self-fulfilling stories." They can be unverbalized guiding schemas (the hero's journey, the outcast) or terse self-talk ("I can't," "Clumsy"). They are not so much unconscious as unexamined, taken as givens, mind-worms turning dark soil over and over.

Negative mantras can be dispelled by the magic of counter-mantras. I discovered this after a summer touring Europe in a rental car with my wife and our two young daughters, ages three and seven. We'd brought along some of our children's sing-along music to keep them occupied. During our family drives, our daughters fixated, as children do, on a few songs they wanted to hear over and over. Their favorite album was *Bert and Ernie's Sesame Street Sing-Along*. Over many, many, *many* repetitions, the album imprinted itself indelibly in our memories. Forty years later, we can still recite the lyrics.

After returning to the United States, I was at work one day when I stumbled and dropped a pencil. The harsh critic in my head immediately and automatically called out, "Clumsy!" Then, unbidden, the Sesame Street album began playing, Big Bird singing,

> *Oh, everyone makes mistakes, oh yes, they do*
> *Your sister and your brother and your dad and mother too . . .*
> *Everyone makes, so why can't you?*

Hearing Big Bird's voice, I couldn't help but smile. A little humor is a good Dharma friend, counterbalancing a superego that takes itself too seriously. This small incident helped me begin to lighten up, ease off on fault-finding, and let go of my delusions of perfectionism. The Buddha can take many forms—even that of a big yellow Muppet.

RITUAL AND REVERENCE

Mantras, like Muppets, offer forms for the formless to express itself. Mantras appear in all religions, even when they're not explicitly identified as such. When a series of words is recited so many times that the meaning of the words disappears into its sonority—especially when the words are in a language that's not in daily use—they accrue many of the same characteristics as mantras. The Latin of the Catholic mass and the Aramaic of the Jewish mourner's kaddish lend awe to their orisons through words familiar but mysterious. Without the distraction of meaning, the tones of our prayers evoke reverence undiluted by the analytics of thought. Chanting together with others, hearing many voices merging in the sounds of the syllables, provides a comforting ritual at times of grief and distress.

Reciting prayers or mantras is ritualistic. Being powerful, rituals are double-edged. Baptisms and circumcisions, naming rituals, consecrations, and sacraments give us a connection to something larger than ourselves, easing our life journeys through the transitions of birth, adolescence, death. However, rituals can also be harmful. They have been abused to entrench rigid authorities' demands for obedience, to mutilate adolescents at the first signs of puberty, and to justify continued oppression. Rituals can also be hollowed out by hypocrisy: as verse 38 of the *Tao Te Ching* says, ritual ceremonies can become "mere husks of sincere faith."

Modern society, in socializing us to idolize the individual, often makes us allergic to collective rituals. Where our culture promotes the virtues of self-efficacy and autonomy, rituals are designed to subsume these in a shared sense of communion. In a materialist society where spiritual practice is not reinforced by societal norms, we may shy away from anything touched with a tinge of the sacred. We may mistrust activities that ask us to put aside our skepticism, our cherished sense of irony, and our bitter friendship with alienation. Plunging into a ritual requires a leap of faith. But faith, these days, is often in short supply.

Faith requires daring. It takes us along spiritual paths where we must be willing to let go of our precious personal control. For rituals like mantras to be effective, we need to let go of our tight hold on I-mind and commune with OMind. To do so, we need to supplement self-efficacy with surrender and substitute flexible willingness for stubborn willfulness. We may fear losing ourselves in the process, but we exaggerate the risk. Autonomy does not require omnipotence; easing our grip on ourselves is a prerequisite to liberation, peace, and ease.

While some mantras are designed for specific purposes, times, and places, all mantras can accompany us wherever we go. When I hike in the mountains by myself, I often tire of my own poor company and sometimes get physically fatigued while there are miles still to go. In these situations, I take up the Heart Sutra's mantra, reciting it silently while I fit my steps to the earth's shapes and the mantra's rhythms: "GYA TE GYA TE PARA GYA TE." The mantra meets me, moves me, merges the mind's breath with the body's awareness at each place and time, and gives me energy to go on.

Mantras help us forget ourselves. When we immerse ourselves in a mantra, there is no separation between sound and self, between action and intent. If we're chanting with others, our voices merge even while they remain our own. If we're reciting a mantra by ourselves, we are not alone: together with the mantra, a-lone becomes all-one.

RECITING A MANTRA

The Buddha praises the power of the Surangama mantra for many purposes (recall that Manjusri used the mantra to free Ananda and the Matanga woman from a sexual enchantment). One specific use of this mantra is to dispel evil karma. The Buddha says,

> The mantra can enable people who have broken their precepts to regain their purity . . . when they begin to recite the mantra, that karma from their precept-breaking offenses will melt away as snow is melted by boiling liquid.[3]

For millennia, Buddhists have gathered every month under the full moon to renew their bodhisattva vows. The ceremony begins with an avowal of our karma, wiping our slate clean and so enabling us to recommit to the precepts with whole hearts. Though it's not part of the Zen tradition I'm most familiar with, I've added a recitation of a short form of the Surangama mantra to the bodhisattva ceremony, just after we make a full avowal of our karma. Invoking the mantra so "past offenses melt like snow" helps me experience atonement transformed into "at-one-ment."

In the arising and passing away of each syllable, attunement to each moment liberates us from birth-and-death. This "magic" works best when it's done with one's whole being. When reciting this (or any) mantra, breathe deeply; summon the mantra's voice by sounding its syllables from the bottom of your diaphragm (from your belly, hara, lower dantien). Intone the sounds continuously, without pauses or spaces in between until you've exhaled completely and entirely emptied yourself. Do this breath after breath, round after round.

As you continue the mantra, let go of "you" reciting "it." Merging is auspicious; giving voice to the syllables enables them to carry you along. This holds true whether you recite the mantra silently or vocally, but the mantra is stronger when you can hear the sounds echo and reverberate out loud, and especially powerful in concert with others. Something about the sounds themselves helps our hearts reverberate.

When we chant vigorously with every cell in the body, our beings vibrate like a drum, and our minds ring like a bell. When the chant streams inexhaustibly from our center, its voice circles back and rejoins our own. When we chant with every level of our being, the mantra touches all those levels, replenishing and refreshing us.

In the next section of the sutra, titled "Levels of Being," the Buddha describes many different kinds of beings.[4] He tells us that "putting into practice this [Surangama] mantra of the mind . . . gathers together the beings with whom the Thus-Come-Ones have strong affinities." Reciting the mantra, we collect the many different beings that constitute ourselves. In this way, chanting the mantra actualizes our bodhisattva vow to liberate all beings.

Mantras are mind-protectors. As we chant the Surangama mantra, we summon ten qualities that stabilize the mind, described in the sutra's depiction of the fifty-seven stages of the bodhisattva path:

1. *Confidence.* The vigor of the chant stimulates our sense of confidence, dispelling doubt.
2. *Recollection.* We gather together ("re-member") all parts of ourselves and their karma.
3. *Clarity.* While chanting, our usual habits and delusions don't arise to fog our awareness.
4. *Wisdom.* Clear and calm, the mind is naturally wise.
5. *Samadhi.* Focused on the mantra, chanting concentrates the mind.
6. *Resolve.* The rhythm of the mantra propels us forward, never back.
7. *Protection.* Immersed in the mantra, the mantra enfolds us, secures us in suchness.
8. *Reflection.* The sounds of the syllables echo, bringing us back to ourselves. Mirroring gives rise to compassion.
9. *Steadfastness.* Protected and reflected, practicing the mantra, we abide in the unconditioned where we can never lose ground.
10. *Roaming playfully.* Steadfast in precepts, we are able to go anywhere and do whatever is called for. This stage of stabilizing the mind is called "Accomplishing What One Wishes."

In addition to stimulating these wholesome qualities, the Buddha promises that the Surangama mantra provides multiple concrete benefits—protection from war, evil spirits, illness, and much more:

> People who read the mantra, recite it from memory, write it out, wear it on their bodies, keep it in a safe place, or

> make offerings to it will not be reborn into poverty or into lowly circumstances or in an unpleasant place. . . .[5]
> Where the mantra exists, the celestial dragons will be pleased and the weather is clement, the harvests are abundant, and all the people are happy and at peace. . . .
>
> People will not suffer untimely deaths, nor will they be bound, fettered, or shackled. Day or night they will sleep peacefully, free from evil dreams.[6]

Furthermore, the Buddha promises that reciting this mantra from memory "even protects beings whose minds are scattered and disorderly and lack samādhi."

Sound good?

PROMISES, SKILLFUL MEANS, AND PRACTICE

I wrote this chapter at the height of a political campaign season, when candidates were outdoing each other in the promises they'd make to their electorates—more services *and* lower taxes. The promises of the Surangama mantra may seem similarly unbelievable. The sutra differs from campaign pledges, though: it makes its pledges not from a desire for personal gain but from a compassionate desire to alleviate suffering.

Buddhist scriptures offer inducements to practice in the service of introducing people to the Way of liberation. These enticements are usually justified as "skillful means." Most religions offer something of the sort—favorable treatment for the faithful in this world or, failing that, in heaven or a subsequent reincarnation. Mind-body practices pledge healing and health benefits; the glitter of perfect enlightenment feeds our curative fantasies; the bodhisattva ideal whets our double-edged savior complexes.

I feel uneasy about such lures. I'm more comfortable with Zen's exhortations to practice without any gaining mind. However, each person enters practice through the gate that calls to them, and each gate has its perils. Even "no gaining mind" can hinder us if we grab at purity.

My Taoist qigong teacher, Master Hui Liu,[7] sometimes teased me about Zen severity: "Oh, you Buddhists! Always going on about suffering, old age, death. We Taoists say, 'Live a long life! Be happy!'" She did this in the spirit of *wu-wei*, the Taoist (and Zen) practice of meshing full effort with full release.

The key to wu-wei lies in forgetting yourself to find yourself. Practicing wu-wei through reciting a mantra arouses deep trust unconstrained by expectations. This Way potentiates possibilities and invokes magic moments.

So why not give reciting the mantra a try? The complete mantra consists of 554 phrases, but here is an abbreviated form:

CHI TUO NI

E JIA LA

MI LI ZHU

BO LI

DAN LA YE

NING JIE LI[8]

Roam playfully!
You need lose nothing but your faith in disbelief,
and need gain nothing but trust
in the honesty of wonder.

14

Levels of Being

Truth of Consequences

There is a game, Truth or Consequences, in which participants either answer a question or, if they fail to do so, must perform a humorous physical stunt. It was a popular TV show and can provide a lot of fun at a party.

The play of karma—the truth of consequences—is not always so enjoyable. We often don't like how karma manifests in the stories we make of our lives, dramas tragic and comic.

Invoking the Surangama mantra, our karma "melts away as snow is melted by boiling liquid." When snows accumulate, though, massive glaciers carve deep declivities through granite walls. It takes a lot of boiling water to melt a glacier.[1]

This next section of the sutra describes in great detail the "geography" of esoteric Buddhism: its levels of being. The Buddha identifies the following:

- Twelve classes of beings bound to the cycle of death and rebirth depending on the nature of their inclinations, hindrances, illusions, and so forth

- Three gradual steps that ease beings onto the path of awakening
- Fifty-seven stages of the bodhisattva path
- The seven realms of the hells, ghosts, animals, humans, ascetic masters, gods, and *asuras* (demigods or titans)

It's beyond the scope of this book to examine the levels of being in detail. Instead, I will focus on how all beings in the seven realms, because they are submerged in attributes of the conditioned world, are subject to the karmic consequences of their actions. Failing to fully recognize the fundamental unconditioned Ground of Being (OMind), they are unable to go beyond the duality of existence and nonexistence. Bound to the cycle of death and rebirth, they get caught up in activities leading to eons of rebirths. Snared by delusion, they

> may wish to return to what is real, but to wish for the real is already a falsification. The true nature of the suchness of reality is not a reality that one can seek to return to.[2]
>
> . . . constantly torn between their tendency to commit offenses and their tendency to refrain from committing offenses, they continue to be bound to the cycle of death and rebirth.
>
> . . . such beings are pathetic and greatly to be pitied. [But] you all should understand that *you are responsible for your own deluded actions. Your true nature that is capable of full awakening is not to blame.*[3] [my italics]

These beings are you and me. As my teacher Sojun said in one of his Dharma talks, we're constantly transmigrating through these worlds: "Sometimes we're a fighting demon, sometimes we're a hungry ghost, sometimes we're in the hell realm, sometimes we're in the heavenly realm. And this goes on day in and day out. And to know, 'Oh, now I'm in the hungry ghost realm,' or, 'Now I'm in the fighting demon realm' [helps us ask] 'How do I just become a human being?'"

COMING TO TERMS WITH KARMA

Becoming a human being requires that we acknowledge our all-too-human karma. It's difficult to transform unwholesome habits if we don't acknowledge them first. Many modern meditation practitioners, though, have difficulties with Buddhist teachings on karma and transmigration.

The word "karma" can be misconstrued and misused. Some Buddhist practitioners point out, correctly, that the doctrine of transmigration has historically been used to support the social and political oppressions of caste. Some practitioners recoil from karma as a potential source of moralistic blaming and shaming—"If your practice were more pure, you wouldn't have gotten cancer." Others have difficulties reconciling the emptiness teachings of *anatta* (nonself) with how individual actions can be carried from one life to the next. Practitioners wedded to scientific-materialistic worldviews equate death with the cessation of brain activity and regard any contemplation of what happens after death as speculation at best and superstition at worst.

We don't know what death is—or whether death even "is" anything. Our discriminating I-mind evolved to cope with things, seeking to get a hold on the situations it encounters. I-mind has difficulties grasping nothingness,[4] where there's no "thing" to grasp, so I-mind keeps assigning essential qualities to nothingness.

Treating death as a permanent state makes a nothing into a something, an absence into an abiding presence; we project *thingness* onto death.

Whichever realm we're in, whether it be godly or ghostly, we project the habits of our minds onto the world. We put the feelings we have onto and into others. (Psychologists call this projective identification: "I was feeling lonely, so I called my friend to cheer her up.") By doing this, we're continually creating heavens and hells. Whenever we blame others for our feelings and fate, we're avoiding looking at our own karmic contributions.

Whatever death is or is not (or both is and is not), however karma does or does not operate, our actions have consequences. If you go out into the rain without an umbrella or a jacket, you'll get wet; if you stay out in the sun too long, your skin will burn. Whether we approach the Surangama as literal gospel, myth, or metaphor, it offers helpful reference points for practice. By describing how karmic acts lead to specific hellish sufferings, the sutra vivifies our awareness.

For example, according to the sutra, those who engage in falsehoods and insults wind up in hells completely covered with filth; those who entice and entrap others in life find themselves bound by ropes. Hungry ghosts are reincarnated as the kinds of animals eaten by people; venomous animals, when they regain human form, are reborn among people who are vicious. People who are vicious and incite hatred find themselves in the hells where they are dismembered, beheaded, pierced, and flogged. Positive actions lead to rebirth in higher realms: people who "do not seek what is everlasting and cannot yet renounce their love and affection for their spouses . . . [but] if their minds do not turn to thoughts of sexual misconduct . . . develop a certain purity and radiance. . . . Such people become gods in the Heaven of the Four Kings."[5]

Heaven and hell, like life, are what we make of them. Whatever our beliefs about transmigration and karma, most of us experience circles of thoughts and feelings that propel us through repetitive cycles of states of being.

THINKING AND FEELING

According to the Surangama Sutra, our actions acquire karmic consequences because our habit-paths are intertwined with thoughts and feelings. Specifically, emotional desire produces bodily fluids that have a tendency to sink downward. Thoughts are mental activity, so their nature is to take flight and transcend upward:

> The fundamental nature of all beings is truly pure, Ānanda, but because of their wrong views, they develop deluded habit-patterns . . . While beings are alive, they follow their natural inclinations, and upon their deaths, they follow the various currents of their karma.
>
> - If pure mental activity alone is present in their minds, they will soar upward and will be certain to be born in the heavens . . . if pure mental activity is dominant in their minds but some emotion is also present, they will still soar upward, but not as far.
> - If their pure mental activity and their emotions are equal in strength, beings will neither soar nor fall. They will be born in the human realm. The brighter their thoughts, the greater their intelligence will be; the darker their emotions, the duller their wits will be.
> - If beings have more emotion than pure mental

> activity, they will be reborn in the realm of animals. If their emotions are of greater weight, they will become fur-bearing beasts, and if their emotions are of lesser weight, they will become winged creatures.
> - If emotion is seventy percent of their mental activity and pure thoughts are thirty percent, they . . . will be reborn as hungry ghosts. . . .
> - If emotion is ninety percent of their mental activity and pure thoughts are ten percent, they will enter a hell where suffering is intermittent. . . . When they are ruled entirely by emotion, they sink into the Unrelenting Hell.

Most people's views of affect and cognition are not so different from the sutra's. The sutra divides heavenly thoughts from heavy feelings; our modern society likewise dichotomizes them as we struggle to reconcile the passions of our ids with the ideas of our egos. Some people idealize cognition as being "above" emotion. Other people insist that feelings hold more truth and more of "the native hue of resolution" than does the "pale cast of thought." Both views rest on untenable assumptions.

The depiction of feelings and emotions in popular culture, such as Pixar's film *Inside Out*, and introductory psychology classes is not so different from the Surangama's description of emotions:

> Habit-patterns that are internal involve beings' internal autonomic processes. When they are influenced by emotional desire, Ānanda, and their feelings accumulate steadily, they generate fluids associated with emotion. Thus when beings think of delicious foods, their mouths water.

> When they think of others who are no longer alive, whom they may have cherished or may have hated, their eyes fill with tears. . . . When they think about sexual acts, their procreative organs, whether male or female, will secrete fluid in response.
>
> Emotions differ, Ānanda, but all are alike in that they are associated with secretions.[6]

Psychology texts and popular science substitute "hormones" and "neurotransmitters" for the "secretions" of the sutra but view emotions similarly. The usual assumption goes something like this: an external stimulus makes a part of the brain light up. This causes changes in the body, which result in an identifiable, basic emotion flowing "inside" us. These feelings drive all complex organisms because, under emotional pressure, the only choices are to express them, wait them out, suppress them, channel them, or somehow counteract them. Humans have "higher-level" brain functions, which help us modulate these feelings; meditation helps strengthen the executive mind's control over the primitive limbic brain.

This view of emotions is an illusion. It contributes to our suffering by fostering a (false) sense of self ("I am the person who is feeling this") and alienating us from ourselves (emotions can be experienced as forces out of our control, separate from the person who is subject to its "invasion"). Treating emotions as a set of universal, hardwired set of primitive primary responses, each with its own "fingerprint" of feeling—fear, anger, lust, and so forth—is not so different from medieval notions of "humors," even if we look to the amygdala rather than the liver and substitute neurotransmitters, hormones, and electrical currents for bile, phlegm, and blood.

Instead, modern neuroscience is finding that there are no such "things" as internal fixed feelings.[7] Emotions are contextual; they emerge as interpretations of the perpetually fluctuating internal and external environments in which they arise. The same brain pattern can lead to different emotions; different brain patterns can result in the same emotion.

We can interpret the same somatic signal in different ways. When we feel our hearts beating fast, we may take it as an indicator we're thrilled, falling in love, or frightened depending on whether we're on a carnival roller coaster, on a date with an attractive potential partner, or in the wilderness and stumbling upon a grizzly bear. Conversely, the same emotion can elicit different physiological responses: terrified by a threat, we can react by freezing or fleeing. Context (such as whether a person is alone or with someone else) can magnify an emotion (e.g., fear) through contagion or alleviate it through companionship.

We try to sort out our sentiments, but we are often unclear where they come from or exactly what we're feeling. As Chuang Tzu says,

> Joy, anger, grief, delight, worry, regret, fickleness, inflexibility, modesty, willfulness, candor, insolence:
>
> music from empty holes, mushrooms springing up in dampness, day and night replacing each other before us, and no one knows where they sprout from.
>
> Let it be! Let it be!
>
> It is enough that morning and evening we have them, and they are the means by which we live.[8]

I like Chuang Tzu's image of mushrooms springing up in the dark. We identify mushrooms with their fruiting bodies, because that's how they appear to us in their most obvious (and most transient) form. Fungi, in fact, are widespread networks of mycelia, threadlike filaments intertwined with the lives of plants and worms, traversing acres of dark soil. The stalk and cap emerge at nodes of an ecological matrix: like ourselves, they are one more manifestation of the Thus-Come-One.

Similarly, emotions are the fruiting bodies of the hyphae connecting the multiple internal and external energy states of our situation; they are the colors of our lives refracted through the prisms of our being. We run into difficulties when, instead of relating to our emotions as the "means by which we live," we treat them as either invasive aliens or badges of identity.

When we treat emotions as other than ourselves, we sometimes employ them as excuses: "I couldn't help it! I didn't mean to do it, but I felt so angry." Sometimes we blame others: "I didn't mean to do it, but *you* made me so angry." Other times we put ourselves in charge: "I refuse to let you make me angry. I refuse to let you do that to me; I'm going to stand up for myself!" Other times we identify with our emotions: if I tell myself "I am a loving person," I set the conditions for making myself feel guilty if I push away someone who is causing pain by stepping on my toes. (On the other hand, identifying as "I am a loving person" may make it easier to tolerate someone stepping on your toes, for better or worse.) Whichever route we take, we get enmeshed in judging the good and bad of our emotions, justifying or guilt-tripping ourselves and others according to our habit-patterns.

Feelings and thoughts are not separate from each other; they are the means by which the brain translates the raw data of experience to awareness. Feelings and thoughts are different languages with a common root: our being in the world.

Our emotions and ideas are inextricable from our environment in surprisingly concrete ways. Psychological research[9] has shown that we assess other people as more and less convivial, depending on whether the temperature of the beverage we're holding in our hands is warm or cold. We're more likely to be fearful when we're in the dark; our circadian rhythms alter the efficiency of our thinking along with our sleep-wake cycle according to the rhythms of sunlight. We are usually blissfully unaware of our susceptibility to conditions, preferring to think our thoughts and feelings are all our own.

All these judgments, though, are imprinted with an "I." We are tilted by our inclinations, distorted by our illusions of "me" and "you," by the false boundaries we put between ourselves and the world. These delusions are the roots of karma; when emotions and beings become "things," one thing leads to another.

Thinking and feeling, we go round and round in habit-patterns that reinforce themselves. How do we find our way out of these ruts, to embark on the bodhisattva path for liberation from the creation of suffering for ourselves and others?

LIBERATION'S PATH

Dharma is the antidote to karma.

In discussing the Buddhist precepts in chapter 11, we touched on the Noble Eightfold Path: first we need to become aware that suffering exists, that we are responsible for our own and others' suffering, and that this need not be endlessly inescapable. It helps to be mindful of what we're thinking, feeling, and doing.

By itself though, awareness will not bring enlightenment. As the sutra notes:

No practice is entirely continuous,
So even mindfulness perforce arises and must halt.
An intermittent practice's results are intermittent.
How could awareness guide all beings to enlightenment?[10]

Insight is insufficient without action. Relying on personal willpower to raise awareness asks I-mind to catch its own tail, which can be exhausting. Meditation without changing how we conduct our lives will not extinguish the conflagrations of living and dying. If we are sincere in our intention to realize the Way, we need to get real.

Once we recognize that some habit-energy is causing problems for us and others, we can begin to cultivate countervailing wholesome behaviors. Psychologists have found this is usually more effective than trying to repress a harmful behavior through sheer willpower. An alcoholic who decides to stop drinking is wise to avoid going into bars, but if you're feeling lonely on a Saturday night, it helps to have arranged beforehand to meet a friend at a bowling alley or movie theater.

When we smile gently, our lips won't set themselves in a fierce scowl; when we share our food with someone, we're less likely to overeat; when we open our hand in kindness, we won't make a threatening fist. One of my favorite practices that I do throughout the day is noticing and releasing any tension in my hands. Letting the hands soften reduces my stress, making it easier to enjoy being with others.

Buddhism offers the paradigms of the four immeasurables (sympathetic joy, equanimity, compassion, and kindness) and the six paramitas (generosity, ethical behavior, patience, vigor, concentration, and wisdom) to illuminate our path. Just as we can train our muscles through regular exercise, we can train our thoughts and feelings by exercising wholesome habits. It's important to not restrict our cultivation of the immeasurables and the paramitas to meditation sessions or sangha gatherings: we need to put some effort into planning how to translate them into specific actions during our everyday lives. If I want to develop my capacity to be generous, I can set aside some money each morning, put it in a separate pocket, and look for an opportunity during the day to give it to someone. If I want to develop patience, I can decide I will make the time to let my car come to a complete halt at a stop sign.

In the Surangama Sutra, the Buddha suggests that instead of letting ourselves be carried along by our streams of perceptions, thoughts, and feelings, we can intentionally embark on the path of practice-realization that is both our source and our destination. We can turn reacting into doing and doing into being. In essence, the method is to go to the enlightened basis of whatever we encounter. Another way of saying this is: turn everything to the Dharma.

When hot or cold, go to the enlightened basis of hot or cold.[11] When in pain, go to the enlightened basis of sensing pain; when happy, go to the enlightened basis of happiness. The Dharma is not some abstract ideal: it appears through our concrete experience of sights, sounds, smells, tastes, touches, and thoughts. The Dharma is not far away; it is never anywhere but here.

When we are attached to what "I" am thinking, feeling, seeing, hearing, and so forth, we are in the realm of delusion. Snared by mental objects, we treat the objects of our thoughts, feelings, sights, sounds, tastes, and touch as things—and thus turn our selves into things as well. Objective information about a thing, though, cannot be the measure of a being. You are not your shoe size or your IQ, your opponents' ideology cannot be bypassed by any length of a tunnel, and your lovers are not delineated by the gifts they give nor the diameters of their disappointments. To think otherwise is to place true nature "out there," project ourselves onto every self-object, and, instead of the joys of mutual co-arising, experience the alienation of lonely separation, gain, and loss.

The technical term "outflows" (Pali *asava*, Skt. *asrava*) carries various connotations in Buddhism. It can refer to any state or influence that arises through unenlightened contact and thereby contributes to suffering and delusion. In the Surangama Sutra, it refers to desires, illusions, or defilements that "flow out" from the mind to objects of mind and thereby bring karmic consequences and incur suffering.

In the chapter on the sound of the bell, the Buddha taught us how to turn around our outflows: instead of mistaking hearing for sounds, to go to the enlightened basis of hearing. Avalokiteshvara described the experience: "sounds and silence ceased . . . awareness and the objects of my awareness were emptied . . . my mind ascended to unite with the fundamental, wondrous, enlightened mind of all Buddhas . . . and my power of compassion became the same as theirs."

We can apply this same practice not just to the sound of the bell but to all of the six senses (taste, touch, smell, sound, sight, thought) and to all the skandhas (forms, feelings, perceptions, formations, consciousnesses). We can apply this simple method to any of the varieties of our attention, be they wide or narrow, scanning or focused; to any of the qualities of our experiences, be they painful, pleasurable, or neutral; and to any inclination, urge, or intention. The method is simple: we turn each to its enlightened Dharma basis. When we let go of our self-centeredness and let things "just be," we realize every object and thing is being itself. We discover our own-being arises with the self-becoming of all being. All arise in, and give rise to, mind.

> The body arises through the mind;
> The mind arises through the body.
> A thought arises through the mind
> The mind arises through a thought.
> A feeling arises through the mind;
> The mind arises through a feeling.
> All being arises in the mind;
> the mind arises through all being.

When we approach the skandhas from a self-centered perspective, the karmic outflows of our actions take us further from our true selves. As soon as we treat any being as an object, we turn ourselves into objects and become subject to karma; as soon as we turn around the outflows and enter the dance of the Dharma, there are no inflows nor outflows but emptiness. *Here* the Way arises, without any hindrance. No fears exist, and we are released from suffering to suchness.[12]

When we turn all outflows to the Dharma, we leap past many and one.[13] I-mind and OMind complete each other in being ever-ordinary. Forgetting ourselves, we find ourselves in how all five skandhas, in their own-being, are emptily ungraspable and are intimate with the heart of wondrous understanding: *just this*, the Tathagata, the Matrix of the Thus-Come-One. The *Tao Te Ching* describes just this:

> *Immersed in flow, no starting and no stopping*
> *no placing claims, no holding on*
> *no merit and no fault.*

15

Fifty Demonic States of Mind

Accumulating Nothing

In this penultimate section of the sutra, the Buddha warns us against mistaking surface serenity with deep enlightenment: "This subtle clarity is not the true mind. It is, rather, like a rapidly flowing stream that seems at first glance to be calm and still."

I shiver when I recall the time I attempted to ford an innocent-looking creek swollen with spring snowmelt from the Olympic Mountains. The placid surface concealed fierce currents below; a single misstep was enough to make me lose my balance and knock me off my feet. Although the waters were only thigh-high, the undertow sucked me down, and the weight of my backpack hampered my movements. I thrashed about while the stream threatened to spit me out into the rapids of the major river it joined nearby. I barely managed to shuck off the restraining straps of my pack and regain the shore.

Seasonal streams can be avoided. Impermanence is inescapable, making all security ephemeral at best and often a sham. Vimalakirti reminds us, "The Dharma is not a secure refuge. A person who enjoys a secure refuge is not interested in the Dharma but is interested in a secure refuge."[1]

Meditation practice can increase resilience and promote health, but it will not shield us from old age, sickness, death, and disappointment. Meditation practice offers no guarantees against breaking our hearts (one might even say the heart cannot blossom fully until it breaks open). Cultivating awareness of the breath does not prevent us from choking on wildfire smoke and pollution, nor does it inoculate us against pneumonia.

The Dharma is not docile; if it were, it would exclude a substantial portion of our existence in the conditioned world of the trichiliocosm. The lion's roar of the Buddhadharma is not the voice of a *tame* lion.[2] The unconditioned Matrix of the Thus-Come-One is unmarked by any abiding characteristics: one cannot tame that which cannot be grasped. When, regardless, we attempt to clutch it tight, we create hells and heavens, realms of hungry ghosts and gods.

UNSEEN DANGERS

The Buddha warns that whatever realm we may be in, so long as mental activities continue, so does delusion:

> It is through such mental activity that life is perpetuated. . . . Merely thinking about climbing up to the edge of a precipice can cause your feet to ache. . . .
>
> From this you should know that the body which you now have is an instance of the illusion of solid matter. . . . A sense-perception caused by deluded mental activity can affect your physical body. You now experience what is pleasing and beneficial and what is displeasing and harmful. These . . . are an instance of the illusion of sense-perception.[3]

> Demons may arise within you from the five aggregates. Or a celestial demon or a ghost or a spirit—perhaps a mountain spirit or an animal possessing ghost—may come to possess you. If your mind is not clear [of delusion] when this happens, you may well take a burglar to be your own child.[4]

We humans habitually become attached, not only to our children but also to our demons. We know smoking and drug use harm us and those around us, but once addicted, it's not easy to stop. Teenagers pick at their pimples even after seeing that it scars; elders relish recalling youthful follies. Professionals are often reluctant to relinquish cherished techniques, even when they become outmoded or turn out to be harmful. Spiritual leaders who pin their identities to the forms of their affiliations are likely to recommend their practice to everyone, even (or especially) when they find themselves struggling to comply with the rituals.[5]

It's important to recognize the potential dangers of meditation practice.[6] I am glad to see more people in our society meditating, but I am concerned this sometimes happens without sufficient awareness of the risks involved. Meditation is not always benign; especially when it becomes a profitable product, we can't expect it to remain unadulterated. Some workshops teach meditation without either screening participants beforehand or providing for follow-up afterward. Meditation (hopefully) leads to fundamental changes in the ways we live; leaving people to practice on their own without giving them fair warning of the challenges they're likely to face can leave them floundering.

Traditionally, spiritual practices are embedded within a supportive context: an ongoing community of fellow practitioners, teachers, or spiritual guides; a coherent body of readings for study;

established practice forms; and precepts for governing behavior. In Buddhism, meditation occurs within the triple jewel of Buddha, Dharma, and Sangha. Extracting one component in isolation alters its meaning and diminishes its efficacy. In worst-case situations, it can cause psychological and emotional harm.

Every person is unique, so it's impossible to know how a particular individual will respond to a particular intervention. Anything that has enough power to help has enough power to harm, so there's always some risk involved. Even a seemingly benign relaxation method will initially be met, in a significant number of people (about 15 percent), with relaxation-induced anxiety.[7] Good intentions don't ensure good outcomes, no matter how apparently benign the intervention. There are no magic pills or surefire techniques.

Any methods we employ to modulate our minds need to be accompanied by changes in the way we live. If I strain a muscle while exercising, I can take an analgesic to alleviate the pain, but I would be wise to learn how to modify the exercise so my efforts at strengthening don't tear a tendon. The Surangama Sutra offers numerous practice methods, but techniques are inefficacious unless accompanied by a healthy way of life that permeates all our activities.

We put some care into maintaining our bodies. At the end of a long day or waking up from a night's sleep, we have a stale taste in our mouths: we floss and brush our teeth to refresh our breath, stimulate our gums, and prevent the buildup of plaque on our teeth. Meditation is like this for the mind. If I don't meditate regularly, I can feel the plaque from my ideas and impulses, my feelings and deeds, accumulate. To continue with the metaphor, even simple activities like flossing and brushing can damage our gums and fail to protect our teeth if we aren't practicing them properly. It's a good idea to regularly consult a dentist who can detect if we're flossing and brushing properly, alert us if we need to change our oral hygiene practices, and provide some remedial procedure if necessary.

Our psyches are at least as difficult to maintain as our mouths. Even if we brush and floss regularly, a steady diet of junk food is likely to make us ill; even if we meditate regularly, unless we act according to the precepts, we're likely to suffer. In spiritual practice, we sometimes need teachers and sangha members to tell us where we're stuck or when we're missing something. It's not easy to examine the dark places of our minds; it calls for practice our whole life through.

SKILL IS ALWAYS INCOMPLETE

Dayan (Wild Goose) qigong was traditionally passed down from master to disciple. When Yang Meijun learned it as a teenager and reached some level of proficiency, her teacher told her, "Practice sixty years more, then you can teach." When Grandmaster Yang's disciple, Master Hui Liu, adapted qigong for American students at the Wen Wu School, she found it was possible to provide the introductory basics of its first sixty-four movements in about four months to students who were willing to practice daily and come to lessons several times a week. When I teach there, it's common, at the end of four months, to hear a student say, "Great! We finished the set! When do we start learning the second set?"

Some years ago, I was teaching one of the more difficult movements to a class and, to encourage them, said, "Don't feel frustrated and impatient with yourselves. I've been practicing this movement for about fifteen years; I think maybe I'll be close to getting it in another ten years or so." My teacher, Master Liu, happened to be passing through the room and overheard. She paused, smiling sweetly at me. "Oh no, Bob, not ten more years," she said. "Whole life, Bob. Whole life."

When Master Liu's husband, Sifu Y. C. Chiang, was ninety years old, a collection of his calligraphy was published, and in the preface he wrote,

> *I learned to write calligraphy since the age of five;*
> *at age seventy, my brush finally became obedient;*
> *at age eighty, my brush still cannot express my intention;*
> *now at age ninety, I feel there is still much more to learn.*

This is a good attitude to cultivate toward any spiritual practice. Eihei Dogen wrote something similar: "When dharma does not fill your whole body and mind, you think it is already sufficient. When dharma fills your body and mind, you understand that something is missing."[8]

In the Surangama Sutra, the Buddha warns his listeners that when they become skillful enough in meditation to be able to enter deep samadhi,

> When you abide in this state, having entered samādhi, you will be like someone who ordinarily can see clearly but who finds himself in a dark place. Your essential nature will be wonderfully pure, but your mind does not yet emit light.[9]

This comes as something of a shock. We are nearing the end of the sutra—shouldn't we be closer to seeing the light? What more could be left to say? Indeed, at this point in the sutra the Buddha seems to feel he's said enough:

> Then the Thus-Come-One prepared to leave the Dharma seat. Rising from the Lion's Throne, he placed his hand on the table before him.
>
> . . . But then, moving his body, which was the color of purple-golden mountains, he sat down again.[10]

The Buddha has intimately communicated the teaching of Thusness, taught the nature and location of the mind, unveiled the illusions of the skandhas, introduced the Matrix of the Thus-Come-One, provided instructions for practice and precepts for wholesome behavior, issued a protective mantra, displayed the entire cosmos, and described the fifty-seven stages on the bodhisattva path. He starts to rise, but, recognizing that his followers will face dangers if they think their understanding is complete, the Buddha sits back down. Still incomplete!

The Buddha now goes into considerable detail, warning his listeners about fifty dangerous states of mind. The demonic states of mind cover a wide range:

- Those associated with sense-perceptions that invoke overwhelming sorrow, manic joy, infinite serenity, or boundless sexual cravings
- Those associated with forms that enable practitioners to leave their bodies; hear voices; see throughout all space, even in the dark; have visual hallucinations of buddhas; and become immune to pain

- Those where adepts gain the ability to see inside their own bodies (to the point where they are able to pull intestinal worms out of their bodies without harming themselves or the worms!)

The Buddha warns us that if we are excessively severe in practice, we will experience overwhelming sorrow at the sufferings of all beings: we will "pity a worm like a newborn child." If we feel an urge to rapidly excel in our practice of the Dharma, we will develop an inflated sense of superiority. If we lack steady discernment, we will feel content with what we have already achieved and go no further. We can lose our way; we may experience states of aridity or longing, or memories that will not fade away. If we lose sight of the method suitable to our level of practice, we may become despondent, feeling we haven't accomplished anything or not as much as we should have.

These are just a few of the fifty demons. All of these states of mind can occur to people who come to practice bearing no obvious psychological hindrances. They are riskier yet for the many (probably most) people who come to practice suffering from some mental distress. Then we're in the situation where (as the sutra says) "the innkeeper is befuddled, so his guests can do as they please."

STATES OF MIND

States of mind are not mere moods. States of mind are complex constellations of ideas connected to emotions, connected to images of self and other and to the ways we interact with the psychological, biological, and material world. Our states of mind map the world into contours shaped by our beliefs, paint our relationships in the colors of our desires, and form our feelings to match our delusions.

The nervous system is continually making physiological and psychological adjustments to respond to the fluctuations in and around us that mark our transient existence. These are all moments of I-mind, arising from (and supported by) the mind-ground of OMind. They vary in how they fit circumstances and whether they help or hinder skillful responding, but no state of mind is essentially good or essentially bad: all are merely natural. As Chuang Tzu puts it, "There is nothing that is not so, nothing that is not acceptable."[11]

The psychoanalyst Mardi Horowitz demonstrated how paying attention to shifts in states of mind can clarify patterns during psychotherapy; in everyday life, we traverse these shifting states moment by moment.[12] For example, as you read these words, you (hopefully) are in an "open learning" state of mind characterized by an idea ("this may be helpful to explore"), a feeling (curiosity), and a role relationship model of yourself as an "interested reader-student" and myself as an "author-teacher." The sounds, sights, and tactile sensations of your physical environment may have receded into the background. This mention of your physical environment, though, might trigger a transition in your state of mind. Perhaps you become aware of noises, such as a neighbor's vacuum cleaner. You may then feel annoyed by this digression and slip into an "annoyed skeptic" state of mind—one in which our roles change as you become a critical consumer ("Why is he going on about this?") and I become a boring pedant. If so, in this new state, the exterior world might feel a little more intrusive, and your interior being might experience some increased susceptibility to sensations of tiredness, muscle aches, or hunger.

It's important to cultivate awareness of our states of mind, not just the objects of mind, as we meditate. When we notice the mind is wandering and bring the mind back to some focus, we can do so in a "striving student" state, a "dutiful practitioner" state, a "frustrated perfectionist" state, or a "kindly healer" state. From a psychological standpoint, it's helpful to become aware of our self-talk in order to alter what we say to ourselves (and others). However, changing the *tone* of the self-talk is more fundamental than changing the content, since it generalizes—one mind tone can pervade many habits. If we self-correct from a compassionate state of mind, we'll benefit even if we get it "wrong"; if we self-correct from a harshly critical state of mind, we'll continue to suffer even if we get it "right."

So long as we adopt Chuang Tzu's "everything acceptable" state of mind, we don't cloud our awareness; we aren't attached or averse to any element, so feelings and thoughts come and go much like guests checking in and out of a host's inn. Usually, the host can remain silent and still behind the reception desk while staff take care of the administrative details. In a similar way, when meditators in samadhi are fully awake and free of delusion, they understand that everything they are experiencing is just a passing state of mind. The Buddha assures us that in this case they "will not become confused. Eventually the state will disappear of its own accord," and they need not worry about demonic states:

> Celestial demons, shape-shifting ghosts, and succubus-demons will all come to disturb your samādhi. But despite their furious rage, they are subject to the stress of entanglement with perceived objects, while you abide within wondrous enlightenment. Therefore they can do you no harm

> any more than wind can blow light away or a knife cut water. . . . They can visit you only briefly . . . when you are absorbed in meditation, fully awake and free of delusion, how will the deeds of these demons be able to affect you?[13]

Unfortunately, as anyone who practices meditation discovers, there are times when even though we are absorbed in meditating, we are *not* fully awake and free of delusion. We get caught by states of mind distorted by picking and choosing, delusions born of desire and loathing. Then people

> may be dulled and confused by these experiences, and they will no longer be capable of taking a proper measure of themselves . . . they will become further confused, and in their failure to know themselves, they will make the claim that they have reached the level of a sage.[14]

This is when danger comes. To continue with the hotel metaphor, if one of the guests or a member of the staff decides *they* are the host and tries to take over, the smooth functioning of the place will be disturbed.

> If he does think he is a sage, he will be open to a host of deviant influences.[15]

> . . . this good person . . . may come to abide in a state of purity, and his mind will be at peace. A feeling of joy may suddenly well up within him. He will take such pleasure in this state of mind that he loses control of it. This state is called "feeling what one takes to be serenity but lacking

> wisdom to exercise self-control." If he understands this state, he will not suppose that he has become a sage. *But if he thinks that he has become a sage, [the state] will become demonic and will take over his mind* [my italics] . . .[16]

BEFUDDLED INNKEEPERS

One of the quirks of our mental functioning is that each component thinks it's a sage. Our thoughts insist, "I figure things out, so I'm in charge. Do what I say." Feelings are perhaps less argumentative but more overwhelming: when we're joyous, we forget pain ever existed. Ecstasy is unlikely to pay heed to common sense, and pessimism paints everything in shades of gray.

States of mind that have a negative valence—fear, doubt, depression—can be very persuasive. Their succubus-demons can convince us that things will *always* be this way. In torpid gloom we still think we're sages, though of an opposite, negative sort: depression can turn us into oracles of nihilistic emptiness, certain that life really is meaningless and worthless. Fear feels forever, as if it will never end, except in calamity or rescue; we're certain our forecasts of catastrophic consequences are true predictions, so we close ourselves to countervailing evidence offered to us by those who (unwisely) dispute us.

It's important to take our states of mind into account when we practice. If you are going through a sticky, depressive episode, you might benefit more from aerobic exercise than from sitting unmoving, mired in despondency. You might still go to the retreat center but spend less time on the cushion and more time working actively on maintaining the practice place (it's a good time to dust the shelves, sweep the walkways, and rake the leaves).

States of mind where we feel "up" can also befuddle the innkeeper. It's hard to convince someone with bipolar disorder to get treatment when they are in a manic phase for the simple reason that what looks like mania to others feels really, really good and intensely appropriate to the one in the frenzy. Similarly, it can be hard to convince someone of the dangers of ecstatic meditative states of mind—especially when the practitioner mistakes ecstasy for enlightenment.

The Surangama Sutra warns us of the lure and the danger of pursuing special states, such as being able to read others' minds, to leave the body to roam freely, and to have psychic knowledge of others. It can be perilous to seek deeper levels of even seemingly benign states such as concentration or sustained merging with oneness. It can lead people to self-proclaim enlightenment and solicit followers. Generally speaking, when someone lays claim to some special enlightenment, it's a sign they're caught by delusion—especially if they insist, "I'm enlightened, and you're not."

The Surangama Sutra reserves its most severe warnings for those who declare themselves to be sages on the basis of achieving some "advanced" state of meditation:

> When they encounter these states—each one according to what he craves, each one confused by his long-cherished habits—they will choose to abide in one of these states, which they will suppose is the final and serene place of refuge.
>
> They will make the claim that they have completed a full and supreme awakening. This is an egregious lie, and because of it—once the karma of their present state has been exhausted— . . . they will fall into the Unrelenting Hell.[17]

It's important to not fall into the trap of thinking we are fully, supremely awakened. If we have grandiose confidence in ourselves, we're likely to overstep our bounds and harm others. If, on the other hand, we try to hold tight to our supposed awakening, we are worrying that having acquired supreme perfect enlightenment, we might lose it. Worrying about losing something that cannot be gained or lost is a sign of foolishness.

We'd be foolish to call ourselves sages. Nevertheless, we'd also be foolish to disavow our intuitive wisdom.

WISDOM

Zen practice relies on our fundamental awakened nature. We run into a different kind of devil if we say, "Everyone is fundamentally enlightened," but don't believe that can really apply to us. If we don't have faith in our enlightenment, it will be hard to follow the Buddha's advice to be a light unto ourselves.

If we don't acknowledge that we have a little wisdom, we'll keep looking for it everywhere but at its source. Certain we are not sages, we run the risk of settling for whatever level of understanding our self-image says we dummies are worthy of. This takes us off the hook of living up to our enlightenment; we can always excuse our shortcomings by saying, "I'm only human."

We're all more human than otherwise,[18] but we also are all buddhas and bodhisattvas—as well as hungry ghosts, animals, and gods. Our practice greets all beings—all the denizens of our minds, all the world's spirits and forms—with kindness and compassion. We invoke this wisdom at the opening of the sutra of loving-kindness, the Metta Sutta:[19] "This is what is accomplished by the one who is wise, seeking the good, being peace." A few lines down, the sutra says, "May we be wise but not puffed up."

It's wise to not puff ourselves up, thinking we're sages. However, we mustn't recuse ourselves from the process of learning to be wise. The Surangama Sutra's heroic journey to wondrous understanding is a journey for wisdom; the paramitas and the bodhisattva way are skillful means for cultivating wisdom.

Dale Wright, in his book on the paramitas, summarizes the Mahayana perspective on wisdom[20] (I've punctuated the original with bullet points):

- Wisdom . . . is the ability to face the truth and not be unnerved or frightened.
- It is the capacity to be disillusioned, but not disheartened.
- It is the ability to consider the contingency and the groundlessness of all things, oneself included, and not turn away from that consideration in fear.
- Wisdom means setting aside illusions about oneself and the world . . . it entails willingness to avoid seeking the security of the unchanging and to open oneself to a world of flux and complex relations.

I cannot say what wisdom is. I'm embarrassed to even have the effrontery to address the question, but I also feel the issue is inescapable and requires all our best efforts.

The Surangama Sutra reminds us that the key to wisdom is humility. A major roadblock in our potential for wisdom is arrogance. When we think we're sages, we invite demons to be our companions. When we reject sagacity, we invite ignorance to supplant the inquiring mind of not-knowing.

I'm pretty sure wisdom is simpler than I conceive of it, that it does not let itself be deterred by desire or fear. I have faith that wisdom enjoys laughter and refreshes itself in reverence and awe. I find a useful rule of thumb for approaching wisdom in a saying by the Jewish sage Ben Zoma who, around the first or second century C.E., wrote: "Who is wise? One who learns from all people."

The voice of the One who is wise is not always easy to hear, so I endeavor to remind myself that every being I encounter is my teacher. I look for ways to train myself to recognize the sage in everyone. With this intention, I extracted some of the *Tao Te Ching*'s descriptions of the sage and collated them. The result reads almost like a poem—or perhaps a mantra to ward off demons:

The sage rejects nobody and no thing
lets go of overdoing
is not caught in extremes
lives free of excess.

Thus the sage is straightforward but does not overreach
is an edge but does not cut
is a sharp point but does not stab
is a light but does not dazzle.

Sages know themselves but make no show of themselves
love themselves but are not full of themselves
take action without holding on to the fruits
accomplish tasks without dwelling on merits or worth
make no claims on others

accumulate nothing

The sage has no set mind but simply is
the ordinary mind of all people.

To the good they are good,
to the not good they are also good.
This is the goodness of nature.

To those who are true they are true;
to those who are untrue they are also true.
This is the truth of nature.

As for the sage's presence in the world:
one with It, mind's auspicious merging.

People strain to focus their ears and eyes;
sages have a gentle smile for all.

16

The Merit of Teaching the Surangama Dharma

Reverence and Joy

After the Buddha finishes his warnings about demonic states of being, Ananda stands up and asks one more question: "When the five categories of delusion, based on the five aggregates, disappear, do they do so all at once or in a specific sequence?"

By this time, even Shakyamuni's patience is starting to run out. He responds, "I have already explained this to you with the example of untying my scarf. What is it that you did not understand, so that you ask me about it again? You should thoroughly understand the source of deluded acts of mind, and then you should transmit this teaching!" Nevertheless, with infinite compassion the Buddha offers a brief summary. The five aggregates are simply the development of five kinds of deluded mental activity: (1) the illusion of solid matter (form); (2) the illusion of sense-perception; (3) cognition creating an illusory understanding of the cooperative functioning of mind and body; (4) the uninterrupted succession of thought after thought that characterizes mental formations; and (5) the false mental impressions lying within what seems to be the clarity of consciousness.

> This subtle clarity is not the true mind. . . . Until your six faculties merge and become interchangeable, you will never be able to put an end to your deluded mental acts.[1]

> . . . In the subtle, true, wondrous understanding, in the fundamental, awakened, perfect purity, no death or rebirth remains, nor any defilement, not even space itself.[2]

Where there is not even space, there is (in the words of the Heart Sutra) no realm of mind-consciousness, no ignorance and no extinction of it, no suffering, no origination, no stopping, no path—and no more questions! The Buddha then offers his listeners some final words of encouragement:

> "Ānanda, even in an infinite number of eons I could not fully describe the benefit that beings will gain from reciting this Sutra and from holding this mantra in their minds. By relying on this teaching that I have given you, and by practicing just as I have instructed you, you will go directly to full awakening without creating any more karma that would lead to entanglement in the demonic."
>
> The Buddha had now finished speaking this Sutra. . . . All who were there felt great joy. They bowed in reverence and departed.[3]

As we reach the last chapter of this book, before we bow in reverence and depart, I hope it is clear that the sutra is not confined to finite words appearing on a set number of pages (or, for e-books, a specific number of kilobytes).

Your (and my) experience of the sutra and this book's exploration arise as the forms, feelings, perceptions, formations, and consciousnesses of your mind—but *that* is not your mind!

Just this is The Mind of the Great Sage of India. It is intimately transmitted, unlimited by then and now, here and there.

In writing this chapter, I struggled for days to find fitting words to cap our study of the Surangama Sutra. During this time, I had a head cold that made it difficult to think or write clearly. I wanted to find some inspiring summary, some morsels of wisdom to convey at this book's conclusion. I feared if I failed to do so, this project we've undertaken together might feel unsatisfying to you. Eventually I realized that my mind was befogged not so much by the cold bug as by the viral vicissitudes of desire. I was caught in all the congestion that accompanies ego-attachments and aversions.

Both my wants and my fears are delusions. Accomplishment and failure, worthwhile and useless are false dichotomies. As we saw in the previous chapter, as our skills increase, we realize there is so much more to learn. Wisdom recognizes that its understanding faces limitless horizons. Believing that our study and practice could have a beginning and an end is pure illusion, caught in the suffering of birth-and-death.

LOOKING BACKWARD: ILLUSIONS

When I look back on our engagement with the Surangama Sutra, I find three pervasive themes. The first is how everything we see, hear, feel, and think is an illusion. In the penultimate chapter of the sutra, the Buddha summarizes the ways we get caught in five delusions of the mind:

- We are caught by the illusions of solid matter—such as the body. "Even thinking about something sour can cause the mouth to water," even though there's no sour fruit in the mouth, no sour lemon in the room, or (if your mouth is puckering) any sour grapes on this page (and hopefully, no sour grapes at having devoted time and energy to reading this book).
- We are caught by the illusions of pleasant and unpleasant. Our experiences are charged by false dualisms of pleasure and pain.
- We are caught by the illusions of seeking and avoidance. Once the thought of a perceived object arises in the mind, the body responds by pursuing and fleeing, dreaming we can obtain what we want and avoid what we don't want.
- We are caught by the illusions that we fail to be aware of—the uninterrupted succession of thought after thought, sensation after sensation. According to the sutra, these wear us down; they manifest as incessant and imperceptible changes of aging and decreasing vitality. Our faces wrinkle, our habits become crusts and then crack.
- We are caught by the illusions of mental clarity. "These states of mind seem pure and unmoving but are not the true mind, since they contain traces of habits and mental activities [i.e., the storehouse consciousness]. . . . Mental

clarity . . . is like a rapidly flowing stream that seems at first glance to be calm and still. Although you do not see it, there is nevertheless a current."

Illusion piled upon illusion! Even the teachings of the Dharma and the Buddha herself are not exempt.[4] Master Hua, commenting on the sutra, offers these profound analogies:

- All karma is an illusion.
- All phenomena are like a mirage.
- All physical bodies are like the moon in water.
- All wondrous forms are like flowers in space.
- All Buddhalands are chimeras, castles in the air.
- All the deeds of the Buddha are like dreams.
- All three bodies of the Buddha are reflections, shadows, transformations.[5]

Again and again, our teachers warn, "Don't get caught in the appearances and appurtenances of the teaching!" Don't mistake the finger pointing at the moon for the moon. The moon is itself, the finger is itself, and this "itself" is ungraspable, because "itself" *is not an object*. As the Vimalakirti Sutra puts it,

> The Dharma is ultimately without formulation, without contrived theories, and without verbalizations. A person who is attached to anything, even to liberation, is not interested in the Dharma but is interested in the taint of desire.
>
> The Dharma is not an object. . . . Not a sight, a sound, a category or an idea. A person who is involved in sights,

> sounds, categories, and ideas is not interested in the Dharma but is interested in seeing, hearing, sensing, knowing and understanding.[6]

We should not even be attached to Buddha. Why be attached to body and mind?

LOOKING BACKWARD: TURNING AROUND THE OUTFLOWS

This brings us to the second pervasive theme of the Surangama Sutra: To free ourselves from illusions, we need to realize how all objects of mind are I-maginations and turn around our outflows. This is a process of turning self-centered forms, feelings, perceptions, formations, and consciousnesses back to their foundational Dharma. Instead of being attached to our projections and dualistic concepts of "inner" and "outer" phenomena, "mine" and "yours," we return all experiences to their empty, enlightened nature.[7] All being is interbeing, so all moments are meetings.

Hearing the sound of a bell, instead of being caught by its sound, we go to the enlightened basis of hearing that is not confined to objects of mind. Similarly, we greet our inclinations and aversions, our pains and pleasures, by uniting them with—returning them to—the nature from which they arise. This is the Matrix of the Thus-Come-One, that which encompasses not only sounds and silence but all the myriad ways we register and respond to the world—including joy, acceptance, compassion, kindness. This is sometimes called "returning to the root," meeting each and all in suchness.

This perhaps sounds overly mystical. Freeing ourselves from outflows is simple: instead of turning away (outward) from anything we encounter, we turn *toward* every experience. Instead of approaching things insofar as what they mean to "me," we do our best to let go of the illusions cast by our aversions and attachments, and approach things as It is.

Every ordinary moment manifests as "just this," illuminating us and the entire universe as the Matrix of the Thus-Come-One. We realize, as Tozan (Dongshan) said at a moment of enlightenment, "I am not It; It actually is me."

Shunryu Suzuki, reflecting on Tozan's expression, said, "'I' am not an object that can be grasped."[8] Nor do any such objects exist. We are all continuously flowing, tossed about by rivers, but we are the river; consumed by fires, but we are the fire.[9] The world cracks open into suchness, where you and I appear as the times of our lives: *here* is the place, *now* the Way unfolds.[10]

Our hearts lift at this, but our I-minds recoil from no-thingness, so we are thrown into doubt. Is "just this" really all there is? We fantasize about a fancier cure, a bigger Truth than life-and-death as it is. Such ungraspable suchness not only slips through our fingers but is completely inconceivable to our discriminating thinking. As verse 14 of the *Tao Te Ching* puts it,

> *It cannot be seen, so we name it unclear;*
> *It cannot be heard, so we name it indistinct;*
> *It cannot be grasped, so we name it insubstantial.*

Words fail. Our practice of the Dharma is an ongoing process of translating ineffable experience into words and actions that seem to be always lacking, because what we wish to express is ungraspable. Our practice of the Dharma cannot be captured in a formula or a mental model because our being is interbeing—activity, not essence.

LOOKING FORWARD: REACHING FOR REALIZATION

Dynamic activity is the third major theme of the Surangama Sutra. What we do matters; our actions have consequences. If we don't align our actions with the precepts, meditation will be a fruitless attempt at cooking sand to make steamed rice. The tones of the Surangama mantra only exert their powers through beings intoning them. No practice, no realization.

The importance of right practice circles us back to the sutra's first theme: don't be deceived! If we think we're enlightened, we'll be misled by demons along the way. If we idealize our practice, we turn it into an idol. That turns our practice into a thing. "Things" are always illusory.

Deep down inside we know there is nothing we can grasp, but we keep groping, much like reaching for the pillow behind us at night. The pillow is another illusion; it's not "really" a pillow, just a sack stuffed with feathers or foam that falls apart easily in pillow fights and restless nights. Still, the cushion is pillowy enough to support our heads and allow us to dream.

We want to be ourselves, but our thing-selves are illusions. To take illusion as unreal is delusion. Illusion is as real as real can be. Our illusion of human entitlement despoils the earth. The illusion of absolute power corrupts absolutely; the illusion of powerlessness lessens us by engendering despair. Our illusion of being either enlightened or unenlightened really makes us suffer.[11]

Descartes, haunted by doubt about whether he could trust in anything being real, took refuge in *cogito ergo sum* ("I think, therefore I am") and bequeathed Westerners with a dualistic oxymoron:

faith in reason.[12] Sengcan might have advised Descartes to have faith in Mind.

We can have faith in OMind—Buddha's Mind, the Matrix of the Thus-Come-One—because OMind is truth itself: thinking and doubt, ergo and ogre, beyond sums and minuses. In contrast, our thinking I-mind's primary mission—"Get a grip on yourself!"—is inherently frustrating: the eye cannot see itself without a mirror.

Everything turns out to be a mirror; when empty mirrors face each other, they shatter into pieces, infinities of reflections.[13] Everything we perceive and think is a mere reflection in the Matrix, an illusion. That doesn't mean it's unreal—it's just not what it seems to be. Our practice is to turn seeming into being, returning thin images of things to their source, moment by moment, continuous flow.

Practice requires us to be fully engaged, but we can only be fully engaged by letting go of ourselves. Letting go of ourselves means letting go of all our aversions and attachments, all our fears and hopes. At our most naked, we find ourselves mutually embracing: reaching *to* each other, reaching *for* each other. Reaching is realization.

REACHING LOVE

In our incompleteness and delusion, we keep reaching for that which lies beyond, within, or among us. We reach to touch our untouchable enlightened nature; we make our enlightenment real by reaching. Realization is not a single satori of ecstatic bliss: not a feeling; not an insight; not a taste, touch, smell, or object of mind.

Realization is groping for, finding, and touching each other—without ever completing any "thing."

How could we complete ourselves or each other when we are not things but the suchness of complete dynamic activity? The Matrix of the Thus-Come-One, enlightened suchness, is not in you, or me, or any thing. This suchness is not outside you, or me, or any thing. It is not between you, or me, or any thing.

When we face this mystery, we bring our hands together and bow with reverence and joy. Reaching for the truth of each other through ourselves with reverence and joy—isn't this love?

LOVE IN THE SURANGAMA

I confess that in the course of studying the Surangama Sutra, I've rather fallen in love with it. Love is the center point of the sutra; like every point it is dimensionless, with infinite potential in its emptiness. The center of the Wheel of the Dharma is empty so the wheel can turn. In its turning, the sutra is lovingly alive.

Every time the Buddha attempts to instruct us in the wondrous, illuminated understanding of the Thus-Come-One, it is an act of love. The sutra's loving is inherent in our practice of it. Each time we study the teaching— even though we never "get it"—it's an act of love.

In the Surangama Sutra, the Buddha teaches the wondrous, enlightened Mind that underlies all, the Mind that transcends "understanding" by intellectual thinking or emotional sensing. He warns Ananda not to equate the mind of "just this" with the mind that grasps at objects, saying, "Ānanda! *That is not your mind!*"

The Chinese (and Japanese) character for "mind" can also be translated as "heart." The Buddha is reminding Ananda and all of us, "*That* is not your heart!" When we treat any being as an object, we reduce an ungraspable being to "that thing." Our hearts rest between each beat, our minds still between each thought, but there is never any interruption to the continuous flowing that animates our heart-minds' pulsing being. Even when our blood flow stops and our EEG flattens, our being does not turn into a thing. Our corpse finds other paths of becoming in the play of birth-and-death, manifesting its own-being in different forms of transformation. Our heart-minds connect the seeming separations of life and death, this and that, you and me, I-mind and OMind, buddhas and deluded beings. Compassion and wisdom mutually embrace and make us whole.

The Surangama Sutra begins by showing us Ananda and a woman from the Matanga tribe embracing. They nearly succumb to a magical sexual spell until Buddha rescues them, dispatching Manjusri to dispel their illusions with the Surangama mantra. Later in the sutra, we hear the sequel: the Surangama mantra freed not only Ananda but the Matanga woman as well. Buddha tells Ananda,

> In previous lifetimes during many eons, you and the young Mātaṅga woman developed affinities with each other, which led to habits of love and devotion. It has not been for one lifetime only, nor even for one eon only. Yet hearing me proclaim the Dharma freed her mind forever from the entanglements of love. Now she is an Arhat, though she had been a mere courtesan, someone who had never intended to undertake spiritual cultivation. But by the hidden aid of the mantra's power, she quickly became one who needs no further instruction.[14]

The Surangama mantra provided a truer love song for Ananda and the young woman than the siren calls of sexual desire. Renouncing meaningless coitus, they released each other to the intimate embrace of the Thus-Come-One. In doing so, they found themselves.

In classical Buddhism, love and sex were viewed as insuperable obstacles to realizing *annutara-samyak-sambodhi* ("complete perfect enlightenment"). Emotional attachment was seen as inevitably creating karmic burdens; householder responsibilities obviously left no space for meditation and Dharma study. In order to realize enlightenment, Siddhartha Gautama had to leave home, abjure the love of a husband for his wife, renounce the love of a father for his children, and relinquish the love of a son for his parents.[15] Gautama, a king's son, had to leave his family and his palace. The Buddha, though, does not (did not, will not) depart nor arrive.

Siddhartha Gautama's personal choice, taken within the cultural context of his time, set home-leaving as the iconic means of realization for two millennia. Buddhist institutions cemented a custom into a command, dividing temple practice from home practice in ways that challenge us today. Today, many (most) of us practice as householders. We have responsibilities to our families, friends, coworkers, and communities. We carry the burdens of possessions, along with the pains and pleasures of love. Does this mean enlightenment is out of reach?

I would argue: no more so than it ever has been or will be. The Surangama Sutra reveals how every seeming thing—every form, feeling, perception, formation, consciousness—is a delusory appearance that cannot be grasped as either existing or not-existing (or both or neither). These very delusions are the gateways to liberation.

That being so, there is no "thing" that is not a practice vehicle; every being we encounter offers a where and when for awakening.

Sexual experience blends life with death, fantasy with all-too-solid flesh, forgetting with fulfilling. Mind cannot be grasped but neither can a lover, no matter how fiercely we try to hold them tight. Meditation, when self-centered, can become a form of masturbation. Sexuality, when practiced with generosity, morality, patience, and concentrated effort can teach the truth of impermanence and arouse wisdom and compassion. When we practice the paramitas at every moment with every one, in our living rooms and workplaces as well as in our meditation halls and temples, we begin to hear the lion's roar of compassion and join our own voice to it with our whole being.

What is love, after all, but meeting all we encounter with utmost sincerity and a trusting heart? When we devote ourselves this way to everyone and everything, with equal respect and appreciation, we let go of self-centeredness. This is how Dogen urges us to practice:

> *Practice with heart,*
> *practice with beyond heart,*
> *practice even with half a heart.*
> *You attain the marrow and are invariably transmitted*
> *dharma through your utmost sincerity and trusting heart*[16]

This is our true nature reaching for itself. We reach for our true nature when we bow at the zendo altar and when we make room for the driver attempting to merge into our lane on the way to work, while playing fetch with our dog and reading our child's favorite book to them for the umpteenth time. We touch the Matrix of the Thus-Come-One in a puppy or a rattlesnake, a pebble or an avalanche, a mud puddle or a marsh-wiggle. When we bring ourselves wholeheartedly to our sweethearts, we meet Buddha whether we are touching each other through a skin-to-skin embrace or through our egos sparring over whose turn it is to take out the garbage.

The practice of genuinely loving each other is difficult: it summons all our illusions, all the bends and breaks in ourselves, all our frightening hurts and cherished habits. The Matrix of the Thus-Come-One is obscured by fifty delusive, demonic states of mind.

The practice of genuinely loving each other is easy: the ungraspable, unknowable mystery of our beloved arouses our wonder and awe, our fondest feelings and kindly compassion. On the fifty-seven way stations of the bodhisattva's path, our egocentric pursuits and evasions are sifted through the mudra of Buddha's smile, and we bow to each other in reverence and joy.

Love, basically, is bowing to each other with reverence and joy.

I like to think there may be another Surangama Sutra in one of the alternate universes physicists say exist, a version that highlights the suchness of love. In that less misogynistic version of the sutra, the Mantanga woman has a name. When the Buddha sends Manjusri to her and Ananda with the Surangama mantra, the power of the mantra dissolves the spells clouding both their minds. She is freed from the demonic state of mind that insists she must seduce in order to succeed. Ananda is freed from the demonic state of mind that insists he must be separated from his fleshly sensations in order to seek the Dharma. They awaken and, seeing each other clearly, fall—or perhaps, arise—in love.

Perhaps they consummate their relationship with sex. Perhaps they redirect their yearnings and join each other in chanting a sutra. Perhaps, being awkward in their first taste of love, they stumble; they leave each other but bring whatever they've learned to their next intimate relationships. Whatever paths they take, once and forever they proclaim the no-thing path of realizing love.

Realizing love comes through in ordinary ways—singeing the toast, eating the burnt slices, offering the nicer ones to others, enjoying the slices offered to you. The Matrix of the Thus-Come-One is a place where I-mind and OMind meet, where mind and body merge, where the self-centered dreams of "me" and "you" embrace and discover—meeting at a moment, touching each other, we touch ourselves— "just this."

I'll conclude this introduction to the Surangama Sutra with the principles I use in my practice of Ordinary Mind Zen.[17] For me, these practice principles render the sutra in a few concise phrases:

Caught in a self-centered dream—only suffering.
Aversion, attachment—exactly the dream.
"Just this"—the ever-teacher.
Meeting this moment—compassion's Way.

ACKNOWLEDGMENTS

This book would not be possible without the efforts of the Buddhist Text Translation Society and their English language translation of the Surangama Sutra with selected comments by Master Hsuan Hua. I am deeply grateful to them and to Reverend Heng Sure, who kindly and generously gave permission on behalf of BTTS, to freely share excerpts from their translation.

My sweetheart and wife, Jeanne Courtney, read early versions of the manuscript and began the process of weaning me from obscure language, run-on sentences, and too-frequent use of colons and semicolons. Jeanne's loving support sustains me, and her ongoing practice inspires me.

I'm indebted to my editors at Shambhala, Matt Zepelin and Breanna Locke, for bearing with me through numerous revisions and assisting me throughout the publication process. Matt, as senior editor, provided valuable writing guidance and, as a fellow Zen practitioner, insightful Dharma observations. Breanna helped me be more sensitive to some of the implications of what

I'd written and helped me get through some of the linguistic and technical thickets I encountered.

My sister, Elana, and her husband, David, generously read and commented on early versions of the manuscript—despite the topic not being their usual choice for reading! Their love, emotional support, and companionship sustains me as we practice with the process of aging. I'm grateful to my daughters for allowing me to share some of their (and their children's) stories and to the joy they bring me through their families, their socially conscious work contributions, and through simply being themselves.

Deep thanks to my friends and fellow Ordinary Mind Zen teachers Diane Rizzetto and Malcolm Martin, for reading early versions of the manuscript and providing encouragement, helpful suggestions, and critiques. Many of my students, here and abroad, have also provided helpful comments on the Dharma talks I gave that formed my earliest attempts to share the Surangama's teachings. I hope I did not confuse them overmuch. My students continue to inspire me through their ongoing practice of meditation and qigong and by their good hearts.

Deep bows to all whose efforts sustain me by contributing to the infrastructure of the food and energy, the material goods, social fabric, and spiritual goodwill I rely on; to all those working to heal the past in the present; and to those who are helping remedy the present so it will not lead to mass extinctions, and so it will allow my grandchildren to live in a wholesome future.

In this regard, I want to acknowledge I wrote this book while living on the Tribal lands of Sacramento's Indigenous People. The history of the Sacramento area, and its people, is rich in heritage, culture, and tradition. This area was, and still is, the Tribal land of the Nisenan People. Sacramento was a gathering place for many local Tribes who have lived throughout the central valley and the foothills for generations and were the original stewards of this land, so I want to acknowledge the Southern Maidu People to the North, the Valley and Plains Miwok/ Me-Wuk Peoples to the south of the American River, and also honor the Patwin Wintun Peoples to the west of the Sacramento River.

May we, each and all, realize wisdom seeking good, compassionately being peace.

APPENDIX I

Hearing Meditation

As in any meditation practice, focus less on what you do and more on how you approach it. Do not try to accomplish anything. Explore.

Settle yourself in meditation. Ease your grip on all involvements. Let the myriad things rest.

AWARENESS OF SOUNDS

- Be aware of the sounds and silences in the space around you.
- Hear each sound as just a sound. Refrain from commenting on it or identifying it.
- The conditioned mind grasps at what is making the sound; when that occurs, notice the naming of it. Let go of the name, let go of what the sound might be, and return to just the sound as a sound.
- The conditioned mind grasps at whether a sound is pleasing or harsh, high or low. When that occurs, notice the

judging. Let go of the judging and return to the sound as pure sound.

- Whenever a thought, feeling, impulse, or sensation (other than sound) arises, notice it, gently let go, and return to sound-and-silence. Let your whole being open to sound.
- We tend to hear in stereo, left-front-right. Extend the sound-space to a full sphere, including above, below, behind, and all around you.
- Within this expansive space, some sounds will come and go in the foreground. Notice how they arise and fall, grow louder or softer, appear suddenly or gradually.
- Within this expansive space, some sounds will seem continuous in the background: perhaps the hum of an appliance, the white noise of traffic, the subtle susurrations of your breath. Notice how these sounds persist while your awareness of them comes and goes.
- Explore when the mind seems to move "out" toward a sound that draws it, then moves toward another. Explore when the mind seems to move "in" toward the center, and "holds" a sound. Explore when the mind "holds" several sounds at once.
- Don't listen just with your ears. Sounds do not reside only in your head; every space in body-mind is a container, an echo chamber. Sound-vibrations are transmitted physically through bones and flesh. Allow sound-and-silence to be in your belly and breast, muscle and tendon, skin and breath.
- Notice how any tension of the body changes the sound of a thought, feeling, or sensation as it moves through skin, flesh, and bones. Notice how any constriction of the mind crimps the tone color.

- Let the mind rest between the sounds. Let the sounds rest within the mind.

AWARENESS OF SILENCE

This is the same as Meditation I, but you practice with silence.

You'll probably notice that however quiet it becomes, silences are relative; there will still be some sound either inside or outside.

Listen for the silence that "surrounds" and "upholds" any sound.

TURNING HEARING INWARD

When the mind has quieted sufficiently, turn your hearing inward.

- Stop the outflows (reaching toward objects of hearing). Listen to yourself.
- Let your whole being act as a sounding board. Vibrations come and go. Vibrations in our hearing range are called "sound"; subsonic and supersonic vibrations are energy waves.
- *Let every experience—physical sensations such as pain or comfort, thoughts and judgments, urges and wishes—come via the mind's gate of hearing.* Let yourself "hear" sights, smells, tastes, touches, thoughts. Perceive every experience as a kind of vibration, a subtle wave.
- Listen without adding or subtracting anything.

GOING TO THE ENLIGHTENED BASIS OF HEARING

When you're ready, let yourself go deeper into hearing itself—go to the enlightened basis of hearing.

- Let go of observing. Let go of exploring.
- Don't try to listen to hearing; merge with nondiscriminating hearing.
- Dwell as hearing.
- Reflect, resound, and resonate without being moved or disturbed by the rising and falling of the waves.

EXTENDING HEARING MEDITATION TO ALL EXPERIENCES

This meditation cultivates an appreciation of suchness, such that objects are not perceived as separate from awareness. It can be applied to any of the six faculties (eyes, ears, nose, tongue, body, and cognition). Any body sensation (e.g., pressure, heat, cold, pain, pleasure) can be "turned" toward its enlightened basis as can any thought, fantasy, or judgment. The practice can be applied to any aspect of any of the skandhas (e.g., emotions, impulses, inclinations, urges, intentions), to the varieties of attention and consciousness.

The Buddha advises us that, by liberating one faculty, it is possible to liberate all six. I've found that after spending a concentrated period of time (at least a few months) with one faculty, it helps to apply the same form of meditation to another faculty or to one of the skandhas. Meditation with each new "channel" of experience deepens my being with the others. Perhaps this is what the Buddha means when he advises us that, by liberating one faculty, it is possible to liberate all six.

APPENDIX II

Meditation with the Center

PRELIMINARIES: LOCATE THE POINTS AND DANTIENS

Familiarizing yourself with the following four points and three levels of the dantien is important to facilitate the main practice that follows. Once you're familiar with them, it's not necessary to look for them each time.

FOUR POINTS OF TRADITIONAL CHINESE MEDICINE

- At the fontanel on the crown of the skull, where the bones knit together, is the twentieth point on the *yang Du* meridian ("governing channel"): this point is called the *Baihui*, or "one hundred convergences." You can find this point by moving your fingers from the top tips of both your ears up to the skull until they meet. You'll find the "soft spot" on the skull there. (Note: don't press too hard.)
- At the base of your torso there is a point midway between the anus and the genitalia (root of the scrotum in males;

posterior labial commissure in females). You can feel this point by bringing your attention to the area while sitting erect on a firm surface, or you can feel for the point with your fingers (again, don't press too hard). This is the first point on the *yin Ren* meridian (conception channel); it's called *Huiyin*, or "meeting of yin."

- Locate your navel (belly button). This is the eighth point on the *yin Ren* meridian, called *Shenque*, or "spirit gate." The point directly opposite on the spine is the fourth point on the yang Du meridian, *Mingmen*, or "life's gate."

THREE ENERGY CENTERS (DANTIENS) OF TRADITIONAL CHINESE MEDICINE

- The *upper dantien* is a sphere occupying most of the skull space, housing and protecting your brain. To get a sense of it, place one hand on your forehead, the other on the back of your skull (the occiput). Squeeze gently. Make some time to become aware of, and explore, the space between your hands. Then you may want to put one hand on the left side of your skull and the other on the right, squeeze gently, and feel the entire space. "Feel your way" toward the center of this space (the center of the brain) while maintaining awareness of the firm protection provided by its boundary bones.
- The *middle dantien* is a sphere occupying most of the chest space, housing and protecting your heart and lungs. To get a sense of it, place one hand on your sternum, bring the other hand around your waist and reach up to wherever you can comfortably reach on the spine directly opposite. Explore the space, its boundaries, and its center,

as you did with the upper dantien. An optional exercise is to place your palms on either side of your rib cage, apply mild pressure, and explore the space.

- The *lower dantien* is a sphere occupying most of the abdominal space, housing and protecting your vital organs. To get a sense of it, place one hand on your navel (belly button), bring the other hand around and place it directly opposite, on the Mingmen point of your spine. (If you can't reach, press your spine against a wall, or ask someone else to touch your spine there gently.) Explore the space, its boundaries, and its center, as with the other two dantiens. You may also wish to place your palms on either side of your waist just above the pelvis, apply gentle pressure, and explore the space.

BASIC CENTERING MEDITATION

FIND YOURSELF WHERE YOU ARE

- Settle into a comfortable, stable sitting position. Let your hands rest comfortably (in a mudra or on your lap, legs, or knees).
- Let the Baihui point (the fontanel) float directly above the Huiyin point (bottom of the torso). This helps align the spine naturally.
- Keep your eyes open but with a soft gaze, "looking within."
- Place the tip of the tongue so that it touches the upper palate as gently as possible, near where the upper middle front teeth meet the gums. Keep the tongue in this position throughout the rest of the meditation.

- *Let go of your hold on all your involvements. Let the myriad things rest.*

GATHER YOURSELF TO YOURSELF

- Keeping the hands and fingers relaxed, but with the fingers gently spread, open your arms and let the hands float up while keeping the shoulders relaxed.
- When the arms are about chest height, begin to gather yourself to yourself by bringing the hands up further until the palms are facing the forehead (close to but not quite touching). Keep the elbows up, shoulders relaxed, and eyes open but soft, "looking within."
- Concentrate on the upper dantien for 5 to 10 seconds or so. Feel the space there. Find its center.

- Let the hands and arms slowly sink, palms facing you, straight down the midline. Allow this to happen naturally, letting gravity do the work, exerting just enough effort so the hands sink softly.
- As the hands sink, let the mind follow within.
- Pause when the hands reach chest/heart level.
- Concentrate on the middle dantien for 5 to 10 seconds or so. Feel the space there. Find its center.

- From here on, you can either leave your eyes softly open, or close them, or leave them half-open.
- Let the hands/palms sink straight down the midline, slowly but naturally, with the mind following within.
- When the hands reach the abdomen with the center of the palms directly in front of the navel, pause.

- Concentrate on the lower dantien for 5 to 10 seconds or so. Feel the space there. Find its center.
- When you're ready, *while keeping the mind at the center of the lower dantien*, bring the hands to the original resting position.

LET THE MIND REST, CENTERED IN THE LOWER DANTIEN

- Do not suppress thoughts/feelings/sensations, but do not let them run away with you.
- When the mind wanders, simply come back—again and again—to center in the lower dantien.
- Whatever arises, notice it, gently let go, and return to your center in the lower dantien.

ENDING

- If you've closed your eyes, open them. Pause.
- Repeat the gathering sequence, but this time without pausing as long at upper and middle dantiens. The hands come to face the forehead, sink down to the chest, and continue down to pause at the lower dantien.
- Pause a few moments to feel your center of gravity, absorbing any helpful calm or energy and letting go of anything you need to let go of.
- Then let the hands and arms come to rest and relax completely.

Do not get up abruptly. Take a few moments to collect yourself before resuming regular activities.

CENTERING ON COMPASSION

Often during self-compassion workshops, participants are invited to place their hands over their hearts to make a moment for compassion. Most people experience some sense of comfort with this. It's possible to increase the effect by paying attention to the *laogong* acupuncture points near the center of each palm. In traditional Chinese medicine, the laogong is the eighth point on the channel of the pericardium, the pericardium being the sheath that protects the heart and helps calm the mind.

Start with the self-compassion exercise of placing your hands on your heart. Pause, and notice what that feels like. Then cultivate awareness of the center of each palm (the laogong points), and paying attention to those, arrange your hands so the centers of both palms align with each other and with your heart-mind, pressing gently on the sternum. The centers of the hands, the heart, and the mind meet: take a few moments to give compassion to yourself. You may experience a somewhat deeper sense of balance and peace.

If you do feel some increase in comfort, it may be due in part to how aligning the points puts the body into a more symmetrically balanced position. If you want, you can experiment to take this one step further.

Start with your hands resting on your lap or by your sides. Relax, then concentrate on the palm of each hand (laogong points). Keeping the mind on the centers of the palms, let your fingers, hands, arms, and shoulders remain relaxed while your arms rise and begin to encircle the space in front of you, as if you were about to hug someone. With the arms still outstretched and relaxed, bring one hand to overlap the other, palms centering, facing your heart. Allowing yourself to feel as if you've gathered some sense of calm or energy within the circle of your arms, bring the centers of your hands toward you until they touch your heart. Press gently, letting any feeling you've gathered go in to permeate the heart and mind.

When doing this, do you get a greater sense of self-compassion? If so, ask yourself, when you reached out beyond yourself, "where" did the compassion come from?

APPENDIX III

Twenty-Five Sages and Their Practice Methods

SIX KINDS OF PERCEIVED OBJECTS

- *Ajnatakauṇḍinya*—contemplation of sound
- *Upaniṣad*—contemplation of visible objects
- *Sublimity fragrance*—contemplation of fragrance
- *Two princes of healing*—contemplation of flavors
- *Bhadrapala*—contemplation of tangible objects
- *Mahakasyapa*—contemplation of objects of cognition

FIVE FACULTIES OF PERCEPTION

- *Aniruddha*—turning the faculty of seeing around and tracing it back to its source
- *Ksudrapanthaka*—turning the faculty of the nose around by contemplating the emptiness of the breath
- *Gavampati*—turning the faculty of the tongue away from the flavors and back to itself
- *Pilindavatsa*—purifying tactile awareness until the body is forgotten

- *Subhuti*—purifying the cognitive faculty by contemplating all phenomena are empty

SIX CONSCIOUSNESSES

- *Sariputra*—returning the eye-consciousness to purity so it becomes radiant with light and illuminates the wisdom and vision of the Buddha
- *Samantabhadra*—returning the ear-consciousness to purity, listening with complete understanding with free and unattached discernment
- *Sundarananda*—refining the breath
- *Purṇamaitrayaṇiputra*—using the sound of Dharma
- *Upali*—observing precepts with body-and-mind
- *Great Maudgalyayana*—returning the mind-consciousness to the wondrous enlightened True Mind

SEVEN PRIMARY ELEMENTS

- *Ucchusma*—contemplating the primary element fire
- *Bodhisattva Ground-Leveler*—contemplating the primary element earth
- *Pure Youth Moonlight*—contemplating the primary element water
- *The Dharma-Prince Brilliance of Lapis Lazuli*—contemplating the primary element wind
- *Bodhisattva Matrix of Space*—contemplating the primary element space
- *Bodhisattva Maitreya*—contemplating consciousness-only
- *Mahasthamaprapta*—mindfulness of the Buddha
- *Avalokiteshvara Bodhisattva*—hearing the cries of the world

NOTES

INTRODUCTION

1. On November 7, 1940, the wind blew through the Tacoma Narrows and produced the resonant frequency of the suspension bridge that spanned the gap. Videos of it oscillating and collapsing are widely available on the internet.
2. Thomas Cleary, trans. *Book of Serenity* (Hudson, NY: Lindisfarne Press, 1990), 377.
3. The short title of the sutra, transliterated into English, is variously written as Surangama, Shurangama, or with diacritics over the *S*, *u*, and *n*. This is an attempt to convey the Sanskrit word *surangama*, which roughly means "indestructible" or "ultimately durable." However, in Chinese this is translated to *shou leng yan*, and the sutra is often referred to by its shortened title, *Lengyanjing*. Throughout this book, I use Surangama for the sake of simplicity.
4. Buddhist Text Translation Society (BTTS), *The Surangama Sutra, with Excerpts from the Commentary by the Venerable Master Hsuan Hua* (Ukiah, CA: Buddhist Text Translation Society, 2009), xiii–xv.
5. The version of *The Surangama Sutra* I use for this book (see note 4) is a single-volume edition. The BTTS and the City of Ten Thousand Buddhas also offer an eight-volume edition containing all of Master Hua's commentaries via their websites.

6. Shohaku Okumura, "Dōgen's Criticism against The Complete Enlightenment Sutra and the Surangama Sutra," *Dharma Eye Soto Zen Journal* 36 (November 2015): 6–16.
7. James A. Benn, "Another Look at the Pseudo-Suramgama Sutra," *Harvard Journal of Asiatic Studies* 68, no. 1 (2008): 57–89.
8. Ronald Epstein, "The Shurangama Sutra: A Reappraisal of Its Authenticity" (presentation at the annual meeting of the American Oriental Society, Philadelphia, PA, March 16–18, 1976).
9. Eihei Dogen, "Turning the Dharma Wheel," in fascicle 74 of *Treasury of the True Dharma Eye: Zen Master Dogen's Shobo Genzo*, ed. K. Tanahashi (Boston, MA: Shambhala, 2010), 693.
10. Benn, "Another Look at the Pseudo-Suramgama Sutra," 57, 89.
11. The titles of the ten sections are as follows: The Nature and Location of the Mind; The Nature of Visual Awareness; The Matrix of the Thus-Come-One; The Coming into Being of the World of Illusion; Instructions for Practice; Twenty-Five Sages; Four Clear and Definitive Instructions on Purity; The Surangama Mantra; Levels of Being; and Fifty Demonic States of Mind.
12. BTTS, *The Surangama Sutra*, x.

1. THE REQUEST FOR DHARMA

1. BTTS, *The Surangama Sutra*, 14.
2. BTTS, *The Surangama Sutra*, 15.
3. What we think of as "the brain" is an abstract generalization, whether it's a plastic model or a functional brain scan derived by averaging activity from a number of brains. No single brain will conform exactly to the abstract summary, and no model will depict the individual brain fully accurately. You and I may share a concept of a grapefruit, but if we cut one in half, you may call it sweet while I taste it as tart. Some grapefruits are so large and pale they're taken for pomelos, while others are so small and pink they may be hard to pick out from a bin mixed with blood oranges. This being the case for grapefruits, why would we think there is a practice path we can identify with a name and follow to some "thing" we call enlightenment?
4. All quotations in this book from the *Tao Te Ching* are my own. I drew on a large number of alternative translations, then compiled and reworded

them. All 81 verses appear in my book *Walking the Way: 81 Zen Encounters with the Tao Te Ching*. (Somerville, MA: Wisdom Publications, 2013).

5. I first encountered the felicitous phrase "laying down a path by walking" as the title of chapter 11 in Francisco Varela, Evan Thompson, and Eleanor Rosch's *The Embodied Mind* (Cambridge, MA: MIT Press, 1993). The phrase has a progenitor in a famous poem by Antonio Machado, "Caminante," which begins (my translation): "Oh wanderer, the road is but your footsteps ..."

2. TEMPTATION AND INTENTION

1. Lee Ross identified "the fundamental attribution error" back in 1977, which means people have a tendency to attribute behavior to personality rather than to external circumstances. He also identified how we harbor a bias in thinking that our perceptions, values, and beliefs are shared more by others than they actually are—the "false consensus" effect. His later work culminated in identification and exploration of what he deemed "'the truly fundamental attribution error': the illusion of superior personal objectivity and its various consequences for interpersonal and intergroup interactions." He summarizes his work in Lee Ross, "From the Fundamental Attribution Error to the Truly Fundamental Attribution Error and Beyond: My Research Journey," *Perspectives on Psychological Science* 13, no. 6 (2018): 750–69, https://doi.org/10.1177/1745691618769855. Due to Lee Ross's recent (June 2021) death, many encomiums and summaries of his work are currently available.
2. Melissa Bateson, Daniel Nettle, and Gilbert Roberts, "Cues of Being Watched Enhance Cooperation in a Real-World Setting," *Biology Letters* 2 (2006): 412–14, https://doi.org/10.1098/rsbl.2006.0509. There is a host of research on similar phenomena, ranging from how people eat more M&Ms when there are more colors (Barbara Kahn and Brian Wansink, "The Influence of Assortment Structure on Perceived Variety and Consumption Qualities," *Consumer Research* 30, no. 4 [2004]: 519–33, http://dx.doi.org/10.1086/380286) to how people are more likely to trust others if they've recently touched something warm rather than something cold (Yoona Kang, et. al., "Physical Temperature Effects on Trust Behavior: The Role of Insula," *Social Cognitive and Affec-*

tive Neuroscience 6, no. 4 [2011]: 507–15, https://doi.org/10.1093/scan/nsq077). An excellent exposition of how conscious "System 2" thinking is affected by automatic "System 1" cognition is Daniel Kahneman's *Thinking Fast and Slow* (New York: Farrar, Strauss and Giroux, 2011). A less technical but entertaining presentation is Jonah Berger's *Invisible Influence* (New York: Simon & Schuster, 2016).

3. Kapila appears in both Hindu Vedic and Buddhist literature. The reference is likely to the Hindu sage who founded the Samkhya school, but it could be to the *yaksha* demon Buddha turned into a guardian-protector or (less likely) to a previous incarnation of the Buddha. Because the Samkhya school is a dualistic philosophy, its association with an evil spell in this explicitly nondualistic sutra (the sutra teaches the same skandhas that confuse students are also gateways to enlightenment) brings an intriguing twist to the material. Note: The Matangas were a tribal people in the India of the Buddha's time.
4. BTTS, *The Surangama Sutra*, 9.
5. Peter Gollwitzer and Gabriele Oettingen, "Psychology of Motivation and Actions," in *International Encyclopedia of the Social & Behavioral Sciences*, 2nd ed., ed. James D. Wright (Oxford, UK: Elsevier, 2015), 15:887–93.
6. BTTS, *The Surangama Sutra*, 89.
7. We need to beware of facile generalizations that purport to identify precursors of modern physics in Buddhist philosophies. The details of the constituents of matter and energy in physics do not align neatly (or sloppily) with Buddhism's five aggregates, six faculties, twelve sites, and eighteen elements. The Standard Model of physics identifies four forces (gravity and the electromagnetic, weak and strong interactions); the seven elementary particles (quarks, leptons, gluons, photos, Z bosons, W bosons, Higgs) come in various types, generations, flavors, and colors, making up sixty-one in total (thus far).
8. Eliot's "The Hollow Men" was first published in 1925. A hypertext version is available at http://aduni.org/~heather/occs/honors/Poem.htm.
9. In the Vimalakirti Sutra, Vimalakirti is a layperson, a householder whose enlightenment is so profound he is able to manifest the Dharma in nondual activity. "He lived at home, but remained aloof from the realm of desire, the realm of pure matter, and the immaterial realm. . . . He seemed to eat and drink, yet always took nourishment from

the taste of meditation. . . . To train living beings, he would appear at crossroads and on street corners, and to protect them he participated in government. . . . To develop children, he visited all the schools. To demonstrate the evils of desire, he even entered the brothels. To establish drunkards in correct mindfulness, he entered all the cabarets." Robert Thurman, trans., *The Holy Teaching of Vimalakirti* (University Park, PA: Penn State University Press, 1976).

3. THE NATURE AND LOCATION OF THE MIND

1. BTTS, *The Surangama Sutra*, 27–28.
2. Roxanne Khamsi, "Jennifer Aniston Strikes a Nerve," *Nature*, June 22, 2005, https://doi.org/10.1038/news050620-7. The actual article is less sensational (R. Quian Quiroga, L. Reddy, G. Kreiman, C. Foch, and I Fried, "Invariant Visual Representation by Single Neurons in the Human Brain," *Nature*, June 23, 2005, 435, 1102–1107). It does not claim there is a single neuron that responds to each particular face. Instead, it asserts that single neurons can serve to represent abstract concepts that integrate a variety of information. This is still somewhat controversial but generally not accepted by most neuroscientists, who instead have been investigating network theories of the brain.
3. It's not surprising that the brain functions via multiple pathways to the same end and that the same path can lead to different ends. This is how most of life works. You can usually drive to your favorite restaurant by many different routes; you can take the same route each time but arrive at your destination to discover the restaurant has been sold and now serves a different cuisine (or perhaps has been converted to a parking lot).

   Meditation practitioners commonly use different methods to evoke samadhi; using the same method each time leads to varied meditation experiences. The corollary is obvious for Dharma practice: no one way works for everybody, and each way will bring fluctuating, impermanent outcomes. Unfortunately, we can lose sight of this when, in our efforts to remain faithful to tradition or consistent to a research agenda, we focus overmuch on the forms of a school of practice or try to manualize a meditation technique.
4. A review of this research, together with an exposition of network brain theories of emotion and the role of environmental context, is Lisa

Feldman-Barrett's excellent (but somewhat misleadingly titled) *How Emotions Are Made: The Secret Life of the Brain* (Boston, MA: Houghton Mifflin Harcourt, 2017).

5. A good brief popular introduction is available at Samuel McNerney, "A Brief Guide to Embodied Cognition: Why You Are Not Your Brain," *Scientific American* (blog), November 4, 2011, https://blogs.scientificamerican.com/guest-blog/a-brief-guide-to-embodied-cognition-why-you-are-not-your-brain/. For those interested in the underpinnings, George Lakoff and Mark Johnson's *Metaphors We Live By* (Chicago: University of Chicago Press, 1980) inspired research such as Joshua M. Ackerman, Christopher C. Nocera, and John A. Bargh, "Incidental Haptic Sensations Influence Social Judgments and Decisions," *Science* 328, no. 5986 (2010): 1712–15, https://doi.org/10.1126/science.1189993.
6. I've truncated the quote because the last two words in the original ("of outflows") might not be clear in this context. The full quotation would be: "All I have done is to become learned, and so I am not yet free of outflows." "Outflows" is a technical term in Buddhism. In the Surangama Sutra, it often connotes desires, illusions, or defilements that "flow out" from the mind and affect other things. We'll encounter the term in subsequent chapters: in chapters 8 and 12, the meaning will be apparent from the context, and in chapters 14 and 16, I'll clarify that "outflows" can refer to any state or influence arising through unenlightened contact that contributes to suffering and delusion.
7. BTTS, *The Surangama Sutra*, 32.
8. There are many translations of this seminal poem. Here, I'm quoting from the one by Richard B. Clarke, available online at hwww.mendosa.com/way.html and in Seng-ts'an, *Hsin-Hsin Ming*, trans. Richard B. Clarke (Buffalo, NY: White Pine Press, 2001).
9. Barry Magid points out, in *Ending the Pursuit of Happiness: A Zen Guide* (Boston, MA: Wisdom Publications, 1980), that most of us come to meditation practice with "curative fantasies," so we pursue a (false) vision of a mind that will provide us with an idealized freedom from the natural ups and downs of life.
10. Dogen, "Sangai-Yuishin: The Triple World Is Only Mind," in *Shobo-*

genzo Book 3, trans. Gudo Nishijima and Chodo Cross (Bristol, UK: Windbell Publications, 1997), 37–42.

11. "Ego" has a wide range of connotations both in popular usage and as a technical term in psychology. At its most basic, it is simply the Latin word for "I." Some writers distinguish between "self" and "ego." I will use "ego" to refer to all psychological phenomena related to *individual* maintenance and preservation, whether conscious or unconscious.
12. Daniel Kahneman, *Thinking, Fast and Slow* (New York: Farrar, Straus and Giroux, 2011). System 1 maximizes efficiency and minimizes effort. It operates rapidly and automatically by evoking overlearned habits, beliefs, intuitions, and stereotypes. We're generally unaware of System 1 processes, which have an emotional tone—they "feel right." System 2, in contrast, requires intentional effort and explicit analysis. It is slower and more controlled than System 1 and relies on reasoning and problem solving to consciously "make sense" of a situation.
13. One of my editors, Matt Zepelin, pointed out how similar the story of Huike and Bodhidharma is to this interchange between the Buddha and Ananda in the Surangama Sutra. Dazu Huike (Jap. Taiso Eka) lived 487–593 C.E., so the purported interchange would have occurred prior to the appearance of the Surangama Sutra. However, the koans were collected hundreds of years after they supposedly occurred, and it was common in the China of that era to distill different versions of oral tales into prototypical exemplars and predate them. So it's uncertain which of the stories influenced the other.
14. BTTS, *The Surangama Sutra*, 33–34.
15. Eihei Dogen, Genjō Koān, "Actualizing the Fundamental Point," in *Moon in a Dewdrop: Writings of Zen Master Dogen*, ed. Kazuaki Tanashi, trans. Robert Aitken et al. (New York: North Point Press, 1995), 69.
16. I'd summarize my qigong master Hui Liu's teaching with these two words: "just natural!" She merged Taoism, Confucianism, and Buddhism seamlessly through her practice and her everyday actions. Beyond labels and words, Shimu gave herself generously to all she encountered. In doing so, in being completely herself without ever being full of herself, she showed us the way to our true selves.
17. Robert Aitken, *The Mind of Clover* (Berkeley, CA: North Point Press, 1984).

18. Eihei Dogen, "Undivided Activity," in *Moon in a Dewdrop: Writings of Zen Master Dogen*, ed. Kazuaki Tanashi, trans. Robert Aitken et al. (New York: North Point Press, 1995), 85–86. This fascicle was translated by Ed Brown and Kazuaki Tanashi.
19. Keizan Jokin, *Denkoroku: The Record of Transmitting the Light*, trans. F. Cook (Boston, MA: Wisdom Publications, 2003). Keizan is quoting Dongshan Liangjie.

4. THE NATURE OF VISUAL AWARENESS

1. Robert Rosenbaum, "Reflections on Mirroring," in *Encountering Buddhism: Western Psychology and Buddhist Teachings*, ed. Seth Robert Segall (Albany, NY: State University of New York Press, 2003), 143–64.
2. BTTS, *The Surangama Sutra*, 81.
3. A nice historical review is Pierre Sachse, et. al., "'The World Is Upside Down'—The Innsbruck Goggle Experiments of Theodor Erismann (1883–1961) and Ivo Kohler (1915–1985)," *Cortex* 92 (2017): 222–32.
4. BTTS, *The Surangama Sutra*, 54.
5. I don't want to confuse the argument here, but strictly speaking, not only is visual awareness not an object, neither the finger nor the moon are either. In Mahayana Buddhism, no "thing" exists with a core, immutable essence. All objects are transitory appearances. Some trends in contemporary science suggest treating all living organisms as events and all nonliving things as processes.
6. Dayan (Wild Goose) qigong is one of the oldest forms of the art. Tradition says it was created during the Jin dynasty (around 300 C.E.) by a Buddhist-Taoist monk, Dao An, as an aid to meditation and good health. For many years, it was passed down from master to disciple until, after the Cultural Revolution, Grandmaster Yang Meiiun began offering it publicly. Dayan is an especially comprehensive form of qigong—just its first set involves a sequence of sixty-four movements. It emphasizes *wu-wei* (effortless effort) and principles of traditional Chinese medicine (TCM). I've been fortunate to learn Dayan qigong from Master Hui Liu, one of Grandmaster Yang's foremost disciples.
7. BTTS, *The Surangama Sutra*, 70.
8. Regarding "understanding," also see chapter 6, p. 94. The Buddha says,

"An enlightenment to which an understanding is added cannot be a true enlightenment."

9. BTTS, *The Surangama Sutra*, 81–82.

5. THE MATRIX OF THE THUS-COME-ONE

1. This is the title of Gregory Bateson's last book, *Mind and Nature: A Necessary Unity* (New York: Hampton Press, 2002).
2. BTTS, *The Surangama Sutra*, 90–91.
3. BTTS, *The Surangama Sutra*, 93.
4. National Oceanographic and Atmospheric Association, "Harmonic Constituents," Tides & Currents, https://tidesandcurrents.noaa.gov/harcon.html?id=9410170.
5. For the last hundred years, experiments have forced physicists to grapple with many counterintuitive findings about time. This is beyond the scope of the present discussion, but the interested reader can find a good nontechnical exploration in Carlos Rovalli's *The Order of Time* (New York: Riverhead Books, 2018). Eihei Dogen provided a remarkable Zen perspective in his fascicle "The Time-Being," in *Moon in a Dewdrop: Writings of Zen Master Dogen*, ed. Kazuaki Tanashi, trans. Robert Aitken et al. (New York: North Point Press, 1995), 77–83. This fascicle was translated by Dan Welch and Kazuaki Tanashi.
6. BTTS, *The Surangama Sutra*, 53.
7. BTTS, *The Surangama Sutra*, 72.
8. You don't need to sacrifice a limb to experience this. If you put your right hand in a box that has a rubber hand on top in line with your shoulder and arm, and someone strokes a finger of your real hand (unseen, in the box) while simultaneously stroking the same finger of the rubber hand you are looking at, after a few minutes it will seem like your "real" hand vanishes and the fake hand is your own.
9. A good review of these issues is Michael Heller and James Salzman, *Mine: How the Hidden Rules of Ownership Control Our Lives.* (New York: Doubleday, 2021), 161–200. The book also covers how the same issues that come up in physical ownership of things and bodies also come up in the patents, copyrights, and so forth that are designed to deal with objects of mind.

10. Personal communication from my teacher, Sojun Mel Weitsman, quoting his teacher, Shunryu Suzuki.
11. I want to emphasize that this is not some idealized pretty picture but a description of concrete experience. When I go out to the garden to weed, if I fight the weeds by yanking at them, they break off in my hand and leave their roots intact to sprout again. When I'm able to make the space and time to meet the weeds in the proper conditions—it helps for the soil to be not too damp and soft, not too dry and hard—the whole plant comes up easily. However, when I *try* to meet the weeds and conditions in the expectation that this will make my task easier, it never works out the way I want it to in my self-centered plans.
12. Readers familiar with the *nidanas*—the twelve links in the chain of dependent origination that lead to suffering—will recognize "contact" as one of the links. Sometimes these links are presented as "real," and achieving nirvana becomes a process of breaking the links. In the Mahayana, these are seen as fundamentally illusory, "empty." The Mahayana most frequently treats enlightenment not just as a journey from samsara to nirvana but the realization of (as the Heart Sutra says) "no suffering and no extinction of it."
13. BTTS, *The Surangama Sutra*, 94.
14. BTTS, *The Surangama Sutra*, 128–29.
15. Jorge Cham and Daniel Whiteson, "What Is Space? It's Not What You Think," *Nautilus*, June 22, 2017, https://nautil.us/issue/49/the-absurd/what-is-space. Originally published in Cham and Whiteson, *We Have No Idea: A Guide to the Unknown Universe* (New York: Riverhead Books, 2017).
16. Steven Weinberg, "The Search for Unity: Notes for a History of Quantum Field Theory," *Daedalus* 106, no. 4, Discoveries and Interpretations: Studies in Contemporary Scholarship, Volume II (Fall 1977): 19.
17. It's difficult to conceptualize the emptiness of emptiness. When we visualize "empty" fields, we usually fill them with some "thing," such as space or darkness. Quantum field theory gives rise to virtual particles that pop in and out of existence; it's difficult to visualize "nothing" becoming "something" without imagining some invisible, latent embryo waiting in the dark for its chance to appear.

The closest I've come was on a warm, sunny afternoon, alone at the top of a mountain in Spain between Granada and the Mediterranean Sea. I looked out at a cloudless, brilliant blue sky while the cool breeze at high altitude was stirred by the hot dry winds of the plains mixing with the moist air of the sea. Suddenly, in the empty expanse, a wisp of white appeared, spiraled as a brief strand, and vanished. A minute later, while I looked out into endless blue, another cloud filament curled in a thin thread, stretched itself out into evaporation, and vanished. These manifestations and vanishings continued popping in and out of existence while I watched, entranced, for an hour. Something from nothing, nothing from something, again and again. These were atmospheric expressions, not quantum fluctuations, and they certainly held no sectarian Buddhist preferences. Still, my heart-mind skipped and capered along with them, cavorting as form-and-emptiness.

18. BTTS, *The Surangama Sutra*, 135.
19. BTTS, *The Surangama Sutra*, 137.

6. THE COMING INTO BEING OF THE WORLD OF ILLUSION (I)

1. BTTS, *The Surangama Sutra*, 141.
2. BTTS, *The Surangama Sutra*, 144–45.
3. BTTS, *The Surangama Sutra*, 143–44.
4. The quote is from the seventeenth-century Spanish playwright Calderon de la Barca's play *La Vida es Sueño* [Life Is a Dream] (my translation).
5. Lisa Fazio, Nadia Brashier, B. Keith Payne, and Elizabeth Marsh, "Knowledge Does Not Protect against Illusory Truth," *Journal of Experimental Psychology: General* 144, no. 5 (2015): 993–1002. The article cites many pioneering studies, including the initial findings in Lynn Hasher, David Goldstein, and Thomas Toppino, "Frequency and the Conference of Referential Validity," *Journal of Verbal Learning and Verbal Behavior* 16 (1977): 107–12. The 2015 study adds a rather disturbing element: it demonstrates that repeating statements leads people to perceive them as more truthful, *even when they know better* (i.e., are familiar with accurate information that contradicts the repeated false statements). More recent studies have shown the effect occurs even when the false information

is patently implausible and when subjects are told they are being given false information. The more often information is repeated, the more likely it is to be believed.

6. Keizan Jokin, *Denkoroku.*
7. Since the era of that class, neuropsychological research has emerged that strongly suggests dreams do play a psychological role in the process of memory consolidation and the clearing of day residues. However, the kinds of meanings ascribed by Freudian, Jungian, and Gestalt therapists still seem more of a therapeutic creative act than an uncovering of invariable symbolic meaning.
8. Martin Heidegger, *Discourse on Thinking.* trans. John Anderson and E. Hans Freund (New York, Harper and Row:1966), 90.
9. BTTS, *The Surangama Sutra*, 146–47.
10. Eihei Dogen, "Guidelines for Studying the Way," in *Moon in a Dewdrop: Writings of Zen Master Dogen*, ed. Kazuaki Tanashi, trans. Robert Aitken et al. (New York: North Point Press, 1995), 38. This fascicle was translated by Ed Brown and Kazuaki Tanashi. I have expanded the quotation slightly to include the editor's notes on translating *nensōkan.*
11. Eihei Dogen, Genjō Koān, "Actualizing the Fundamental Point," in *Moon in a Dewdrop: Writings of Zen Master Dogen*, ed. Kazuaki Tanashi, trans. Robert Aitken et al. (New York: North Point Press, 1995), 69.

7. THE COMING INTO BEING OF THE WORLD OF ILLUSION (II)

1. Florence Caplow and Susan Moon, eds., *The Hidden Lamp* (Boston, MA: Shambhala, 2013), 271.
2. *Blue Cliff Record*, case 46.
3. BTTS, *The Surangama Sutra*, 70–71.
4. Craig Holdrege, "Do Frogs Come from Tadpoles?" chap. 8 in *Seeing the Animal Whole: And Why It Matters* (Herndon, VA: Lindisfarne Books, 2021).
5. Reference is to Eihei Dogen's *Genjo Koan*: "You should understand that firewood abides in the phenomenal expression of firewood, which fully includes past and future and is independent of past and future. Ash abides in the phenomenal expression of ash, which fully includes future and past. Just as firewood does not become firewood again after

it is ash, you do not return to birth after death." Eihei Dogen, Genjō Koān, "Actualizing the Fundamental Point," in *Moon in a Dewdrop: Writings of Zen Master Dogen*, ed. Kazuaki Tanashi, trans. Robert Aitken et al. (New York: North Point Press, 1995), 70.

6. The phrase comes from the *Hokyo Zammai* [Jewel Mirror Samadhi] by Dongshan Liangjie, of which there are many translations. Most Soto Zen websites have a version available online (e.g., www.sfzc.org/files/daily_sutras_Song_of_the_Jewel_Mirror_Samadhi), and I've compiled my own version. The phrase I'm quoting is from an older translation by Thomas Cleary, no longer in print. There is a complex, character-by-character translation study available online at https://terebess.hu/zen/HokyoMirror.pdf.
7. BTTS, *The Surangama Sutra*, 164.
8. A paraphrase of Shunryu Suzuki Roshi, as related to me by his disciple and my teacher, Sojun Mel Weitsman.

PART TWO: HEART

1. BTTS, *Surangama Sutra*, 169–70.
2. BTTS, *Surangama Sutra*, 175.

8. INSTRUCTIONS FOR PRACTICE

1. BTTS, *The Surangama Sutra*, 252.
2. Arthur Conan Doyle, "Silver Blaze," in *The Complete Sherlock Holmes* (New York: Barnes and Noble, 1992), 335.
3. BTTS, *The Surangama Sutra*, 182–83.
4. BTTS, *The Surangama Sutra*, 185.
5. BTTS, *The Surangama Sutra*, 186–87.
6. In response to this experience, Cage composed one of the most influential music pieces of the twentieth century, "4'33"." In it, a pianist comes on stage, opens the piano lid, takes out a stopwatch, times four minutes and thirty-three seconds, closes the lid, bows, and exits.
7. One of Eihei Dogen's poems expresses this beautifully:

   The water gouges the cliff and pounds the rocks unceasingly.
   Even from a distance we know how high it is.
   How can the valley stream be blocked?
   It will end up in the ocean as billows.

   Dogen, "Continuous Practice, Part One," in *Shobogenzo*, 351.

8. "Outflows" is a technical term in Buddhism. It can refer to any state or influence that contributes to suffering and delusion arising through unenlightened contact with objects of perception. This is discussed further in chapters 14 and 16.
9. James Green, trans., *The Recorded Sayings of Zen Master Joshu* (Boston, MA: Shambhala, 2001), 42.
10. If you're unfamiliar with the Möbius strip, you can create one. Take a strip of paper, make a single twist in the strip, then fasten the two ends together with tape or glue. If you then place a pencil on the inside of the strip and draw a continuous line without lifting the pencil from the paper, you'll find your pencil moves from the inside to the outside of the strip and back again. Mathematically, the Möbius strip is a one-dimensional space, even though we can manipulate it in our usual three dimensions.
11. As mentioned in chapter 3, note 15. Eihei Dogen says, "The Buddha Way is, basically, leaping clear of the many and the one." Eihei Dogen, Genjō Koān, "Actualizing the Fundamental Point," in *Moon in a Dewdrop: Writings of Zen Master Dogen*, ed. Kazuaki Tanashi, trans. Robert Aitken et al. (New York: North Point Press, 1995), 69.
12. BTTS, *The Surangama Sutra*, 193.

9. TWENTY-FIVE SAGES SPEAK OF ENLIGHTENMENT

1. BTTS, *The Surangama Sutra*, 191–93.
2. In most sanghas, there are many opportunities to discuss practice informally with our Dharma friends, but when we set aside a time and place to talk about it with a senior student, we label it "practice discussion." At Berkeley Zen Center, we distinguished this from formal meetings with a designated teacher, or *dokusan*. However, the usage of these terms varies from sangha to sangha.
3. I'm indebted to my friend Hozan Alan Senauke for this guiding beacon. Hozan has now succeeded Sojun as Abbot of Berkeley Zen Center.
4. BTTS, *The Surangama Sutra*, 248.
5. As noted previously, there are many translations of the *Hsin-Hsin Ming*. Three versions are available at http://dmzencenter.org/wp-content/uploads/2020/04/Hsin-Hsin-Ming-Three-Translations.pdf.
6. Eihei Dogen, Genjō Koān, "Actualizing the Fundamental Point," in *Moon in a Dewdrop: Writings of Zen Master Dogen*, ed. Kazuaki Tanashi, trans. Robert Aitken et al. (New York: North Point Press, 1995), 72.

10. THE BODHISATTVA WHO HEARS THE CRIES OF THE WORLD

1. BTTS, *The Surangama Sutra*, 244.
2. BTTS, *The Surangama Sutra*, 241.
3. Once we begin picking and choosing on the basis of who "deserves" our help, we're on a slippery slope. I'm reminded of Alfred Doolittle in George Bernard Shaw's play *Pygmalion*. Doolittle is an alcoholic and a philanderer who, while acknowledging being "undeserving," says, "But my needs is as great [as anyone else's] . . . I don't need less than a deserving man: I need more. I don't eat less hearty than him; and I drink a *lot* more." George Bernard Shaw, *Pygmalion*, "The Project Gutenberg eBook of Pygmalion," March 1, 2003, www.gutenberg.org/files/3825/3825-h/3825-h.htm.
4. Very few medical practitioners receive adequate training in the neurobiology of pain and its management (in fact, veterinarians receive more hours of training in this area than do medical students). Chronic pain, in particular, is a complex phenomenon; it is not simply acute pain that persists over time. Changes occur in the central nervous system that often make it difficult to determine a specific location or disease process for the chronic pain, but that doesn't make it less real. A common dictum among chronic pain specialists is "The *strain* in *pain* lies *mainly* in the *brain.*" I like to add: "Pain's least, will cease, release, when heart's at peace" as well as "Pain's bind unwinds when mind becomes more kind."
5. *Blue Cliff Record*, case #80. A monk asked Chao Chu, "Does a newborn infant also have six consciousnesses?" Joshu said, "A ball tossed on rushing water." When the monk asked T'uo Tzu what that meant, he responded "moment to moment, nonstop flow."
6. BTTS, *The Surangama Sutra*, 234–35.
7. BTTS, *The Surangama Sutra*, 235.
8. "Centering on Compassion," in appendix II, provides a concrete exercise in reaching for compassion.
9. This koan appears, in slightly different forms, as number 54 in the *Shoyoroku* (*Book of Serenity*) and number 89 in the *Hekiganroku* (*Blue Cliff Record*).
10. A line from the capping verse for the preceding koan on compassion begins, "one hole, emptiness pervading."

11. We are husband and wife, but I prefer to call her my sweetheart. I don't like the word "wife" because the economic and social institutions of marriage have historically been oppressive, especially to women. Can't spouses be sweethearts?
12. BTTS, *The Surangama Sutra*, 259.

11. FOUR CLEAR AND DEFINITIVE INSTRUCTIONS ON PURITY

1. Norman Fischer, *Training in Compassion: Zen Teachings on the Practice of Lojong* (Boston, MA: Shambhala, 2013), 6.
2. Robert Rosenbaum and Barry Magid, eds., *What's Wrong with Mindfulness (and What Isn't)* (Boston, MA: Wisdom Publications, 2016).
3. "Precept," Lexico, www.lexico.com/en/definition/precept.
4. Dale Wright, discussing the paramita of wisdom, in *The Six Perfections: Buddhism & the Cultivation of Character* (New York: Oxford University Press, 2009), 244.
5. Ananda, in the midst of his grief, didn't ask the Buddha which rules were inviolable and which could be modified, so when the community of monks and nuns codified the rules of the *vinaya-pitaka*, "the basket of discipline," at the First Council, they decided to retain all of them.
6. BTTS, *The Surangama Sutra*, 265.
7. BTTS, *The Surangama Sutra*, 268.
8. BTTS, *The Surangama Sutra*, 276.
9. BTTS, *The Surangama Sutra*, 273.
10. Robert Aitken, *The Dragon Who Never Sleeps: Verses for Zen Buddhist Practice* (Berkeley, CA: Parallax Press, 1991), 4.
11. Diane Rizzetto, *Waking Up to What You Do* (Boston, MA: Shambhala, 2006).
12. In reality, each of the precepts interacts with all the others. We take the precepts one by one to provide some focus. In the process, most students begin to develop a sense of the precepts' interbeing. This is the "Te" in Lao Tzu's *Tao Te Ching*. Many people have heard of the Tao, but the Tao manifests through Te, which is often translated as "virtue." In my book *Walking the Way*, I suggest instead we translate *Te* as "rightness."

13. David Rohde, "The Lethal Water Wells of Bangladesh," *New York Times*, July 17, 2005, sec. A, p. 6, national edition.
14. Burton Watson, trans., "Rifling Trunks," in *The Complete Works of Chuang Tzu* (New York: Columbia University Press, 1968), 108–9.
15. My friend Joel Schone provided me with a wonderful example of selfless practice when, inspired by the Dharma of trekking in the Himalayas, he gave up a comfortable job and devoted himself to introducing others to the clarity that could be found there. He offered treks that rarely earned him a profit, devoting his earnings to the welfare of his crews and the people of the villages he visited.
16. Aitken, *The Dragon Who Never Sleeps*, 23.

12. ESTABLISHING A PLACE FOR AWAKENING

1. BTTS, *The Surangama Sutra*, 279.
2. As in verse 16 of the *Tao Te Ching*, quoted at the beginning of chapter 7:

   Return to the root;
   at the root to be still.
   In stillness recover, revive, and endure.
3. BTTS, *The Surangama Sutra*, 282.
4. Eihei Dogen, *Fukanzazengi* , "Recommending Zazen to All People," in *Treasury of the True Dharma Eye: Zen Master Dogen's Shobo Genzo*, ed. Kazuaki Tanahashi (Boston, MA: Shambhala, 2010), 2:907–8. This is a founational meditation text for the Soto branch of Zen and can be found on the Soto-shu website at https://www.sotozen.com/eng/practice/zazen/advice/fukanzanzeng.html.
5. This is another version of the first line of Sengcan's *Hsin-Hsin Ming*, translation by Richard Clarke, used at several Zen centers: Seng-ts'an, *Hsin-Hsin Ming*, trans. Richard B. Clarke (Buffalo, NY: White Pine Press, 2001).
6. The translation is by Ken McLeod, quoted in Repa Dorje Odzer (Justin von Bujdoss), "Tilopa's Six Nails," *Tricycle,* Spring 2018, https://tricycle.org/magazine/tilopas-six-nails/.
7. Personal communication. Catherine says she adapted this from a version by Norman Fischer.
8. I'm paraphrasing the koan. There are many translations. One version by Thomas Cleary and J. C. Cleary, trans., *The Blue Cliff Record* (Bos-

ton, MA: Shambhala, 1992), 226, goes "There is nothing in the triple world, where can mind be found?"—dovetailing nicely with the Surangama Sutra's depiction of mind as neither being inside, outside, in-between, nor without location.

9. Craig Holdrege, "Meeting Bloodroot," *In Context #44* (Fall 2020): 16.
10. The more precise our measurement, the smaller we need to make our measuring device. Because of this, the mathematician Benoit Mandelbrot, in his paper "How Long Is the Coastline of Great Britain," demonstrated mathematically that the boundary of Great Britain has infinite length even though it encloses a finite space. James Gleick provides a nontechnical description in *Chaos: Making a New Science* (New York: Penguin Books, 1987). The original paper (which is beyond my mathematical abilities) is B. B. Mandelbrot, "How Long Is the Coast of Britain? Statistical Self-Similarity and Fractional Dimension," *Science* 156 (1967): 636–38.

13. THE SURANGAMA MANTRA

1. BTTS, *The Surangama Sutra*, 290.
2. Bill Bryson reported feeling something similar: "In some odd way that you don't understand and can't articulate . . . this large, brooding, hypnotic presence has an importance to you at the species level . . . and that in some way your visit here is more than happenstance." *In a Sunburnt Country* (New York: Broadway Books, 2000), 256.
3. BTTS, *The Surangama Sutra*, 303–04.
4. Twelve classes of beings, fifty-seven stages of the bodhisattva's path, and the many forms of life according to Chinese Buddhist taxonomy: heavens and hells; gods and demons; bioluminescent beings, beings born of eggs, of wombs; beings who creep, crawl, fly, swim; beings dull and bright.
5. BTTS, *The Surangama Sutra*, 302.
6. BTTS, *The Surangama Sutra*, 306.
7. Master Liu was also a devoted Buddhist, practicing and teaching at the City of Ten Thousand Buddhas. She integrated Buddhism, Taoism, and Confucianism in her life. Such syncretism is common in Chinese spiritual practice.
8. These syllables were identified by Master Hua as the core of the man-

tra. It's the version I've introduced into our Zen Bodhisattva ceremony. The complete Surangama mantra, parsed into 554 phrases as used at The City of Ten Thousand Buddhas, is available in the full translation of the sutra by BTTS as well as online at www.cttbusa.org/shurangama6/shurangama6_9.asp.html.

14. LEVELS OF BEING

1. While it takes lots of boiling water to melt a glacier, a few degrees of global warming are already causing massive glacial retreat around the world. Whenever I hike in the Himalayas or Sierras, I'm shocked by seeing that where there were once miles and miles of ice, there are now miles and miles of bare rock. The glaciers are the water sources for billions of beings; their loss will have (and is already having) dire consequences. Greed, hate, and delusion inspire fossil fuel consumption that accelerates climate change. We need to heed the cries of the world.
2. BTTS, *The Surangama Sutra*, 315.
3. BTTS, *The Surangama Sutra*, 387–88.
4. I-mind especially objects to its own inessential nature. To acknowledge "things" as ungraspable goes against I-mind's prime directive: "Get a grip on yourself!"
5. However, even the gods at the summits of the twenty-eight heavens—six heavens of desire, eighteen heavens of form, four planes of formlessness—do not "fully comprehend the wondrous enlightened mind . . . [they] eventually will fall back into the cycle of death and rebirth . . . to join other beings whose karmas are similar." The same holds true for the ascetic masters and the asuras.
6. BTTS, *The Surangama Sutra*, 348.
7. See note 3 in chapter 3. Much of what I write here follows Lisa Feldman-Barrett's *How Emotions Are Made: The Secret Life of the Brain* (Boston, MA: Houghton Mifflin Harcourt, 2017).
8. Burton Watson, trans., "Discussion on Making All Things Equal," in *The Complete Works of Chuang Tzu* (New York: Columbia University Press, 1968), 37–38.
9. For example, Kang et al., "Physical Temperature Effects on Trust Behavior."
10. BTTS, *The Surangama Sutra*, 253.

11. The forty-third case of the *Blue Cliff Record* goes (I'm summarizing in my own words, drawing on several translations):

> A student asked Dongshan, "When cold and heat come, how can we avoid them?"
>
> Dongshan replied, "Why don't you go to the place where there is no hot or cold?"
>
> The student asked, "If I do that, what then?"
>
> Dongshan: "When it's cold, cold kills (or "finishes") the student; when it's hot, heat kills ("finishes") the student."

At one December sesshin at Berkeley Zen Center, before we installed heat in the zendo, it was unusually cold for people used to the Bay Area's clement weather. Everyone piled on layers of clothing but shivered in the chill air. Sojun took the opportunity to reminisce about his early days helping to build Tassajara in the remoteness of the Big Sur mountains. Snows covered the single rough access road, cutting off supplies. Sojun told of how they foraged for edible plants and froze while sitting in motionless zazen. "However," Sojun said, "the cold contributes something to your development. It's like apples: the best apples become crisp and sweet only if they weather a good cold snap."

We all listened, entranced. Some of us maybe even went to the place of no hot or cold. Then one of the students raised her hand.

"Yes, you have a question," said Sojun.

"What happens if you're not an apple? What happens if you're a tangerine?"

We all laughed. "Better to be an apple," said Sojun.

(I'd say, "Come taste my tangerine sorbet!")

12. Compare the first line of the Heart Sutra, in the translation used at Berkeley Zen Center: "Avalokiteshvara Bodisattva, when practicing deeply the prajnaparamita, perceived that all five skandhas in their own-being are empty and was saved from all suffering."

To say we turn "from" mind-objects "to" the Dharma can be misleading in the same way that "emptiness" can seem to have qualities of voidness or dark space. Just as emptiness is empty, the Dharma manifests as mind-objects; mind-objects proclaim the Dharma.

13. As cited twice previously, in the *Genjo Koan,* Dogen says: "The Buddha Way is, basically, leaping clear of the many and the one." Eihei Dogen, Genjō Koān, "Actualizing the Fundamental Point," in *Moon in a Dewdrop: Writings of Zen Master Dogen*, ed. Kazuaki Tanashi, trans. Robert Aitken et al. (New York: North Point Press, 1995), 69.

15. FIFTY DEMONIC STATES OF MIND

1. Thurman, *The Holy Teaching of Vimalakirti*, 51.
2. The Buddha shares some qualities with the lion Aslan of C. S. Lewis's *Narnia* books. In those books, children find a doorway to a fantasy kingdom of talking animals, witches, and marsh-wiggles. The children's adventures are religious parables where Christ appears as the lion, Aslan. Aslan is kind, but he can also be fierce; the children repeatedly warn each other to remember: "He's not a *tame* lion."
3. BTTS, *The Surangama Sutra*, 458–59.
4. BTTS, *The Surangama Sutra*, 391.
5. Zen is not exempt. Eihei Dogen's meditation instructions carry the title "Recommending Zazen for All People." This has its downsides, as Barry Magid and I discuss in our introduction to *What's Wrong with Mindfulness (and What Isn't)* (Boston: Wisdom Publications, 2016), 5.
6. See, for example, M. Farias, E. Maraldi, K. C. Wallenkampf, and G. Lucchetti, "Adverse Events in Meditation Practices and Meditation-Based Therapies: A Systematic Review," *Acta Psychiatrica Scandinavica* 142, no. 5 (August 2020): 374–393, https://doi.org/10.1111/acps.13225.
7. F. J. and T.D. Heide Borkovec. "Relaxation-Induced Anxiety: Paradoxical Anxiety Enhancement Due to Relaxation Training," *Journal of Consulting and Clinical Psychology 51,* no. 2 (1983): 171–82, https://doi.org/10.1037/0022-006X.51.2.171; Luberto et al., "OA14.01. Relaxation-Induced Anxiety: Predictors and Subjective Explanations Among Young Adults ." Supplement, *BMC Complementary and Alternative Medicine* 12. no. S1 (2012):053 http://www.biomedcentral.com/1472-6882/12/S1/O53.
8. Eihei Dogen, Genjō Koān, "Actualizing the Fundamental Point," in *Moon in a Dewdrop: Writings of Zen Master Dogen*, ed. Kazuaki Tanashi, trans. Robert Aitken et al. (New York: North Point Press, 1995), 71.
9. BTTS, *The Surangama Sutra*, 396.
10. BTTS, *The Surangama Sutra*, 391.

11. Watson, "Discussion on Making All Things Equal," 40.
12. Mardi Horowitz, *States of Mind: Analysis of Change in Psychotherapy* (New York: Plenum Medical Books, 1979), 130–35.
13. BTTS, *The Surangama Sutra*, 393–94.
14. BTTS, *The Surangama Sutra*, 401.
15. BTTS, *The Surangama Sutra*, 399.
16. BTTS, *The Surangama Sutra*, 406.
17. BTTS, *The Surangama Sutra*, 454.
18. This was a favorite saying of the psychiatrist Harry Stack Sullivan.
19. There are many, many translations of several versions of the Pali Metta Sutta; the one I offer here is the most recent one we use in our sangha. The sutra's central portion—"May all beings be happy, at ease, joyous, safe"—is recited in many settings, including ones offering Zen, Vipassana, and secular mindfulness practice. The full text of the sutra is not as well known but is well worth reading and reciting. It embeds the wish for happiness into a broader context of wholesome behavior (for example, not desiring great possessions, not deceiving others, not wishing harm to others), condensing many of the precepts into a few short paragraphs.
20. Wright, *The Six Perfections*, 244.

16. THE MERIT OF TEACHING THE SURANGAMA DHARMA

1. BTTS, *Surangama Sutra*, 460.
2. BTTS, *Surangama Sutra*, 457.
3. BTTS, *Surangama Sutra*, 464.
4. Referring to the Buddha as "herself" is not a misprint. I'm attempting to point to how dichotomizing gender into "his" and "hers" is fundamentally illusion.
5. BTTS, *Surangama Sutra*, 342.
6. Thurman, *The Holy Teaching of Vimalakirti*, 50–51. I have taken the liberty of combining Thurman's translation with one I have by John McRae, *The Vimalakirti Sutra* (Berkeley, CA: Numata Center for Buddhist Translation and Research, 2004), www.bdk.or.jp/document/dgtl-dl/dBET_Srimala_Vimalakirti_2004.pdf.
7. Heidegger described a similar process of "releasing into openness," and his statement "human nature remains *appropriated* to that from

whence we are called" is evocative of what Buddhism refers to as empty, enlightened nature. Martin Heidegger, *Discourse on Thinking*, trans. John Anderson and E. Hans Freund (New York: Harper and Row, 1966), 90.

8. Personal communication to the author from Sojun Mel Weitsman of an unpublished lecture he had from his teacher, Shunryu Suzuki.
9. Not a direct quote, but a reference to a passage in Jorge Luis Borges's *Labyrinths* that begins "Time is the substance I am made of . . ."
10. Eihei Dogen, Genjō Koān, "Actualizing the Fundamental Point," in *Moon in a Dewdrop: Writings of Zen Master Dogen*, ed. Kazuaki Tanashi, trans. Robert Aitken et al. (New York: North Point Press, 1995), 72.
11. One of my favorite Dogen poems expresses this nicely. It appears in Dogen, "Chinese-Style Poems," from *Moon in a Dewdrop*, 217.

    All my life false and real, right and wrong tangled.
    Playing with the moon, ridiculing wind, listening to birds. . . .
    Many years wasted seeing the mountain covered with snow.
    This winter I suddenly realize snow makes a mountain.

12. Some existentialist philosophers like to point out Descartes's starting point was doubt. The Buddha might go a little further to say Descartes's foundation was in being—being aware through doubt, finding experience itself is ungraspable.
13. Mirrors are ubiquitous symbols in Buddhism, particularly in Zen. Here I'm referring here to Dogen, *Kokyo* [Ancient Mirror]," in *Shobogenzo* 1: 205–21. See Rosenbaum, "Reflections on Mirroring."
14. BTTS, *The Surangama Sutra*, 281.
15. The usual gloss on Buddha's home-leaving is that it was an act of love, a self-sacrifice in the service of saving all beings. Another interpretation is that while he had to leave his social roles behind, this did not mean he stopped loving his family. Either, or both, may be true. But there is very little in the Buddhist sutras to indicate he took his family's feelings into account or discussed his plans with them and attempted to include them in the decision.

    As a psychologist, I can understand how someone like Gautama, who had been sequestered behind palace walls and sheltered from exposure to worldly difficulties, would need to break free of these blinders for his spiritual journey and taste the pains of loss and want.

However, his personal example need not serve as an exalted model for everyone. There is a difference between voluntary renunciation and involuntary deprivation: many homeless people might, for their spiritual practice, need to enter a home (and experience the constraints and challenges that come with it). Some householders need a retreat to deepen their spiritual practice, while for others a retreat is a means of avoidance. Some monks (and psychotherapy clients!) might need to work out their relationship issues in the protected confines of a sangha or a therapist's office, while others might do better to work out their emotional tangles, along with their karma, by dealing directly with their original and current family, friends, and coworkers.

The fact that Siddhartha Gautama left home is not necessarily problematical. Yet when Buddhist institutions' economic and political interests give rise to privileging his personal path into a superior one-size-fits-all, it fosters unnecessary divisiveness and suffering.

16. Eihei Dogen, *Raihai-tokuzui* [Receiving the Marrow by Bowing], in *Shobogenzo*, 1: 72–73.
17. After Joko Beck passed away, several of her Dharma heirs met and developed practice principles for Ordinary Mind Zen. One of the characteristics of OMZ is its flexibility in adapting practice forms to the particular circumstances of sanghas and the teaching styles of their leaders, so there are many versions of these principles, which continue to evolve. I've based my version on one in widespread use, provided to me by Karen Terzano and Diane Rizzetto:

    Caught in a self-centered dream, only suffering
    Holding to self-centered thoughts, exactly the dream
    Each moment, life as it is, the only teacher
    Being just this moment, compassion's way.

ABOUT THE AUTHOR

ROBERT MEIKYO ROSENBAUM, PHD, began Zen practice in 1971 but did not find his root teacher, Sojun Mel Weitsman, until 1989. Sojun gave Bob his Dharma name, Meikyo Onza (Clear Mirror, Calm Sitting). After practicing at Berkeley Zen Center for several decades, Bob received lay entrustment from Sojun. Bob is committed to the lay practice of Zen and is a founding member of the Lay Zen Teachers' Association. In 2010 Bob established a Zen sangha in the Sierra foothills; he has taught in Finland, Australia, Nepal, and India. In 2019 Bob received *denkai* in Ordinary Mind Zen from Karen Terzano. He currently lives and practices in Sacramento, California.

Bob found a natural complement to Zen in the Taoist practice of Dayan (Wild Goose) qigong as taught by Master Hui Liu in the lineage of Grandmaster Yang Meijun. In 1991 Master Liu authorized Bob as a teacher. Since then, at her request, he has brought Dayan qigong to numerous venues in the United States and around the world including yoga centers, medical clinics, and meditation communities. He continues to teach master classes at the Wen Wu School in El Cerrito.

Bob has thirty years' experience as a neuropsychologist, psychotherapist, and behavioral medicine specialist at Kaiser Permanente. He was a Fulbright Professor at the National Institute of Mental Health and Neurosciences in India. Since retiring from clinical work, he has taught professional workshops and consulted with clinics and academic institutions internationally on the topics of chronic pain management and single-session psychotherapies.

In addition to numerous journal articles and book chapters on brief psychotherapy, he is the author of the books *Zen and the Heart of Psychotherapy*; *Walking the Way: 81 Zen Encounters with the Tao Te Ching*; and co-editor (with Barry Magid) of *What's Wrong with Mindfulness (and What Isn't)*. His current book project is on the Metta Sutta.